LOSING ASIA

LOSING
ASIA

• • ••

MODERNIZATION
AND THE CULTURE OF
DEVELOPMENT

•• ••

BRET WALLACH

• Drawings by Susan Trammell •

THE JOHNS HOPKINS UNIVERSITY PRESS
BALTIMORE AND LONDON

This book has been brought to publication with the generous assistance
of the Karl and Edith Pribram Fund.

The Johns Hopkins University Press
2715 North Charles Street
Baltimore, Maryland 21218-4319
The Johns Hopkins Press Ltd., London

Library of Congress Cataloging-in-Publication Data
will be found at the end of this book.

A catalog record for this book is available
from the British Library.

ISBN 0-8018-5170-X

Published in cooperation with the Center for American Places,
Harrisonburg, Virginia

CONTENTS

PREFACE AND ACKNOWLEDGMENTS

I THINK BACK FIFTEEN YEARS, TO THE TIME when I first set foot in Asia. I find myself skimming over Japan and Thailand. I alight in India. Not the great Hindu heartland of the Ganges Plains, but the South. And not just the South but the great plateau of Telangana, its soil gritty and red. The farmers here do not bore wells: traditionally, at least, they excavate them—swing picks into rotten granite until they have dug a cube twenty feet on a side, fissured, leaking, with a pond of precious seepage water at the bottom. They climb back to the surface and see, beyond the fields, only the occasional palm and more granite: gray domes fit for Yosemite but weathered into hills of boulders nested in gravel. Always, or so it seems, the rock by midday is too hot to touch.

I think of tiny rice paddies irrigated by a stream that Americans would hardly call a creek. The simplest of dams: no signs to ward off trespassers, no fencing. A ditch you could jump across. The ditch winding alongside the hot boulders and feeding—often just seeping through mud walls—into fields on the other side. Egrets walk delicately in the paddies, and a farmer wearing only a breechclout walks through the water to broadcast a powder—fertilizer? something more lethal?—that is as white as the birds.

Such places have fascinated Americans for a long time. I

think of Hiram King's *Farmers of Forty Centuries*. A soil scientist whose career had been spent at the University of Wisconsin in Madison, King suspected that American farming was physically unsustainable. Therefore he had gone to Asia, where, as his title implied, Americans could study firsthand an agriculture that was perpetual. Many, many visitors have echoed King's sentiments in the years since 1911, when he published his book. And it certainly is difficult to deny that the traditional agriculture of Asia is in remarkably good ecological balance. Some have tried; my own chief quibble is that many Asian landscapes simply look old because they have been shaped with old technologies.

But my interest in these places is not ecological. From the first time I saw them, it has always been the beauty of these places that has spoken most powerfully to me. How, I sometimes ask myself, could it have been otherwise? A boy from California grows up on huge dams, immense canals, almost limitless fields. They stay with him, so that today I yield to no one in my naive admiration for gigantic equipment. Yet it didn't take five minutes in Telangana to realize that my world didn't touch—for sheer beauty would never touch—these backward parts of Asia.

Ironically, of course, Asia was—and is—struggling with great success to catch up with the West; its traditional agriculture is changing fast, becoming more and more like our own. Who would dare to speak against this transformation? Yet how could I not raise a voice in protest, even if it meant that I was venturing onto forbidden ground?

Is what I have done anything less? For this is a book about the aesthetic cost of modernizing the Asian countryside. A book about our blindness to the destruction of what I consider

---

Rice paddies along the Nizamabad Road, a few miles north of Hyderabad, capital of Andhra Pradesh. The weathered granite is typical of the Telangana Plateau and provides relief from the otherwise dull topography; along with the fine network of small streams that cross the plateau west to east, the outcrops largely control the location of the rice paddies that beautify this otherwise harsh landscape.

the most beautiful places on earth. A book about saving those places. In short, this book is an attack on nine generations of the utilitarian mentality that has shaped—dominated—every discussion of the rural development in Asia. It is a book that dares to question what I have taken to calling the culture of development. One does not criticize such dogmas with impunity.

As soon as I announce my intentions, I see brows furrowing. I recognize the signs, know what they signify. By what right dare I ask millions of people to live lives of drudgery and discomfort? By what right dare I ask those people to live a kind of life that I would surely not choose for myself? To speak of preserving beauty in the midst of such suffering is immoral. It is hypocritical. It is profoundly reactionary.

This is a forceful argument: at least I feel its force. But I also have come to think that its force comes less from logic than from slowly accrued intellectual momentum. After all, I have said nothing about being opposed to development. Nor shall I. Why, then, should anyone assume that in arguing for the preservation of magnificent cultural landscapes I am resisting a moral imperative? After all, the same people who say that economic growth must take precedence over the preservation of beauty are willing to admit ecological limits to growth. They are often willing to concede that traditional cities should be preserved, not butchered. Why, then, should they object to preserving the countryside?

I can hardly settle this matter with one paragraph. But if I could, a new set of critics would arise. They would raise their hands as soon as it became clear that I want Asia to be rich enough that it can afford the luxury of preserving its traditional countryside. This, I will promptly be told, is absurd: the ecological sky is going to fall long before such a thing happens.

Perhaps it's true. And perhaps I should then rest easy. After all, farmers will then continue to build steep terraces: they will have no choice. And perhaps the environmentalists (to give these critics their name) *are* right; certainly I have read jeremiads whose force has made me wonder whether my assessment of our technological creativity is not too optimistic. I cannot, in short, refute the environmental argument as tidily as I would like. I *can* say two things, however. One is that for all the dangers of deforestation, of soil erosion, of degraded air and water quality—for all these things and others—I still think we are likely to survive and get richer in the process. The other is that we should treat the scientific arguments of environmentalists with great caution. I say this because the environmental movement remains at heart a romantic protest against the character of modern life: its scientific arguments should be seen as a cloak worn more effectively to resist the course of progress. I do not say that the science of the environmentalists is wrong because it is a veneer, and for my own part I share the movement's underlying and humanistic sentiments. I do say that we should be especially skeptical about scientific proofs adduced to serve a hidden, nonscientific agenda.

And yet a third group of critics may emerge as soon as it becomes clear that I am seeking preservation and development. Now I will be accused of seeking the gentrification of Asia. And here, reluctantly, I plead guilty. I, too, have groaned at the sign in earth tones and turquoise that welcomes visitors to Taos Pueblo—and directs them to a registration office for check-in and payment of user fees. I, too, know of "listed" barns in Sussex, nobly timbered structures that have been gutted, plumbed, and wired for London brokers. I concede that in "rehabing" Asia we may be left with a shell, hardly more than a tangible reminder of lives more consciously purposeful than our own. I console myself at this juncture with the thought that gentrification need not imply consumerism. A degree of contentment in moderation is, perhaps, less at odds with our inner natures than it is with those who profit by manipulating them.

And I will say further that there is no choice. Reject my vision of an Asia wealthy enough to preserve its traditional landscape, and you are left with a universal Hong Kong or—all in the hallowed name of cultural authenticity—a policy of leaving Asia as it is. The alternatives to gentrification, in short, are worse than gentrification at its most vulgar.

And if this position didn't earn me enough enemies, this is

a book about a forbidden place. Not Asia. I don't mean Asia. *That's* not forbidden. I mean that most of this book is about India, or at least about the greater India that existed in the century or so before 1947. Why, when my title promises Asia? And why "forbidden"? The "forbidden" is simple enough; every bookstore in America has five books on China for each one it has on India. Why? Well, India's not very popular in the United States—hasn't been since the 1920s and *Mother India,* Katherine Mayo's bestseller in which an attack on child marriage became an attack on everything Hindu. Perhaps our antipathy goes back yet further, but I do know that despite our periodic fascination with Mahatma Gandhi we've never recovered from the bias Mayo popularized.

And yet I have no choice but to write chiefly about India. I may begin with China; in fact I will, shortly. I may end by looking at the culture of development as it sweeps across the whole of rural Asia; and I will, eventually. But my central concern in this book is to understand what is happening to the Asian landscape. I want to understand, in other words, how the culture of development has blinded us to the beauty we are destroying. And what is understanding in such matters but history? So it is that I am concerned chiefly with how the culture of development came to Asia, took root there, and grew.

This did not happen uniformly across the continent; on the contrary, it happened differentially. The history could be told through Dutch eyes in the East Indies or through French eyes in Indochina, but it seems to me plain that it can best be told through British eyes in the British Indian Empire. I say this not merely because India had a larger population than Europe's other Asian domains, and not merely because the records of the British are more accessible to American readers than are the records of the Dutch and the French. I say it because the face of Asia today owes more to the influence of the British than it does to any other Europeans. The irrigation works that one sees now from Iraq to Thailand were first advocated by British engineers whose careers began in India. The first improved grains widely grown in Asia were developed by an English couple working at a remote Indian research station.

Even community development, which we probably associate first with Communist China, began in India: only from there—and from the work of the Young Men's Christian Association there—did it diffuse during the 1920s to another YMCA project, this time in China. This is a book chiefly about India, in short, because the technologies and institutions transforming rural Asia today emerged chiefly from India. It is that simple; my hands are tied.

This book could not have been written without the support of a five-year fellowship from the MacArthur Foundation, and I am still indebted to (and perplexed by the identity of) the person who nominated me for it. I would also like to acknowledge the help of the Indo-American Subcommission on Education and Culture, which first sent me to India some fifteen years ago, and of Resources for the Future, which allowed me a follow-on year to wrestle with the materials I had collected. I wish to thank Tom Wickham, who as the first head of the International Irrigation Management Institute hired me and, in so doing, did far more for me than I could do for him. For his help in China I would also like to thank Lee Travers, now of the World Bank but then with the Ford Foundation. I would like to acknowledge, as one of the most remarkable letter writers I have ever known, Robert D'Arcy Shaw of the Aga Khan Foundation, and I would like to thank a number of other people who have talked or written to me about this project, among them Joe Schwartzberg of the University of Minnesota, Jim Parsons of the University of California at Berkeley, Paul Karan of the University of Kentucky, and Anne Matthews of New York University. I heeded their warnings and advice as much as I could.

LOSING ASIA

A CONTINENT AT RISK

IT WAS THE SUMMER OF TIANANMEN, AND THERE were reports of military action near the Beijing airport. The United Airlines flight taking me there from San Francisco was terminated at Tokyo. What did I wish to do? My ticket was reissued with an "involuntary reroute," and I went to Hong Kong to wait. Matters might soon ease up enough for a trip to the southern interior.

It was not to be: after a week I gave up and returned home. During that week, however, I rented a car and took a look at the Kowloon Peninsula.

One day I turned off to the right at the last exit before the highway crosses into China. With that turn I lost sight of all the trucks that, loaded with containers, ply between Shenzhen and Hong Kong's great port. Instead, there was a slow but well-paved road wandering along the shore of Starling Inlet. Across the water to the left lay China; to the right were steep hills that were wooded at their distant tops but rimmed at their bases with bits of settlement—villages with names such as Nam Chung, village ponds with thousands of white ducks clustered at their shores.

That's how I discovered Luk Keng, the village after Nam Chung. My map showed that the road was about to curve back clockwise toward Tai Po and Sha Tin, new towns as vertical as any settlements on earth. If I wanted to stay in the countryside I would have to stop here, in Luk Keng. I parked and started walking, for there is no other way to explore Luk Keng: the main road just touches one end of the village's one street, and that one street is closed to vehicular traffic.

The English-language radio channels were full that day of indignant expatriates outraged by the British government's refusal to grant the "right of abode" to Hong Kong's three and one-half million holders of British passports. But there were no angry voices on Luk Keng's one street. In fact, there were no voices at all, apart from the murmurings of a few elderly Hakka women who were recognizable from the hats they wore: woven and lacquered straw discs sixteen inches in diameter, with a hole for the crown of the wearer's head, covered by a skullcap. The women sat in ones or twos in front of their houses, which lined the side of the street that lay at the base of the sheltering hillside. Houses and women alike looked across that street to the sedimented remains of what had once been a large pond.

There were no commercial buildings in Luk Keng away from the highway intersection—and few enough there: Luk Keng proper was all houses mixed with a few Confucian temples. Most of the buildings were brick or concrete, informally joined together over the years into long rowhouses. New and old had been combined without the least regard for architectural harmony: gray blocks with casement windows and flat roofs sat, common-walled, next to temples whose roofs were dragonishly raked. The street itself was surfaced with concrete but grew narrower and narrower the farther I got from the highway.

After a few hundred yards the lane made a right-angled turn to the left. The paving soon stopped; so did the houses. Now there was a low wooden gate: no real obstacle, but I didn't know the local etiquette and was reluctant to go through. I backtracked to the corner, where a hard-trodden path wound uphill. I started up, at first along a path through a grove of good-sized trees, mostly bamboo. Then, once again and to my frustration, there was another low wooden gate. This time I opened it and within twenty paces was at the top of the hill behind Luk Keng; I saw that I was actually on the crest of a ridge that extended to still higher summits in the distance.

The bamboo disappeared, replaced by terraces that stretched in front of me in amphitheaters on both sides of the ridge. On my right the terraces actually started up from the edge of Nam Chung's duck ponds and climbed far above where I stood. I caught my breath and walked on tiptoe, as if tiptoes would somehow make me invisible and invisibility would somehow prolong the moment. I had escaped Hong Kong, was finally in the great Orient. I forgot the watch on my wrist.

It turned out that there was no need of tiptoes: there was no one at work here to disturb. The irrigation ditches were happily bubbling, but the terraces themselves were covered in weeds—not just on the terrace risers but on the treads where rice should have been growing. There wasn't a panicle of that grain to be seen on the entire mountain. I walked in disbelief past a monument commemorating the concrete lining of the main irrigation ditch: here was proof that the abandonment of these terraces had happened recently. Yet erosion was already overtopping some of the terraces, and slumping had started. Soon the contouring would be smoothed away, and trees would invade and stabilize the slopes.

I shouldn't have been surprised. A few years earlier I had been down in Kuala Lumpur, in Malaysia. I was at a meeting called to discover potential subjects of collaborative research that might be undertaken between Malaysia's Drainage and Irrigation Department and a research institute I represented. The subject of our conversation, I thought, was ways in which to improve the management of Malaysia's irrigation systems, but one of the engineers at the table finally lost patience with my questions and said with some heat that he wasn't worried about moving water: he was worried about keeping farmers farming. Despite everything the government had done for these people, he said, Malaysia's rice farmers were packing up and leaving for factory jobs in Pinang. "Phantom farmers," he called them: they had already walked away, he said, from about half the country's paddy land.

Yet Luk Keng *did* shock me. Here, in terrace amphitheaters, was an example of the most perfect fusion I know of nature and culture; here, bone and rock are more alike than different, and the earth's stability becomes our own. A few miles away in Hong Kong, meanwhile, there were plenty of people enlightened enough to fight to save old neighborhoods and to preserve the colony's remarkable set of wilderness parks. Yet none of them seemed to mind the loss of the last paddies; on the contrary, people seemed to assume that such a loss was inevitable and even welcome.

I went home thinking that I had seen two things of beauty in Hong Kong. One was those terraces; the other was the hats worn by the Hakka women. And I think now of the Muskogee leader I know who recently brought a pair of ballsticks to a classroom at the university where I teach. I asked him why those handmade sticks, of hickory, were the only beautiful things in the room—why the chairs and tables and windows were so utterly devoid of beauty. He said that he understood me but that I was using the wrong words. What the ballsticks had, he said, was spirit, and he meant this very literally: the spirit of the hickory, preserved as he shaped the wood from its original form.

A year later I tried China again. This time I made it without incident to Kunming, the capital of Yunnan, which had been my destination in the previous, troubled year. A few days later four of us set out: me, a driver, a Chinese forester, and an American economist working in Beijing. Our destination was the remote county of Zhenxiong. There had been a lot of rain, and the roads, unpaved, were slick with mud. We overnighted along the way, and the next day the driver, in hopes of getting to the Zhenxiong guesthouse before dark, went as fast as he dared.

The deserted road led through country so remote and mountainous that, with the exception of its narrow floodplains, it has only been brought under cultivation in the last fifty years or so. Some of this new land is reasonably flat, atop plateaus. But Zhenxiong is underlaid by limestone, and farmers lucky enough to have such summits must nonetheless work around residual limestone blocks scattered through their fields as thickly as tank traps. The chief crop on such land is potatoes, grown often in sinkholes cultivated to their umbilical drains.

Over the less fortunate but more common sloping countryside one might expect rice, but though the slopes are terraced they are instead planted to wheat followed by corn, with tobacco on the side. Rice could be grown in abundance if the terraces were irrigated, but they are not, chiefly because there is enough precipitation here for reasonable yields of those alternative crops.

For mile after mile there were no other motor vehicles, and we went so fast that I got no more than a flashing picture of a countryside dark with young corn and equally dark houses. The houses were of unmortared and untreated limestone blocks that weathered into a beautiful and an almost basaltic blackness. Everywhere they were built to a standard plan: a single story, with a pitched roof and a rectangular floorplan that opened to a courtyard on the sunny south. The roofs were of thatch, darkened by unvented coal smoke to a hue as deep as the weathered stone walls. Often the houses stood next to clay barns, used for drying tobacco.

It took a day or so to arrange a visit from Zhenxiong town back to Hengdi, a village that lay perhaps an hour's drive over increasingly mucky roads. There were no public buses here—not even the hand tractors that, hitched to a passenger-carrying cart, go banging along the roads of rural China. Instead we passed young men walking under huge loads of unthreshed wheat; they carried portable chairs with them—poles with a seat on which they could lean back to rest. Other villagers had already done their threshing, and piles of wheat straw were heaped outside their dark limestone houses. The grain had already been milled, and now, as long noodles, it hung outside like laundry drying in the warm sunshine.

It was the strangest sensation, sitting in the jeep and seeing these things: I felt that I was looking straight through the frame of an eighteenth-century European landscape painting. I'm sure there were plenty of sounds out there, but they weren't the sounds I live with, which are overwhelmingly mechanical or electrical. They were the sounds Constable had heard generations ago, sounds the farmers of Luk Keng had heard.

Two black sows and their litters of white piglets meandered down Hengdi's muddy main street. There were single-story shops with a spartan selection of goods and very few customers. The town's one substantial building was a two-story brick structure that had a facing of yellow-painted plaster and, on the pediment of a classical porch, a quotation from Chairman Mao.

Luckily the officials of Hengdi spoke no English, and I, unlike my companions, spoke no Chinese, so while they were courtesy-bound to maintain a conversation I was allowed to drift like an idiot to the edge of the village. And at that moment I had the strangest feeling that rays of light were stretching here from Beijing. Not just from Beijing, but from the Temple of Heaven there.

The Temple of Heaven was where the emperors went to ensure a good crop season, and I suppose they might once in the centuries have thought of this place, or at least of the Yunnan Province of which it is a tiny part. But that's sophistry: the real connection between Hengdi and the Temple of Heaven lies in the geometry of the temple's plaza, which is rimmed with a square wall and then flagged with stones rising at the center in the set of thin circular platforms on whose bull's-eye sits the temple itself, tiled to look like it's roofed in bamboo. Atop its ornate mass an old billboard announces that this is, indeed, the Temple of Heaven. Can a more superfluous sign be imagined? Can anyone ever have read this sign who did not already know what the building was?

But come back to the plaza. Other walled curves come to mind, like Bernini's colonnade in Rome, the one embracing the piazza in front of St. Peter's. But the plaza in Beijing is no social space, no place for a shepherd's flock. This is a place where geometry symbolizes the Chinese world, where the capital stands at the center of creation and reaches outward through an infinite number of rays to the rest of the world. One of those rays came straight to Hengdi, which was suddenly transformed from the remotest and poorest of settlements to a landscape with the purity of an idea.

The next day my companions were busy with official conversations, and the Zhenxiong magistrate took pity on me and provided a jeep for a quick trip some fifteen miles north of town to a feature I had spotted on a large-scale map: a good-sized river that simply stopped at a mountain where, I suspected, there must be a huge sinkhole.

The driver took me north over a summit covered with small white hydrangeas; we descended to the paddy-filled valley of the White Water River. It turned out to be a good-sized stream that ran for perhaps ten miles through a broad paddy-filled valley. Then the river headed straight for a hillside, where it did indeed disappear into the huge sinkhole called Falling Water Cave. The mouth of the cave was perhaps a hundred feet wide and half that high; the cliff behind it rose a hundred feet more before breaking away to a gentler slope. The water, I was told, emerged some dozen miles downstream; some local boys had dared to swim it.

Should I be embarrassed to admit that I thought to myself that it would be a fine place for a luxury hotel, if only the logistics weren't so difficult? I certainly said no such thing the next day, when I had a brief meeting with the Zhenxiong magistrate. It was in a big room in the guesthouse. A dozen aides scattered uncomfortably around the overlarge perimeter; they all held clipboards and stood ready to provide details.

The magistrate was a vigorous man with a Russian degree in chemical engineering. He explained that Zhenxiong County's number one priority was expansion of the traditional silkworm business. The silk factory here in Zhenxiong Town, he said, was working well below capacity; the solution was to get more peasants growing silkworms and to introduce silkworm nurseries and a big-leaf variety of mulberry. Meanwhile, he wanted to increase corn and wheat production, chiefly by applying lime to the fields. (Liming the fields may sound bizarre in this land of limestone, but so much coal is burned that the rains acidify the soil.) He was keen on improved pigs, especially since nearly every one of the county's two hundred thousand farming households already has a pig. And he wanted forestry: he explained that a third of the county had been forested in 1949 but that by 1974 forest cover had fallen to 4 percent. Now it was back to 10 percent, and he wanted that number to grow by 1 percent annually. Foreign aid would help, but he would continue the reforestation work with or without it: "We've got to do it," he said.

He finished and waited for my comments. I think now of all the things I might have said. I might have spoken about Luk Keng and how the last terraces were fading from Hong Kong. I might have told the magistrate about the phantom farmers of Malaysia, too. I might have spoken about the kinds of farming that were replacing them: you only have to travel for two hours from Pinang to see the Muda Scheme, up near Aloh Setar. It's Malaysia's equivalent of California's San Joaquin Valley: everything is straight, from the roads to the edges of the paddy fields and the ditches carrying irrigation water. Everything is on the grand scale, from the quarter-million irrigated acres of the Scheme as a whole to the individual paddies, each one covering thirty to fifty acres.

I might have generalized and said that I saw two trends sweeping across the Asian countryside. One was that the prime farmlands of Asia—the great plains of the Punjab, of the Ganges, of the Yellow River; the valleys of the Irrawaddy, the Chao Phraya, the Mekong—these prime farmlands were going to look more and more like American farms. They would become square, huge, nearly monocropped, and so heavily treated with chemicals that they would stink throughout the growing season. The traditional Asian village in such places would gradually be replaced by scattered houses built by farmers living on the increasingly large and consolidated blocks of land they would cultivate; most of the villagers, whose lives had been these fields, would drain away (I like the hydraulic metaphor) to the great reservoirs that we call cities.

At the same time, I might have said, the Luk Kengs of Asia would disappear: there would be phantom farmers everywhere, as steeply terraced or particularly remote lands were gradually abandoned to scrub and secondary forest. A friend of mine calls it "social fallow" when he describes how the Berbers of Morocco occasionally abandon their terraced Atlas retreats for the charms of Casablanca.

The magistrate, a practical man by any standard, would have been puzzled. "So what?" he might well have asked. What's wrong with these things? Intensification is just what we want, and the retirement of unneeded and economically marginal land is perfectly reasonable.

And then what would I have said? I would have had to go back to Sir Francis Bacon, that trumpeter of a new world. Bacon's language is archaic and difficult even for English-speakers today, but it remains too important for us to ignore: "The end of our foundation," Bacon had written, "is the knowledge of causes and secret motions of things; and the enlarging of the bounds of human empire, to the effecting of all things possible." Indeed.

The knowledge Bacon sought has very nearly transformed the world. In the ruins of scholasticism Bacon had urged us to "reject vain speculations, and whatsoever is empty and void, and to preserve and augment whatsoever is solid and fruitful." We Westerners had listened to him, and a line of intellectual descent extended from him to the Enlightenment, to the utilitarians, and in our own time to the faceless experts upon whom we depend for nearly all things—things whose workings we no longer understand. In the name of knowledge "solid and fruitful" we now have foresters who grow trees like cabbages, orchardists whose citrus groves look like golf-course turf, and horticulturalists who under a chemical cloud draw breath enough yet to brag about the wonders of modern agriculture.

I might have told the magistrate that in the West the weakness of the Baconian philosophy was well understood. I could have pointed to the great Victorian critics, among them Matthew Arnold and John Henry Newman. Cardinal Newman had been no foolishly categorical enemy of Bacon. He had written that the "mission" of Bacon's philosophy "was the increase of physical enjoyment and social comfort," and he conceded without argument our debt to this man and his "method whereby bodily discomforts and temporal wants are to be most effectually removed from the greatest number . . . [while] the gifts of nature . . . [are] brought even to our doors." Yet Newman would also go on to say that in seeking "the increase of physical enjoyment and social comfort" Bacon had "aimed low," and when Newman wrote that the philosopher had "fulfilled his conception and his design" he chose his words carefully. This fulfillment, Newman had written, had been done "most wonderfully, most awfully." His language is archaic, but his thought is modern.

I might have invoked Arnold, remote as he now seems, though to me yet admirable. Arnold, too, had been prepared to concede much to Bacon: "How necessary," Arnold would write, "is the present great movement towards wealth and industrialism, in order to lay broad foundations of material well-being for the society of the future." Yet what a colossal error it was, Arnold went on, to imagine that such progress was sufficient to produce a great society. "Never," Arnold wrote, "did people believe anything more firmly than nine Englishmen out of ten at the present day believe that our greatness and welfare are proved by our being so very rich." It was not so, Arnold argued: the England of his day would, a hundred years in the future, "excite the love, interest, and admiration of mankind" far less than the England of Elizabeth, "when our coal, and our industrial operations depending on coal, were very little developed." On that point, I fear, Arnold has been proven wrong; we have become very nearly the Philistines he dreaded. Is it not true today, as in Arnold's day, that "faith in machinery is our besetting danger," for we treat it "as if it had a value in and for itself." Indeed we do, and indeed we may still ask with Arnold what man is to do, "after he has made himself perfectly comfortable."

I might have told the magistrate how these discontents had expressed themselves, not only in the religious faith of Newman and in Arnold's devotion to his own sense of culture, but also in the romantic conception of the natural world as a place whose value far transcended its worth as a storehouse of resources. That would have brought me, I suppose, to Wordsworth and a Nature that is mankind's

> best and purest friend; from her receives
> That energy by which he seeks the truth,
> From her that happy stillness of the mind
> Which fits him to receive it when unsought.

From lines such as these, I might have said, the wilderness preservation movement had been born: from lines such as these an American Congress almost against its considered judgment had been led to create a Yellowstone Park, a Yosemite, and dozens more. Lines such as these, I might have said, had made it possible for some governments to ban outdoor advertising and to prohibit land uses that, though profitable, spoiled the beauty of the countryside. Lines such as these had inspired planners and designers from the days of Ebenezer Howard and his garden cities to Frank Lloyd Wright and his antiurban utopia, Broadacre. True, such plans had rarely been implemented, but the same romantic inspiration had led hundreds of stockbrokers to buy New England farms and had led literally millions of Americans to buy suburban homes. Every advertising agency on Madison Avenue knew the power of appeals to Nature.

I might have turned to Asia and said that the Baconian philosophy had taken deep root there through the British administrators who, early in the nineteenth century, had consciously made India a laboratory for experimentation with utilitarian principles. English had been introduced as a medium of instruction, and with it a whole intellectual universe had been transplanted: engineers would soon be trained on the banks of the Ganges, and they would be followed by agronomists and social planners. None of these institutions disappeared with the end of the Raj; indeed, they would be coupled to and reinforced by new international organizations. We think here chiefly of the World Bank, but the first of these organizations was the United Nations Food and Agriculture Organization, which was created even before the British left India. A conference had been held in 1943 to organize the FAO, and the resolution passed at its conclusion called for "the uninterrupted development and most advantageous use of agricultural and other material resources." The phrase sounds trite and worn to us now, but that is so only because it is so perfectly Baconian in content, so much a part of what has become our mode of thinking.

The magistrate might well have said that China had never been colonized, but I then would have asked him what air he had breathed in Moscow. Where had Chinese Communism come from, if not from a German intellectual who lived in the British Museum and was buried only a few miles from it now? What was the great tradition of scientific socialism if not the application of Bacon's rationality to the entire domain of social organization and the relations of nature and society?

What Asia needed was an equivalent to the great Victorian critics. Perhaps that equivalent might be found in such traditional beliefs as Taoism or the geomancy still practiced in Hong Kong. Perhaps, alternatively, China's great traditions of landscape painting could be considered not only as the stuff of high culture but also as an inspiration for contemporary land-use planning. No need for Wordsworth here: every magistrate in China needed only to be taken out to the Ming Tombs, where—particularly in the ruined ones, not those that have been restored—one might be taught a lesson on the grandest scale about form and siting. Burial mounds, forests, enclosing walls, and gates: all come together in these tombs to create a symbolic cosmic axis upon which one can stand and feel the oneness of the earth.

What would be the result of such a cultural reformation? The magistrate of Zhenxiong might then work to preserve the character of his county's traditional landscape. He might seek to control urban encroachments on the countryside, might control the use of materials other than limestone and perhaps mud brick in Zhenxiong's villages, might insure that landscape architects were involved in plans for new roads and power lines. He would wonder when the infrastructure would support tourism, wonder when he could begin taxing tourists and plowing the revenue back to subsidize traditional practices.

Of course I said none of this. I said not a word about Sir Francis Bacon or his critics. Not a word about efforts to preserve the aesthetic qualities of the Western countryside, or about Western ideas taking root in Asia. Not a word about the need for a reaction to those ideas, or about the techniques the Chinese might use to preserve their own countryside. Not a word, I say: not me. Whatever I did say I have forgotten, and I am sure that everyone else in that room has too. Looking back, I am inclined to think that we not only stand on the shoulders of our intellectual ancestors but go where they would take us.

THE SPIRIT OF THE PLACE

I THINK BACK NOW TO THAT MUSKOGEE LEADER and his inspirited ballsticks. Whatever the difficulties we might have in understanding the language of Francis Bacon, I think we have no trouble with the fundamental concepts of his philosophy. Our real problem—I speak chiefly of Westerners now—lies on the other side, lies in understanding the non-Western world and the landscapes created by non-Western peoples. I've already pointed to the special quality of those places: once as I stood tiptoe between the amphitheaters of Luk Keng, again as I strolled to the edge of Hengdi and felt those rays from Beijing, a third time in describing the power of the Ming Tombs. Yet it is by no means easy to say precisely what it is that I'm talking about.

I do know that I first felt it in 1981 at a place called Ramappa, or sometimes Palampet, from a nearby village of that name. This was in southern India, at the eastern edge of the Telangana Plateau. I was with a group of irrigation engineers, and we were not more than a few miles south of the Godavary River, across which begin the rough and still wild mountains in which Kipling a century ago set his Mowgli stories. The engineers took me to a medieval reservoir called Ramappa Tank. (That use of the word *tank*, which at first sounds so odd to Americans, is straightforward, for the word is of Indian ori-

gin and simply means reservoir.) We toured the five thousand
acres of paddy it irrigates. The engineers took me also without
warning to a temple, very nearly in ruins, that lay near the
dam. Its stone floor, as well as its roof-supporting columns,
were broken by earth subsidence, and the whole structure
seemed supported mostly by concrete blocks, which had been
mortared into crude pillars sometime in the 1920s.

Perhaps it was the shiny basaltic Nandi that first caught my
eye; it seemed almost alive, this bull waiting patiently outside
the temple for its rider Lord Shiva to step outside. Perhaps it
was the carefully carved friezes, with I suppose hundreds of
tail-in-trunk elephants marching right to left. I can't be more
specific; all I know is that I knew I wanted to come back to
this place, alone.

It took me a decade to get back. Finally, in 1991, I managed
to fly to Hyderabad, rent a car, and drive out the hundred
or so arid, rocky, and sporadically paddy-brightened miles to
Warangal, the nearest town. The next day I drove thirty miles
farther, toward the wild Godavary. Before getting to the river,
I turned off the lonely highway at a junction that was being
used for a weekly market. I happened to come on the right
day, and hundreds of pedestrians, who had already walked
miles to get here, were now milling past piles of foodstuffs
and flamboyantly bright cosmetic powders. There were long
lines of tethered bullocks, their horns painted bright blue;
there were desperately bleating kids being dragged off from
mothers they seemed to know they would never see again.

A one-lane road branched off to the left. I took it and passed
along the base of a long, flat-topped ridge, forested in young
teak. Part of the ridge had been breached by natural forces,
and it was in this breach that the long-vanished Kakatiya kings
had built Ramappa.

When the dynasty fell the dam had failed or been destroyed, and Ramappa remained empty until it was restored
early in the twentieth century by a British engineer working
for the nizam of Hyderabad, in whose dominions Ramappa lay.
Hence the more-or-less modern sluice gates at both ends of
the dam. Hence, too, the sign explaining that the reservoir had

been built originally in 1213, that it had been reconstructed in 1919, that it had a "waterspread" of nine square kilometers, and that it irrigated 4,860 acres.

A mile before the dam I drove through Palampet, a village with a population of perhaps five hundred people. They were all living in one-story buildings, generally poor-looking, though the village lanes did have power lines strung on concrete poles. The lanes headed straight to the surrounding fields, which were dry and in stubble when I saw them; each morning, however, lines of milking buffaloes were led to those fields for grazing; in the evening they came back to enclosures in the village.

Once there had been money in Palampet. You could see it from the large but abandoned houses behind now-collapsed stone walls. The nearby forests still sheltered the militant radicals who a generation earlier had butchered many of the wealthiest local landowners. The rest had got the message, and now there was only a vestige of the old contrast beween rich and poor. It was most evident in the village shopkeepers, who were dressed in spotlessly white cotton shirts and skirts and who stood next to massive grain-measuring scales. Behind the scales were tiny rooms jammed floor to ceiling with baskets of tomatoes and green chillies, onions and eggs. An impressive inventory for a village as poor as this? Yes, but this was January, on the eve of a harvest festival when people would buy luxury foods even if they had almost no money. I would have liked to ask these merchants if they feared night visitors, but it didn't seem tactful.

I continued on toward the dam, where I would stay overnight, and on the way I realized there were a dozen temples here, most of them more completely ruined than the main temple, to which the engineers had taken me a decade before. Roofs had collapsed, walls were penetrated by roots, inner sanctums were filled with litter, and phallic symbols of Lord Shiva had been knocked over. Even so, the temples were powerful buildings, so massive that from some angles they appeared to be natural outcrops of massive and horizontally bedded rock. In the interval since my first visit the Archaeological Survey of India had begun reconstructing some of the structures. Unfortunately, to my taste, the work had brought with it fencing, turf, and flowers, along with pioneer guides and hawkers. Still, compared to India's really famous temples, the nuisance was minimal: I could be alone merely by sitting decerebrate for five minutes and ignoring every plea.

And so here I was, back in the main temple, alone. Perhaps the building was fifty feet square, but it had no walls, had not been built with walls. There was only a floor, much disrupted by subsidence, and a heavy roof supported by a set of intricate columns. Many of them were broken, but they were still standing in a gridded array. The effect was to create two horizontal planes, with me sandwiched between.

Most of the columns were of light-colored rock, carved into a complex shape so that they looked like sections of stacked rectangular blocks, octagons, and discs. But in the center of the temple were four shiny black columns, even more elaborately carved and from a kind of rock apparently transported hundreds of miles to the site. These four columns surrounded a patch of floor in the center of the temple that was occupied by a massive circular stone, a very low platform perhaps ten feet in diameter and once used for ritual dancing.

This circular platform faced a doorway into a small room, closed most of the time. Though this room was the functional center of the temple, dedicated to Lord Shiva, it was visually unimportant: the focal point of the temple was that round stone surrounded by the four black columns. The circle defined a point in the horizontal plane already bounded massively by floor and ceiling, and the power of this bounded point just *radiated*, so that sitting in the temple I felt drawn or pulled to the surrounding countryside, and not just in one direction but to every point of the compass.

I walked to the edge of the temple, which is heavily decorated not only with elephants but with sinuous and half-naked female figures. Normally they might be described as mildly erotic, but looking up at them I felt no eroticism at all. Instead

I heard silent words: "No, not sexual experience," the figures seemed to say: "but this: the greater self you know only through sexuality."

Now I realize that I am speaking here of architecture rather than of landscape; the same charge might have been leveled against me a chapter ago when I mentioned the Temple of Heaven and the Ming Tombs. But I would argue that the architects of all these places were consciously striving for an effect and that the effect they wanted was to make us understand our place in the cosmos. In a sense I suppose they are no different from the masons who built Chartres, but the European cathedral builder wanted to lift us above the corporeal world. The Asian architect, it seems to me, wanted us to be absorbed in the world we already know, and he wanted this precisely because he himself was so absorbed.

We can point to a similar mysticism in the West, not least among the Romantic poets and their literary descendants. But this kind of absorption in place is so completely foreign to the modern outlook and to the spirit of economic development that I want to dwell on it further. I want to see if we can get any closer to a true understanding of the aesthetic quality of the Asian landscape whose power is so strong. I want to dwell on it further because it is those landscapes I want to preserve, not merely the temples that teach us about our place in them. Soon enough we shall come to the ideas with which we are so much more comfortable, the ideas that I have labeled as the culture of development.

But this is a case of "easier said than done," for though there are plenty of places in most Asian countries where Western

---

The interior of the main temple at Palampet or Ramappa, near Warangal in Andhra Pradesh. The shrine lies just off the sketch to the right and is fronted by four black columns, two of which are shown, along with a hint of the stone disc that forms the temple floor in front of the shrine. The ceiling and floor, together with the central disc, place the visitor at the center of a plane so massive that it makes visitors sense their lives not in opposition to physical reality but in and part of it.

influences are hardly visible at first glance, there are very few, I've found, where a visitor can stand still and feel Asia as it was before the Western wind began to blow.

I remember one brave effort of mine to find such a place. Forty years ago an Indian village called Rani Kheri was studied very nearly to death by Oscar Lewis. Not yet famous for his Hobbesian studies of Latin American poverty, Lewis was then working for the Ford Foundation, which was supporting nearly a hundred expatriates, who were mostly working on rural development in the country. With commendable acumen the Foundation decided that, since it was working to change half a million Indian villages, there might be a modicum of wisdom in having an anthropologist explore how at least one Indian village worked. Good thinking! Hence Oscar Lewis and *Village Life in North India.*

The Rani Kheri that Lewis described lay fifteen miles west of Delhi and two miles off the Rohtak Road. It was approached by a cart track motorable during dry weather, and it was surrounded by several hundred acres of fields. The two crop seasons were the summer, with sorghum and millet, and the winter, with barley and wheat. During the winter, Lewis wrote, farmers depended on canal water and a dozen Persian wheels, those elegant old wooden machines, with a bullock yoked to a wheel mounted like a little merry-go-round. Gear teeth on that wheel mesh with those on another wheel set vertically, and over that second wheel a chain of buckets is draped to hang into the pool below.

The villagers, Lewis continued, were dominated by the famous farming caste known as the Jats, who worked so hard and long that they were reputed by folklore to give their children toy plows. The wealthier Jats lived in substantial brick houses, with decorated doorways opening onto the village's unplanned lanes and revealing to passersby courtyards rimmed with rooms on three sides. Most of the villagers lived in much simpler structures: mud-brick rooms, typically without ventilation. They shared these houses year-round with their livestock, whose dung was faithfully collected and made into discus-shaped patties kept in neat stacks shaped like pup tents. There was not a single commercial establishment in the village, Lewis wrote, not a single motor vehicle, and visitors were still rare enough that they attracted a crowd of children.

Not bad, I thought: it might do as one approximation of timeless India. I was dead wrong, and readers will guess why as soon as I say that Delhi today has at least eight million people. Why I wasn't smarter I cannot say. Perhaps because a large-scale map published by the Survey of India in 1970 showed on the western side of the Capital District a large agricultural swath starting some ten miles west of the city center and extending to the Haryana State border, something less than ten miles farther west. At fifteen or so miles from the city center, in other words, Rani Kheri was shown surrounded by fields, just as Lewis described it. The only apparent difference between the village of Lewis's text and the village shown on the Survey's map was that Lewis's old cart track had been replaced by a straight road that started at the main Rohtak Road and headed north, passing a few hundred yards to the east of Rani Kheri.

But 1970 is far away, and I went out along a Rohtak Road lined at first with three-story apartments, oil-storage tanks, and prohibited military areas. By the Rani Kheri turnoff, the buildings had declined to a single story with lots of roadside trees, but the feel remained urban. The old cart track to Rani Kheri was indeed abandoned, but the new road was now dotted with brick walls for residential compounds. Piles of brick awaited laying on staked-out lots.

So much for fields! Here, not two hundred yards from Rani Kheri, were two real estate offices. Their signs, in English, said Royal Properties, telephone number 5471771, and Kanshik Properties, with plots for sale as well as flats and something called "farm houses"—presumably houses for the hobby farms that, new to India, have recently begun appearing around Delhi.

At the spot where the new road comes closest to Rani Kheri I found a bus stop, end of the line for Route 921 of the Delhi Municipal Bus Corporation. Along the link road to the village itself there were a dozen or more shops, some renting videos, others selling ready-made clothes. There were grocers with potatoes and tomatoes and onions, with rice and bread and biscuits, eggs, coolers for soft drinks, jars of small candies, pens and paper, lightbulbs, disinfectant, and infant cereal. There was the Deep Chand Memorial Public School (its perplexing motto: Education Is Life), and there was a doctor. None of this, of course, was in Lewis's account.

The old Jat houses that Lewis describes still stood, but only a very few mud-brick buildings were left, and even the pup tents of dung were now often clad in black plastic sheeting. There were plenty of big new houses, too. Turned ostentatiously outward, they boasted large plastic water tanks on their third-story roofs, which also had TV antennas. (By now, I am sure, someone has a satellite dish to pull in Hong Kong's Star network.) The streets they fronted still twisted confusingly, but they were paved with concrete gutters and gratings; they were lit with fluorescent tubes; there were even motor vehicles in the village now—not only heavy trucks but Indian-made Suzukis. Singly or in small groups, old men sat around hookahs, as Lewis had said they did, but as in Hong Kong's Luk Keng village during working hours, there were few young men.

I walked through the village several times and then out into the surviving fields. It was winter the first time I did this, and the fields were mostly in wheat, but I know from another visit in summer that fodder crops have replaced sorghum: the villagers have begun selling milk to the Delhi market. Village agriculture has become a business, in other words, rather than a subsistence activity. And the farmers are rich enough to have replaced their Persian wheels with motor-driven pumps.

Rani Kheri, in short, is now almost a garden suburb of Delhi. On the way back to the city I measured some distances and found that the village was separated from urban Delhi by no more than a one-mile-wide greenbelt, already under attack by land developers. So much for one doomed attempt of mine to find pristine India. I tried again, this time some 1,200 miles to the south. Leaving the penumbra of the national capital and the national heartland of the Ganges plains, I flew two hours to

Madras and drove southwards through the intensely cultivated fringe of the southeastern coast. Not Telangana this: the peninsular rim is densely settled, intensely cultivated. And here, during the First World War, Gilbert Slater, India's first professor of rural economy, had undertaken some pioneering studies of Indian villages. One of the places he studied was a village called Eruvellipet. One of his students came from this place and is even given credit in Slater's *Some South Indian Villages*.

Slater talks there about going by train south from Madras to Villupuram, which lies west of Pondicherry. For the last eight miles of his trip he travels by bicycle and—when that fails— by bullock cart. Eruvellipet, he says, lies on the highway south to Madurai, and the road is lined with trees whose products are auctioned to the villagers. On the lefthand side of the road, as one enters from the north, there is the quarter of the untouchables, with unplanned paths wandering between circular mud huts under thatch roofs. On the righthand side of the road is the higher-caste village, with two good parallel roads turning off the highway at right angles and forming a rectangular block, with the highway at one narrow end and a connecting street at the other. The houses on this side of the highway are rectangular, with courtyards and a characteristic recess in the frontage wall, a recess that forms a shady platform on which much of Indian domestic life transpires. Slater talks of the village lands, of irrigation and the rice economy, and of the village's low labor productivity. India, he says in one telling sentence, is "a very rich country, inhabited by very poor people."

I went to take a look. This was January, and the rice harvest was in full swing, with women cutting the grain with sickles and, under headloads, marching off to threshing grounds. It was a good harvest, and the people at the threshing grounds were happy. Lifting handfuls of the unthreshed stalks, men swung them like an axe against a cylindrical stone that looked like an elephant's foot. The grain flew in clouds and was raked by women into perfectly circular piles perhaps twelve feet across and—as high as unhusked rice will stack—five feet tall. At one threshing ground I counted six such piles, along with much larger piles of straw. Straight Brueghel, I thought, despite the noise coming from a radio whose speaker could not accommodate the power forced through it.

Long stretches of road were bordered by fields of stubble and by blanket-sized patches of threshed grain, neatly spread to dry and carefully watched by women and children. The rice when dry would be bagged in jute sacks weighing 220 pounds when filled—the hundred kilograms that make the measure called a metric quintal. The straw, perhaps mounded next to a big mango tree, would be tightly tied with a net so that the top of the stack was perfectly domed. Against one such stack there leaned a bamboo ladder with a dozen mortised rungs fitted without a single nail.

Other farmers were further ahead in the annual crop cycle. They had already transplanted the next crop's seedlings into wet paddies, the moisture evaporating into a sweating sky. That meant irrigation, and at one point I stopped at a large open well, almost like a small flooded quarry.

The surrounding fields were being irrigated by a man and

two bullocks. They pulled a rope strung over a pulley that was mounted between two posts inclined over the water; an exotic copper bucket, with a long fabric spout attached to its base like an elephant's trunk, hung from the other end of the rope. The animals took ten steps forward to lift the bucket and ten backward to let it return to the water. The man who drove them also controlled a second rope that let the "trunk" down when the bucket came to the top of the well: perhaps ten gallons of water gushed out into the head of a small channel leading to the rice paddies. It was a beautifully coordinated operation, for the man sat down on the main rope just as the bullocks reached the forward position; his movement gave the rope a tug, made the bucket swing a little bit so it would empty entirely through the trunk. For some minutes I stood listening to the music of the pulley, of the gushing, of the man grunting at the bullocks, of the gallon or so of water that splashed back into the well at each cycle.

When I got to Villupuram, the town where Slater had got off the train from Madras, an old steam locomotive sat fired up

Two images of rice. Both were taken near Tirukkalikudrum, which is south of Madras and just inland from Mamallapuram, but both might as well have come from almost anywhere along the southeast coast of India, where moisture and heat favor this grain over all others. Tractors are still rare here and combines are unknown, but mechanical threshers are gradually replacing manual threshing floors like this one.

on a siding. I followed Slater's directions onto the Madras-Madurai highway, and headed south to the South Pennar River, where his bicycle had bogged down in deep sand. There was a good bridge now, and I drove across.

A few miles later I came to a village. Was it Eruvellipet? I asked several people, but my pronunciation was so wretched that they did not understand what I wanted. Certainly the streets didn't conform to Slater's description, but perhaps things had changed. I turned down one of the few lanes not piled with mountains of rice straw. It was straight, unpaved, and lined with rectangular, good-sized homes of mud and thatch. Electricity went into most of them; there were streetlights; at one point two men came rumbling past me on a throaty Indian Triumph motorcycle. And that was not all: there were mechanical rice threshers at work—three or four men and a Caterpillar-yellow mobile machine, perhaps six feet high by twelve feet long. The men removed its wheels and put it on the ground, where the machine ate armloads of grain from a nearby stack. A pile of threshed but unhusked rice slowly grew. When they were done, the men levered the machine off the ground, put its wheels back on, and headed for a new customer.

But was it Eruvellipet? The question was settled when I drove a few miles farther down the highway and found a highway sign: Iruvelpattu. Obviously *this* was the place, differently transliterated. And, just as Slater had written, the village straddled the road, with huts on one side and solid houses on the other. I hesitated to walk through the untouchable quarter: even in the better parts of an Indian village I am always slightly uncomfortable, not because the villagers are hostile—they never are, in my experience—but because I fear that I am slumming. Still, it was plain from a distance that the untouchables' houses were hidden in compounds rimmed with six-foot gates of roughly woven twigs.

The upper-caste village, on the other hand, was organized around the very same block of which Slater had written: there had been no expansion in seventy-five years—hardly any visible change except for concrete power poles with fluorescent tubes. Here were the lane-fronting walls of mud brick, each house presenting to the street not only a doorway but a built-in bench perhaps a foot and a half high, four or five feet deep, and shaded by the roof thatching. On one such platform a woman with elegant earrings and a nose plug was grinding a poppy-yellow bean paste in a stone mortar and pestle. In Madras I had seen electric grinders available for about a hundred U.S. dollars; here in Eruvellipet a hundred dollars is a fortune, and the woman pulled the pestle round and round with that immemorial sound of stone rolling on stone. Another porch was occupied by two goats; a third, by the man of the house and his toddler son.

The real shock lay around the corner, on the more southerly of the two main streets. Here was a stretch of at least 150 feet bordered by an iron fence. At the center of that span was a gate and a thatched-over walkway leading perhaps forty feet to a two-story white house. Its roof line was trimmed with a parapet, and its entrance porch was supported by massive wooden columns that were solid, darkly handsome, and artistically tapered from a diameter of perhaps eighteen inches at the base.

Bean-paste preparation at Eruvellipet. The work is being done on a front porch, not six feet from a main village lane, and the stone produces a satisfying, rolling sound. At times the work must be numbingly tedious, so contemplating it we are left profoundly ambivalent.

What was such a mansion doing here? There was a gate-keeper who spoke no English. He let me pass, accompanied me to the columned porch, and sat me down. I admired the columns and stared at five framed photographs hanging over the doorway and showing proudly turbaned men.

The owner came out: Mr. Appaji, with more flesh than any of the villagers around the corner, lighter in skin color, and dressed in immaculate white. A 1953 graduate of Loyola College in Madras, he explained that the center photograph—the most regal of the lot—was his grandfather, who had built this house in 1901 and who had owned a thousand acres spread over four or five villages.

Land-reform laws in recent decades had come down hard on Mr. Appaji: today he owned only a hundred acres. Sixty of those were irrigated with a tube well, which had replaced the manual devices of his grandfather's time. Forty were unirrigated, though unirrigated land was of such comparatively low value that when I initially asked how much land he owned Mr. Appaji simply said "seventy acres," as though forty unirrigated acres were worth ten irrigated ones.

Almost every Indian knows the word *benami:* it describes the nominal land transactions by which many, if not most, large ownerships have been divided among family members and friends so that the legal land ceilings are evaded. Certainly the inadequacy of India's land reform greatly exercised the World Bank's Wolf Ladejinsky. He was the man who had shaped the land reform of post–World War II Japan. In the 1970s he was working in India for the World Bank, and he is said to have once tried to explain the importance of genuine land reform to Indira Gandhi—and never to have tried *that* again.

So, despite land reform, Mr. Appaji's house was very well maintained, and he had plenty of servants. There was little Western furniture, other than the porch chairs on which we sat, but Mr. Appaji had a telephone and a television. The most spectacular thing he had, I thought, was a spotlessly clean stable, with fifteen milking buffaloes and cows standing on pavement and shaded by tile-roofed mangers. The animals and their calves ate green fodder from neat bunkers; there was a concrete watering trough filled by a tap. I have never seen such facilities in India except at experiment stations, and I was reminded of the contrast between this setup and the Lahore dairies that a young and thoroughly disgusted Rudyard Kipling had once described.

At first I thought that Slater had been blind to miss the Appaji household, but I went back and found that the mistake was mine: Slater had indeed seen the Appaji house. He writes, unmistakably, that there is one house in the village that is "imposing, with two stories, a flat roof, a covered approach, ornamental iron gates and pillars adorned with paintings." He further notes without comment that the average village landholder owns one acre but that the largest landholder in the village owns six hundred. And he says that the large landholders of the village are all members of the Reddy caste, identifiable by their lighter skin color. When I asked Mr. Appaji if he knew of a Mr. E. V. Sundaram Reddy—Slater's student—he said that he did indeed. Reddy was now dead, Mr. Appaji said, but he had been a prominent lawyer, and a relative.

Surely I should have been able to do something with Eruvellipet, find here some opening into the pristine countryside I wanted. Granted, pristine India was not an India with telephones and straight village lanes; there is even a question of whether the pattern of one large landowner and many small ones is a consequence of British rearrangements. But there was plenty here to work with, plenty to prod a visitor into seeing India as it had been.

Yet I was stuck. I had met Mr. Appaji and been treated courteously; I had walked the village block and taken a batch of pictures; I had satisfied myself that much of what Gilbert Slater saw in 1916 I could see in 1991. But I could go no further. There was no place to stay in the village, and the usual idiotic itinerary had me driving miles more that day. I didn't know quite what to do except leave Eruvellipet, which I did with a feeling that this was pretty stupid, walking away from something with potential.

But I had learned long ago that things seem to work out in India, if you relax. As it happened, with the vaguest of plans I went to Bangladesh, where I quit retracing the steps of academics and began visiting the places where writers had lived when they were children. I would visit Narayanganj, which is Dhaka's port city and the place where the young Rumer Godden lived; then I would go fifty miles north to the small town of Kishorganj, home of the youthful Nirad Chaudhuri.

At first things went badly. I was lucky enough to find the old Godden home, heavy with the atmosphere of a ruined mansion. An old and long-unused lawn roller sat in one corner of a big garden; an immense classical facade and its veranda shutters were in poor shape—the garden literally moving upstairs, tendril by tendril. Old armoires were now filled with the files of the government ferry corporation clerks who occupied the building. The building itself was swallowed up in the city of Narayanganj, with a jute mill on the river side and endless concrete blocks on the other. For my purposes, there was nothing.

Nor did I have better luck at Kishorganj. Chaudhuri's *Autobiography of an Unknown Indian* is filled—as are its lengthy sequel and his other works—with a keen astringency, an almost militant rejection of every form of sentiment. Yet he makes an exception for Kishorganj and writes of the boy he was, who walked barefoot along dusty lanes and who felt sorry for people condemned to wear shoes and feel nothing. Kishorganj, moreover, is still a small place, with tin-roofed shacks on either side of a town-dividing creek. But the town no longer has a good neighborhood on one side, a bad on the other. The mat-and-thatch huts in which Chaudhuri lived are gone, and if I understand the town correctly from Chaudhuri's description, the site of Chaudhuri's father's hut is now occupied by some large brick houses, trimmed with wrought iron and barbed wire.

It was about this time that, discouraged by my inability to find a pristine India, I picked up a guidebook called *Buildings of the British Raj in Bangladesh*, written by the archaeologist Nazimuddin Ahmed. In it there is a description of the Silaidaha Kutibari, the home in which the poet Rabindranath Tagore lived as a young man. Ahmed writes that there are "few

places in Bangladesh which can equal Silaidaha in its en-
chanting natural beauty and its unspoiled rural landscape." I
would probably have paid no attention, except Chaudhuri calls
the oceanic Tagore the greatest of all Bengalis. Such praise
from Chaudhuri is almost inconceivable, and it tipped the
scales. I decided to take a look.

Silaidaha is not the easiest trip to make. The nearest town
is Kushtia, and getting that far involves first of all a sixty-mile
drive west from Dhaka through heavily irrigated lowlands to
the Brahmaputra. From there you can choose between a southerly route with a short ferry ride across the Brahmaputra and
then—at least in 1991—an insane drive of infinite duration
over about a hundred miles of road under construction. The
northern route calls for a longer ferry ride across and up the
Brahmaputra, then a drive some sixty miles west to the town
of Pabna, followed by a second but short ferry across the
Ganges.

Pabna is just about the only place to stop for the night along
this second route, and it was a good place for me to look
around. Bangladesh, after all, has such a hopeless reputation:
endless calamities and infinite destitution. But a two hours'
walk there at dusk cured me forever of thinking of the country
as that "international basketcase."

Piles of magenta mustard seed were spread out to dry on
outdoor pavements; later, they were brought to mill rooms
dark with belt-driven machinery expressing an oil that made
my eyes smart. Next door were carpenters, some splitting and
sawing logs, others screwing planks together to form the seats
of cycle rickshaws. There was a concrete-casting works, with
piles of pipe and ornamental screenings and squat toilets that
it had produced. There were shops where men assembled cotton undershirts with treadle sewing machines; others where
the same machines were sewing automobile seatcovers. There
were electricians rewinding electrical motors. There were
merchants selling sandals, and others selling hand tractors.

Off Pabna's main road and in the residential quarters of the
town horticulturalists grew flowers in plots fenced with sharp-
ened bamboo stakes; nearby, there were houses from whose

windows came the sound of the BBC. Young men literally crowded around a big table in the town library, which itself was one of the dozens of mansions abandoned at the partition of India in 1947. Rabindranath Tagore's family, like Nirad Chaudhuri's, had been part of the Hindu elite; indeed, the Tagores had once been among the wealthiest families of Bengal: Silaidaha was only one of their properties when Rabindranath was sent there by his father in the 1880s to be the estate manager. Tagore had spent the better part of twenty years there, and he returned to it to translate into English the poems that, published as *Gitanjali,* won him the Nobel Prize for Literature in 1913.

The Ganges ferry beyond Pabna is a comparatively simple matter: hardly more than an old barge with a strapped-on motor. But the river itself is much reduced from its historic size by the construction upstream in India of the Farakka Barrage, which diverts a large part of the Ganges to another distributary, the Hooghly, which flows past Calcutta. The barge chugs across the reduced Ganges peaceably enough, at least in comparison with the strong flow of the Brahmaputra, and there is a fine view of the nearby and mile-long Hardinge Bridge, which was opened in 1915 and remains the bravest of all the British efforts to lace Bengal with steel.

The first time I came to Kushtia it was in April and by the misbegotten way along the highway under construction. Exhausted, I threw myself on the mercy of the deputy commissioner. He was kind enough to ask in only a slightly patronizing way if he was correct in surmising that I "required a room, a cool room, I believe." He also asked if I required alcohol. (In this teetotal country he was offering vodka, left over from the visit of a Russian diplomat.) The deputy commissioner reached out a languid arm—his own house was not air-conditioned—picked up a phone, and arranged air-conditioned accommodation at the Kushtia District guest house.

I wanted to see Tagore's home as early as possible the next morning, so my driver and I left the guest house at first light, just before six. A baker down the street was furiously kneading dough for his morning customers. With some hesitation we made our way to an unbridged river, whose small amount of water was a trickle in the middle of several hundred yards of sand. The driver was from Dhaka and had not been here before. He was nervous, especially when told by people crossing the river on foot to drive right across. When we approached the water he took on board a guide who could show us where to drive through the axle-deep water.

Now we were on what turned out to be an island, bounded by this sandstream on the west and by the Ganges on the east: ahead, on the island, lay Silaidaha and the Tagore home. From neither this nor my subsequent winter visit, when I stayed on the island itself, do I remember a single other motor vehicle on the island. There were some trucks—even buses. I can see them crossing the sand. But I cannot remember them on the island.

Tagore's house stands some seven or eight brick-paved and single-lane miles beyond the crossing. It is close to the Ganges but as a building is not particularly interesting: wooden, red, with two stories, laid out on a square about forty feet on a side. It has verandas on the upper floor, a hipped roof, and a cupola capped with a steeple. It also has a most peculiar wall: red brick with a white cap that undulates like a snaking jump rope.

I had thought that the house might be locked up or used as a private residence, but I underestimated Tagore's reputation, even in Muslim Bangladesh. In fact the house is now a museum, run by the government. It is well maintained, though with an emphasis on wall displays of photographs. Most of the original furnishings are gone; the most interesting relic is an ancient lawnmower with the embossed name of a manufacturer in Newburgh, New York. The most interesting room in the house is actually the cupola, barely big enough for a desk but walled with shutters that still open for a view to the Ganges. It was here, apparently, that Tagore sat while he wrote the poems that entranced William Butler Yeats. I myself thought of John Muir and his cupola in Martinez, California.

I went outside and started walking. And there, on a lane close by, was a boy about ten years old, dressed in a Western undershirt and a Bengali wraparound. He was standing with his feet buried a couple of inches in the dust. I thought of Nirad Chaudhuri, and of my compromising sandals.

Here were houses, too, like the ones Chaudhuri remembered. Gabled or hip-roofed, they were mostly covered with corrugated sheetmetal. The walls, however, were either mudded mud brick or simple reed matting. Chaudhuri had written of such things—not only of the sheetmetal, which was replacing thatch by the turn of the century—but also of the mudbrick and reed-mat walls. Today, as then, the walls were scrupulously maintained, so the buildings look forever new, their colors indistinguishable from the earth on which they stand. In a fine book called *An Indian Attachment*, Sarah Lloyd writes of Punjabi farmers "growing" their houses, and you know what she means when you see houses of mud and sticks that have been dug and chopped from the land they stand on.

The extensive pumping facilities developed for irrigation east of the Brahmaputra have not reached out to Silaidaha, so most of the island's fields produce only one crop annually. That's why when I first came, in the hot weather, most of the fields were fallow, with hard and light-brown clods. A whiff of onions came through the air from one field that did get water from a well, but the only activity I saw was men coming to prepare the fallow fields. Like the boy, they wore only undershirts and wraparounds. Each man led a pair of bullocks, and each man carried a plow and a mallet. The plows could not have weighed more than forty pounds: they consisted essentially of three pieces of wood—one for the handle, one for the share, one to reach to the yoke. The mallet was more interesting. Long-handled and with a solid cylinder of wood as a hammer, it puzzled me until the men went to work, smashing clods one at a time.

In a few months the fields would be flooded for rice: that was why the paths that ran through the fields were elevated perhaps eight inches above the level of the ground. After the floods had come and long gone, I returned a second time. The ground was still mostly fallow, but on the few irrigated fields I saw this time people were busy with a sugarcane harvest. This was not the stout kind of cane typically found in India; it was so spindly that the stalks growing in the field were tied together in bundles of nine.

Cane crushing was handled on the spot, with two metal drums set vertically and driven by a bullock walking round and round. Canes were thrust one at a time between the revolving drums to produce a trickle of straw-colored juice, which was collected in five-gallon tins quickly emptied into a furnace with a dozen or so uncovered boiling pans. Not one of the pans held more than a gallon of liquid, but a man sat above the furnace with a long-handled ladle and poured fluid from one pan to another with the nicety of titration. From the last pan he periodically drew off a heavy brown liquid. There, in yet more tins, the local process ended—short of the solid blocks of brown sugar produced so commonly in rural India.

Most of the houses in the neighborhood were not bunched in hamlets but stood as isolated homesteads marked by mangoes, palms, and great stacks of rice straw. I approached one that covered perhaps half an acre, but the compound was well screened by a beautiful herringbone-woven reed fence, and I could hardly see anything beyond the hipped roof of corrugated metal, supported by walls of mudded mud brick pierced by tiny windows with bamboo grates. I saw no one inside the compound except a few women at work in an outdoor kitchen, and I turned away.

I came to another farmstead and, nearby, a simple bridge across a dry wash. I sat down on the bridge railing to watch a couple of bullocks nibbling straw from a large, coarsely woven basket. Nearby, there was a haystack from which the animals had nibbled until it was almost undermined; beyond, there were huts on smooth, shaded dirt.

Two or three young men came up and stared. One of them, it turned out, had studied at a college in Kushtia, and he struggled with his English to explain that the farmstead in front of us belonged to a relative, a poor man—but I was welcome to look.

And so I walked around that immaculate courtyard, which had buildings on all four sides. Each was raised on a mudded platform about two feet high, and each was built of mats and thatch—no mud brick here, except for the platforms. Against one wall stood a bicycle and a couple of utensils—a bowl, a water pot, a bamboo pole. Against another wall leaned one of those plows, as elegant as a fishing rod. In a corner between two buildings there was a screened-in kitchen, a patch of ground on which a girl perhaps ten years old squatted to tend a few pots. She wore a Western-style dress, yellow like cornbread.

The young man now wanted to take me to his own home, which was a couple of hundred yards away. A dozen people were soon crowded into a small room, which was furnished with only a bed and a bench. Resorting occasionally to his English-Bengali dictionary, I gathered that though he was a college graduate he had no job. I avoided the foolish question about working the family's land, for as soon as we made it to his house he disappeared for a moment and returned wearing a long-sleeved shirt.

His mother appeared in widow's white and through her son half-insisted that I eat breakfast. She reappeared in a few minutes with a large bowl of leathery puffed rice, sweetened with crude sugar. It was fine, but the family was disappointed and I hope no more than that when I repeatedly declined the water they offered.

I thanked them and wandered alone along the river. Music far away on the Pabna side drifted across, so little impeded that when I first heard it I thought that a man standing in the shallows in front of me must be holding a tiny radio. I think now of one of Tagore's untitled poems, *Gitanjali* 74:

> The evening air is eager with the sad music of the water. Ah, it calls me out into the dusk. In the lonely lane there is no passer-by, the wind is up, the ripples are rampant in the river.
>
> I know not if I shall come back home. I know not whom I shall chance to meet. There at the fording in the little boat the unknown man plays upon his lute.

The Ganges here is calm all the time, now that the Farakka Barrage is in place. Certainly when I saw it the water's surface

The Ganges near Kushtia, Bangladesh, not far upstream from the river's confluence with the Brahmaputra. The great river and the rice and sugarcane fields behind the viewer are nearly as quiet today as they were early this century, when Rabindranath Tagore sat in the cupola of his home a few hundred yards away and translated *Gitanjali* into English.

offered a perfect reflection of the small boats that moved up and down, sometimes with motors, sometimes with sweeps, sometimes with one man walking on the shore and pulling a rope attached to the top of the mast.

In the Silaidaha evenings I saw almost no electric lights; one small electrically driven gristmill shut down by dark. Oil lanterns were ignited in people's homes and also on the rear axles of the cycle rickshaws clustered at the occasional road crossings. It was a long time until the sun rose, and children gathered at dawn around small bonfires lit to repel the chill made worse by the damp.

The sun rose magnificently, and I think now of *Gitanjali* 57, where Tagore writes of "Light, my light, the world-filling light, the eye-kissing light, heart-sweeting light!" The difference is that I see a spectacular sunrise and Tagore sees divinity. It's like the Muskogee ballsticks, and there's not much doubt about it, for Tagore continues (*Gitanjali* 59):

> Yes, I know, this is nothing but thy love, O beloved of my heart—this golden light that dances upon the leaves, these idle clouds

sailing across the sky, this passing breeze leaving its coolness upon my forehead.

It would be a mistake, I think, to take these lines metaphorically. I think they are absolutely literal. That is why Tagore seems so obsessive to us, for little else matters to him but the glimpse of divinity. "Under thy great sky in solitude and silence," he writes in *Gitanjali* 76, "with humble heart shall I stand before thee face to face?"

What makes all this so difficult for us is not Tagore's faith (we're used to dealing with that) but his sense that we are in a universe inconceivably full of life, growing in every direction—and going nowhere. *That's* where he sticks in our craws. Oh, we know better rationally, but we insist that progress somehow not only makes us comfortable but makes sense; we insist that the universe will somehow sanction our strenuous efforts so that we don't have to worry about why we're so busy. Not Tagore: he will have none of this nonsense; he shames us in our narrowness.

I imagine that he must have been sitting in that little Silaidaha cupola when he looked across the island toward the river and wrote in one of *Gitanjali*'s last poems (92):

> When I think of this end of my moments, the barrier of the moments breaks and I see by the light of death thy world with its careless treasures. Rare is its lowliest seat, rare is its meanest of lives.
>
> Things that I longed for in vain and things that I got—let them pass. Let me but truly possess the things that I ever spurned and overlooked.

You can climb up to the cupola yourself. You can swing open the shutters on all sides. Here he sat, you may think, when he wrote in *Gitanjali* 96: "When I go from hence let this be my parting word, that what I have seen is unsurpassable."

THE WESTERN WIND

A WORLD THAT IS FULL OF LIFE BUT GOING
nowhere: that's the outlook that gives Westerners so much
trouble. We don't all respond to it in the same way, of course.
E. M. Forster, in *A Passage to India*, has Mrs. Moore step into
the Marabar Caves, sense an empty form of that same existen-
tial drift, and panic. Men of action disdain such a luxury. I
think of George Nathaniel Curzon, the most imperious of the
viceroys and the last to be sent in Victoria's lifetime. No soft-
ness for him: "To me," Curzon would say in a speech he gave
in 1904, "the message is carved in granite, it is hewn out of
the rock of doom—that our work is righteous and that it shall
endure."

"Right," I say, and my mind wanders to the marble busts
scattered around the old coronation grounds north of Delhi,
wanders to the assorted statues of Victoria and Edward
piled up behind the Lucknow museum. "It's Ozymandias
time."

But, of course, I am wrong: the work of which Curzon spoke
has endured. One walks off a jetway in Madras or Bombay or
Delhi, lifts luggage off a carousel, turns on a hotel television
and chooses BBC or CNN. I'm not saying for a moment that
India is a Westernized country or that Curzon would be happy
with India as it is today. I am saying that the progressive men-

tality brought to India by the British has survived the passing of their empire—and thrives in Indian hands.

But how did the Western wind begin to blow? That is what I want to explore. I want to go back before Curzon, back to the India of Ramappa and the India of Silaidaha on the Ganges. I want to see the first breezes sweeping over that world, "unsurpassable." The best general guide I know is Eric Stokes, who explored this question in his book *The English Utilitarians and India*. Stokes says that the East India Company's situation had changed in two major ways early in the nineteenth century: on the one hand, its trading monopoly was ended by Parliament in 1813; on the other hand, the company's domain expanded rapidly—from hardly more than Bengal in 1765 to, by 1837, the Raj nearly at its maximum extent, minus chiefly the Indus Valley. The time was ripe, in short, for a major reform in administrative structure.

Stokes then sketches the two approaches to governance that had dominated early-nineteenth-century India. On the one hand, and represented by Lord Cornwallis as governor-general, was the Whig ideal, under which India was to become another Britain, with a politically minimalist administration overseeing an Indian landed gentry. In opposition to this approach was the liberalism that was perhaps best represented by Governor Thomas Munro of Madras. Here, British loyalty was not to the great landowners but to the peasants, who embodied simplicity and traditional wisdom.

Both of these styles—and here Stokes came to his real theme—were gradually pushed aside by the arrival in India at this critical time of a group of men devoted to the utilitarianism of Jeremy Bentham. Bentham, as it happens, very nearly worshipped Francis Bacon, and if Bentham is best known in England today for rationalizing jurisprudence, he was also very much interested in what we would now refer to as the alleviation of poverty. General prosperity was, in fact, only another element of the society that Bentham wished to devise, a society that we would now recognize as a welfare state, rationally conceived to maximize pleasure and minimize pain.

Bentham's influence in India was enormous. There is nothing inferential about this: Stokes points out that a banquet was held in 1828 to honor William Bentinck upon his appointment as India's governor-general. Jeremy Bentham attended the banquet, and in an address Bentinck looked squarely at him and said: "I shall not be governor-general. It is you that will be governor-general."

Nor was Bentinck alone. The East India Company's examiner—in modern terminology its chief executive officer—was for many years James Mill, father of John Stuart Mill and among the most devoted of Bentham's followers. Bentham knew it and late in life wrote that "Mill will be the living executive—I shall be the dead legislative of British India." Bentham's hand can be seen even behind Lord Dalhousie, whose term as governor-general in the 1850s was a perfect frenzy of economic development—so much so that the Indian Mutiny of 1857 has often been explained as a reaction to the shock of the changes Dalhousie introduced.

A few years later, in the wake of that upheaval, the East India Company was pushed aside and the crown took over the direct rule of India. (The change was expressed in part through the newly created position of viceroy, a title assumed by later governors-general.) The announcement was made in Queen Victoria's Allahabad Proclamation of 1858. She had asked Lord Derby, who wrote the proclamation, to "breathe feelings of generosity, benevolence, and religious feeling." And he gave her a proclamation of real eloquence: "In their prosperity will be our strength; in their contentment our security, and in their gratitude our best reward. And may the God of all power grant to us, and to those in authority under us, strength to carry out these our wishes for the good of our people."

Underneath that warm flow, however, the cold hand of Jeremy Bentham grew stronger year by year, along with the government of India itself—capitalized to this day and indeed a leviathan. Stokes traces Bentham's influence as far as Curzon, not the Curzon who spoke of "the rock of doom" but the Curzon who in his farewell speech evaluated his administration and said: "If I were asked to sum it up in a single word, I would say 'Efficiency.'" Bentham would have been proud.

But all this is disturbingly general; even Stokes's three hundred pages are too general for my taste. What I need is something concrete, an example of this new mentality in action. And that is why not long after visiting Ramappa I turned around and went southwest 150 miles from Hyderabad to a town called Shorapur, which lies in Karnataka State almost halfway to Goa.

About halfway out, the highway came to a topographic break. I had been traveling across the red-soiled plateau of Telangana, studded with exfoliation domes of ancient granite. I looked down several hundred feet now and saw a black plain covered with a mantle of the heavy clay that is famous, in India as it is in the southern United States, for cotton. The clay is derived from weathered basalt, and the volcanic landscape stretches far to the north and all the way west to the sea and Bombay. There are no more domes; in their place are lava-capped ridges.

From this vantage I could nearly see Gopalpur, a village studied by Alan Beals in the same years that Oscar Lewis was working at Rani Kheri. Most of Beals's book is concerned with Gopalpur's social organization, but Beals does devote a chapter to the physical character of his village. He describes Gopalpur as lying a few miles from the highway and being accessible only by cart track. There are, he says, no especially noteworthy buildings or monuments—only some dozens of houses, generally on a rectangular format typically thirty feet by forty. The houses are built of stone and mud and are fronted with a veranda and a double door, guarded by carved horseheads projecting just above and on both sides of the door. (The horses are a common motif in this part of India; there are more in Shorapur.) Inside these one-roomed houses, windowless but skylight lit, cattle feed on hay; behind the animals, on a raised platform, there are millstones and doors leading to a kitchen and a room for bathing.

The buildings, Beals continues, are fortresses used for storage and cooking; people actually live on the verandas. Most of them sleep on cots placed in front of the houses, though for crop protection the old men sleep in the fields—out past the thorn fences that rim the village. The crops they guard are sorghum on the heavier soil, millet on the sandier, and a scattering of mangoes.

"Gopalpur?" I asked some people at a bus stop and had just reached the farther limits of my Kannada. No one was willing to hazard a guess, especially with my hopeless pronunciation, but one man traveling with two young girls asked for a ride to a village some miles ahead, and he read the Kannada road signs as we proceeded. A mile or so later he pointed to a sign. It apparently said "Gopalpur," and it certainly indicated that something lay three kilometers to the left. I told him I'd pick him up on the way back, and he and the girls got out.

At first the road was better than a cart track, but it soon degenerated, and on the edge of deep sand I finally parked and started walking: I could see a village of some sort perhaps half a kilometer ahead. It was shrouded in trees, mostly the dark green of mango, lush alongside the stubble of sorghum through which I walked, sweating heavily.

My wish for invisibility was granted for longer than usual this day. I slipped in through screening thorns and walked down an unpaved lane. There were no vehicles of any sort except carts. The buildings were rectangular, single storied, and of stone and clay, though often the stone was immense granite slabs. As Beals had suggested, the houses were fronted with porches supported by unsawn posts and beams; cattle nibbled near stacks of sorghum straw; chickens poked; the silence was colossal.

Three or four minutes passed; the loudest sound was the film advancing automatically in my little camera. Eventually I heard voices, but they were very subdued and coming from behind walls. Then the sound of a treadle-operated sewing machine: a woman at work on her shaded veranda. She sat on a granite bench on the unpaved ground; overhead were massive and rough-hewn beams to hold the shading roof; projecting over the doorway into her house was a pair of elaborately carved wooden horseheads.

She didn't notice me, and I slipped by, past a temple which I knew from Beals must be to the monkey-god Hanuman. Overhead, electric wires draped: *that* was something new. Close by, there was a metal water tank: not more than a few hundred gallons but filled by an electric pump. That was new, too. I came round a corner and was suddenly seen by a dozen people all at once. None of them spoke any English, though I was able to establish that this place was indeed Gopalpur. And now people wanted their pictures taken. A woman sitting on a veranda and stitching a quilt. A family portrait with men, women, and children, all in traditional clothing except for the store-bought shirts of the men. There were, I realized, no stores in Gopalpur, and apparently no government buildings.

Beals wrote that the villagers believed that they were "now second-class citizens of the world." He wrote about the things that could be done for them: improved crop varieties, irrigation, fertilizers, credit. In a reference to the violent radicalism found in the Hyderabad countryside he asked whether the transition from "the old order to the new is to be peaceful and orderly or bloody and disorderly." But there has been little or no transition. Apart from the draped wires and the water tank, what is new? Perhaps the sewing machine; probably the improved road. Blame remoteness or the apparent difficulty of developing irrigation facilities here, but the Gopalpur I saw was hardly different from the one Beals knew.

For that matter, it is hardly different from the villages known to Philip Meadows Taylor. Meadows Taylor, as he has always been known, was the man responsible for my coming to Shorapur. Alone, Taylor for the better part of twenty years ruled much of the country around Gopalpur. He provides, in short, a microcosm of British rule in India.

Shorapur sits exotically in a bowl-like depression atop a ridge. I could hardly see the town's lights until I arrived on the edge of night, and it was plain how the place could have functioned, as Taylor put it, as a "very stronghold of freebooters."

There was a wretched hotel near the bus station, but I found a better place on the far side of town: the Upinn Deluxe had just opened its doors. Hot water was available by bucket, the cook in the courtyard produced reasonable food on his camp stove, the young owner-manager spoke passable English, and there was almost-cold beer.

None of this had existed when Meadows Taylor had arrived with the title political agent. That would have been in 1841, shortly after the death of the raja of Shorapur, who had left his state and half million subjects deeply in debt to the nizam of Hyderabad. That was the situation that had brought Taylor's predecessor here: an effort by the British to clean up the state's finances so that the debt to the nizam could be paid. The job had been impossible for this Captain Gresley, who found himself enmeshed in a political contest between the Rani Ishwarama, who had been the dead raja's senior wife, and Pid Naik, who was the dead raja's younger brother. The rani had charge of the dead raja's son, one Enkatappa Naik, who at seven years old was eleven years too young for ascending to the throne. Pid Naik, on the other hand, had a son whom he wished to place on the throne at once.

Cliques gathered about both the principals, though it was hard enough to work with either of those individuals alone. The rani, Taylor would write, was "dissolute to a degree—in fact a very Messalina," while Pid Naik regularly "gave himself up to fits of intoxication." Enkatappa Naik, on the other hand, struck Taylor as a good boy, much troubled by his mother's open but unexplained hostility, which seems to have arisen from a prophecy, verified by astrologers all over India, that the boy would die in his twenty-fourth year.

The death of Pid Naik in a paralytic seizure simplified matters, but the rani kept Taylor busy with her own machinations until she died, two years later, in 1847; Taylor wrote that she was only forty but "seemed seventy, haggard and wasted." For a while, things were calm: "No intrigue! no suspicion! no combinations!" Enkatappa Naik came to the throne at last, and Taylor was sent to another posting.

Then the Mutiny broke out, and Enkatappa Naik chose the losing side. When British forces approached Shorapur he fled, only to be arrested shortly in Hyderabad. In jail there, he told

Taylor bitterly how he had been unable to resist his own people, who had called him "a coward and a fool" for not rebelling against the British. He had finally done so, he said, and now he was sentenced to die. Taylor wrote that the sentence was commuted to four years' banishment but that on the first day of his trip to his place of seclusion Enkatappa Naik shot himself in the stomach, fatally, with one of his guards' pistols. Taylor calls it an accident but notes that, accident or suicide, it occurred one day short of Enkatappa Naik's twenty-fifth birthday. The prophecy, he states categorically, had been kept an absolute secret from the boy.

Taylor was sent back to Shorapur as commissioner, while decisions were taken that led, finally, to the state's dissolution and incorporation as part of the dominions of the nizam of Hyderabad, in which the state remained until those dominions were dissolved after 1947.

Such is the sum of Taylor's political work in Shorapur, and from the weakness of Enkatappa Naik it may be judged finally a failure. Yet it is not politics that chiefly interests us: it is Taylor himself and the work he did over many years in Shorapur to improve the lives of its people.

It is a classic story, beginning with Taylor's own birth in 1808 in Liverpool and his Dickensian schooling and apprenticeship. At sixteen he had been shipped off alone to Bombay, where he was apprenticed to a merchant whose business collapsed almost as soon as Taylor arrived. Taylor now played his one high card, his mother's family relationship with the chief secretary of the government of Bombay. This Mr. Newnham wrote to the Resident at Hyderabad and secured for Taylor, still sixteen, a commission as a lieutenant in the nizam's army.

Between 1824 and 1841, when he moved to Shorapur, Taylor slipped back and forth between military and civil service for the nizam. He maintained good relations with the succeeding Residents—and such good relations with the prominent Hyderabad banking firm of Palmers that in 1840 he married Mary Palmer.

Taylor's career never advanced very far, partly because the opportunities in the nizam's services were so much more limited than those available to a young man working for the East India Company. In particular he always regretted that as a police officer he had been on the verge of cracking the secrets of the ritual cult of stranglers known as the Thugs. Then he had been transferred, and the fame had gone to Captain William Sleeman. Taylor's only reward had been to write *Confessions of a Thug*, which enjoyed great success both in India and England. It remains readable chiefly because of Taylor's intimate knowledge of how the cult functioned; its chief defect is that Taylor gives it a wholly unnecessary fictional apparatus.

Early on, Taylor was put in charge of large numbers of people. The secret of his success, he wrote, was to like them, treat them fairly, but never become personally close. He recalls, for example, the time when, aged eighteen, he was in charge of the bazaars of Bolaram, a Hyderabad suburb. The merchants were adulterating their flour with sand. Taylor ordered "reliable men" to buy samples of flour from each shop. He then tasted the flour himself "and found it full of sand as I passed it under my teeth." He ordered the merchants to appear before him. " 'Now,' said I, gravely, 'each of you are to weigh out a seer (two pounds) of your flour.' " Was it for some pilgrims, one of the merchants asked? " 'No,' said I, quietly, though I had much difficulty to keep my countenance. 'You must eat it yourself.' " The merchants offered to pay any fine Taylor wished to impose, but "at last, some of them actually began to eat, sputtering out the half-moistened flour, which could be heard crunching between their teeth." Taylor says that he heard no more complaints of bad flour.

Still in his mid-twenties, ill with fever, Taylor was sent to the Nilgiri Hills, where, amazingly, he met both the governor-general, William Bentinck, and a member of his council, none other than Thomas Babington Macaulay. Amazingly, I say, not only because both men were so senior but because I want to discuss Taylor as an exemplar of British utilitarianism in practice, and a stronger link to that philosophy can hardly be imagined than through Bentinck and Macaulay. Bentinck, of course, was the governor-general who had said that Bentham would rule through him, and Macaulay stands today not only as a historian but as an opponent of Newman and Arnold—a defender of Francis Bacon.

It was Macaulay who wrote of ancient philosophy that "it could not condescend to the humble office of ministering to the comfort of human beings." Before Bacon, Macaulay wrote, "the great work of improving the condition of the human race was still considered as unworthy of a man of learning." Was there any real contest between the schools? "We should say that the aim of the Platonic philosophy was to exalt man into a god. The aim of the Baconian philosophy was to provide man with what he requires while he continues to be man. . . . The former aim was noble, but the latter was attainable." Nothing if not pithy, Macaulay would return to that idea a paragraph later and write that "an acre in Middlesex is better than a principality in Utopia."

Both Bentinck and Macaulay made enormous impressions on Meadows Taylor. Of Macaulay, in particular, Taylor wrote that "his seemingly boundless knowledge of life, his acquaintance with history and philosophy, his fiery zeal in argument, and his calm eloquence in oratory, opened to me new subjects of thought for future study. Oh, if I had been among such men always, I thought, I should have been very different!" And when in retirement Taylor looked back upon his career, he still had high praise for Bentinck: "his commencement of that system of progress which is now bearing ample fruit." Interestingly, his highest praise at that time was reserved for Dalhousie, the governor-general of the 1850s. To him Taylor attributed "the most practically useful and single-minded rule that India had ever possessed. . . . he improved everything he touched. To him India owes electric telegraphs, railways, extension of practical education, large irrigation projects, roads, and the removal of many disabilities under which natives suffered."

The list is a good summary of what Taylor, all by himself, did in Shorapur. First off, he strode into the presence of the Rani Ishwarama and demanded an account of the state's finances. The rani, he wrote, was as slippery as an eel, but "I said I would not leave her till I had her determination from

her own mouth ... and I doggedly kept my seat." The rani
finally capitulated, and in time Taylor was sleeping at night
with the keys to the state treasury under his pillow.

But managing the debt and watching the young Enkatappa
Naik were only the beginnings. Taylor went out to the villages
and reorganized the tax structure whose abuses had led to
widespread land abandonment and falling revenues. He introduced improved cotton seed and indigo. He took up civil engineering so he could build dams to store irrigation water—and
he became so good at it that, late in life and retired in Dublin,
he was made a member of the Institution of Civil Engineers.
He became interested in roads—"I had to study road engineering as well as I could"—and built miles of road with carefully maintained widths and gradients. And he worked hard
on afforestation—"planted many thousand of mango and tam-
arind trees."

Within Shorapur town Taylor set up the state's first courts
of justice; later, in another posting, he set up prisons, where,
he boasted, he did not "allow the women to be idle." In Shorapur he opened a public dispensary where he himself served as
vaccinator, and he established schools. Meanwhile he did the
research that after his retirement would emerge in illustrated
volumes about the architectural antiquities near Shorapur.
Somehow Taylor found time to serve for a decade as Indian
correspondent for the London *Times*. Recreation? Taylor ordered a telescope and took up astronomy, and he often sailed
on one of the lakes he had built—sailed on it in a boat of
"tolerably long dimensions" that he designed and had built of
"teak, copper-fastened."

What was driving him? The question brings us back to Eric
Stokes and to the mentality of the British in India. One may
think of Curzon or, to take an example from Taylor's time, of
Henry Lawrence, who lay dying in 1857, victim of the Indian
Mutiny, yet who was conscious enough to command that his
tombstone should bear the words "Henry Lawrence, who tried
to do his duty." So it does still: a flat stone in a park in Lucknow. Gilbert and Sullivan would later mock the phrase, but for
Lawrence, like Taylor, it was not empty.

Taylor, in short, was a representative man who probably worked no less or more than his peers. At the same time it is true that in Taylor's case there was also an element of desperate loneliness, for his wife Mary died in 1844, three years after their arrival in Shorapur. They had already lost two children; Taylor sent the two surviving ones to England. Taylor never remarried, and he writes of Shorapur that there was "no society, no one to speak to from first to last." Of course, it was a self-imposed isolation, characteristic of the Raj throughout its history, when "mingling" was rigidly limited. Yet it does help us understand how Taylor managed to get so much done.

Eventually his health collapsed, and in 1860 he reluctantly resigned from the nizam's service. He retired and during the next sixteen years poured out Indian romances as well as more sober volumes. In 1878 he made a last trip to India, but his health failed again, and on his return he died at Menton, where the French Riviera meets Italy. There he was buried. One of his daughters took care to prepare his memoirs for publication.

And what about Taylor in Shorapur today?

The morning after my arrival I walked back down to the bazaar, which lines the single main street crossing the bowl of the town. In the center of the town and behind high gates I passed the palace of the old rajas, now a school—each floor of its central tower given over to a single classroom. Students coming and going are dangerously crowded into a single steep circular staircase.

Away from its main street, the town quickly degenerated into lanes and paths, mostly twisting and hilly and winding past doorways like those in Gopalpur: exotic doors from which almost life-sized horseheads projected. I saw none of the modern housing that has done so much to change Rani Kheri: here in Shorapur I remember only double doors leading into courtyards, stone-flagged, with verandas on all sides. In one spectacular case the house exterior was a bright blue, the doorway darkly oiled, the interior verandas stacked double.

Here and there I thought I saw signs of Taylor's hand. Massive paving stones and an ancient mango border hinted that a road on the south side of town was his. Unmaintained, the road was being undercut on one side by runoff, and the surface was so rough that people were actually walking on a parallel track. On the other side of town Taylor had planted "a double row of fine young trees, which gave ample promise of fruit," but of these I could find no evidence.

The most striking signs of European civilization in Shorapur's residential neighborhoods had nothing to do with Taylor: they were the cycle rickshaws fitted not with seats but with a barrel for domestic water. Each one had a sign indicating the name of the bank that had financed these ventures in microenterprise.

I entered a girls' high school in hopes of getting directions to the house Taylor had built for himself here in Shorapur. The principal insisted on my having tea, but he was not quite compliant enough to give me the directions I wanted. Instead, he insisted that I should see someone else, someone who would be able to help me. It was a classic demonstration of the feudalism surviving in India, for the man the principal wanted me to see was not a local agent of government but an elderly Pid Naik, descendant of the raja's brother in Taylor's time and now the senior member of the family. Pid Naik, however, turned out to be too ill for a visitor. I was duly sent to his younger brother, one Venkata Naik, eighty-three years old but in good health.

Now Meadows Taylor had always believed that the countryside around Shorapur could be reclaimed by an immense canal that would take water from the left bank of the Krishna River and bring it out in a canal that would curve counterclockwise to flow upstream against the tributary Bhima. Nothing came of this idea in Taylor's lifetime or for a long time afterwards, but in the 1980s India, with help from the World Bank, began building just such a scheme: two million acres to be irrigated. And now I was guided away from Shorapur and down to the surrounding plain where work on that project was continuing in earnest. We went through fields that must once have looked like those of Gopalpur but which were now green with peanuts and dark with soil moisture. The student who was my guide directed me into the driveway of a modest house. I was ushered into a sitting room: whitewashed, clean, with rattan furniture and family photographs. About ten minutes later Mr. Naik appeared.

I asked for directions to "Taylor Manzil," which is to say the Taylor mansion; also for directions to the lake where Taylor had sailed his boat. Mr. Naik arranged guides to both, but in the meanwhile we talked about the family's fortunes. Things had not gone so badly. After the Mutiny the family had lost its ruling status, but for another century it was treated as part of the nizam's nobility and received the land taxes paid by the villages of the former state. That is why Mr. Venkata Naik knew Hyderabad so well: he had a house there, he explained—had even gone to school there. Warmly he recalled a Mr. Perkins, an Episcopal missionary from Iowa, who had been one of his teachers seventy years before.

Mr. Naik had gone to Britain, had graduated from the University of London, been a barrister in the 1930s. He had returned to Hyderabad at the outbreak of the Second World War and practiced law until the nizam's state was forcibly incorporated into India. During the 1960s he had served in Delhi as a member of Parliament. Now, in retirement, he was a farmer. His old village revenues were long gone, and like Mr. Appaji in Eruvellipet he said that his landholdings were nothing compared to what they had once been: in this case some two thousand acres had been reduced to two hundred and twenty, divided between him and his three sons.

Still, Mr. Naik had the blessing of the new Upper Krishna Project: all his land was irrigated. In the summer—the wet season—the irrigation canals were closed, and he grew a sixty-five-day millet that he harvested while the farmers in Gopalpur watched their sorghum grow. Then, when the dry season came, the canals were turned on, and he grew cotton and peanuts in a two-year rotation. The canals themselves were rotated so that water was available one week in three; during the "on" week the farmers along each channel followed a fixed rotation schedule, calculated in proportion to the size of each holding. It was a rotation deliberately designed to discourage rice paddies, which every farmer would cultivate if given the choice, but some farmers had already dug ponds on their land so they could save water from their irrigation period and thereby have a steady water supply that would let them grow the forbidden crop.

We took a walk through the fields, then returned to his house, where Mr. Naik made a phone call to arrange guides. I took my first guide back to the girls' school, then went to a gas station where I picked up another one, who would take me to Bonal Tank, where Taylor had sailed his boat. On the way we stopped at the grand fortifications that rim the far side of Shorapur: miles of stone walls whose narrow walkways gave me vertigo, along with splendid views of the prodigiously rocky ridge they encompassed.

The Bonal Tank, Taylor wrote, was "a noble sheet of water," as much as fifty feet deep, with a dam more than a mile long and a waterspread of six square miles. So it remains. Hoping to find a plaque, I walked to the rough spillway that comes out of the dam and feeds a canal still irrigating perhaps two thousand acres of fortunate rice. The rocks of the spillway were slippery, but, still hopeful, I stripped to get across to the far side. (We had already picked up a local villager who took my camera while I picked my way through the water.) On this side, too, there was no plaque, but I did drop all decorum on this hot day and went for a swim. I had no company, and I suppose Taylor's ghost was disapproving.

And Taylor's house? Back in town I had tentatively spotted an empty building that I thought might be what I wanted: the hairs on the back of my head had prickled when I explored it. But I was wrong, and if I had studied Taylor's memoirs more carefully I would have known better where to look. He writes of his house that "the view was certainly very fine; and as the site was 400 feet above the town, it would not only be cooler, but more healthy than below."

Sure enough, Taylor Manzil stands high above the town, on the north side. No doubt it *is* cooler and healthier than the site I first looked at, but what Taylor never says about the house is that its location was also symbolic of his position. How many angry eyes must once have looked up from the town below!

Taylor Manzil is now a government resthouse and a study in shabbiness. Once surrounded with flower gardens, it is now rimmed by bare ground. The building itself is intact: no surprise since Taylor built it of granite blocks eighteen inches by five by eight. It has a single story, rectangular in plan, with a semicircular portico overlooking the former garden and the town. The portico roof is supported by a modest colonnade, over which is a small stone bearing the words "Taylor Manzil" and the date "1842."

I went inside and found a single central room, oval and divided by a twelve-foot arch into two living rooms; smaller rooms lay to both sides of this main oval. It was, in fact, just as Taylor describes it. Even the roof appeared original and sound, though Taylor had got its wooden beams "for nothing, for there was a lot lying at an old fort in the Nizam's country."

Late in the afternoon I drove west a few miles to a river, a tributary of the Krishna. There was a new bridge, and beyond it a crossroads. Inevitably, there was therefore a collection of tire-repair shops and tea stalls. I bought some apple juice and walked back alongside burning mesquite, flaring in the night sky so that in the morning it might be more easily cut for firewood. There were clouds of gnats, but they didn't bite. Fields of rice lay beyond, irrigated, I think, from Bonal Tank. The river itself was broad and shallow, but it had a current swift enough to pull me along forcibly when I went in. I deliberately waited in the river for full darkness, and I got my money's worth, for returning to the car I found that I had no lights. I proceeded back to Shorapur slowly, the occasional bicycle appearing out of the darkness a few seconds after I heard its clattering or its bell. I thought of an inscription on a cloister wall at Westminster Abbey: "Here are commemorated the Civil Services of the Crown in India; let them not be forgotten for they served India well."

.. 4 ..

IRRIGATION

SOME READERS WILL SAY THAT I AM MAKING
altogether too easy an opposition, too facile a dichotomy between the stagnation of Indian tradition and the dynamism of
the British. For all his love of India, they will say, did not
Rabindranath Tagore condemn Indian poverty? Did he not
create a school to help his people? And, on the other hand,
didn't British officers commonly view progress skeptically?
Did they not often believe that Indian peasants were as happy
as the people of England?

It is all perfectly true: I have indeed exaggerated the contrast between India and the West, between the bastion of tradition and the army of progress. But that does not mean that
there was no army at all. It only means that the army was not
monolithic, and I mean to show now just how powerful that
army was, powerful in changing the character of rural India's
landscape not through the work of individual men like Meadows Taylor but through the work of government departments
and professional institutions saturated with Western notions of
progress. Often enough there would be men in these institutions who appreciated Indian tradition, men whose own ac-
complishments were like grafts on native stock. Yet time and
again the work these men did would be overwhelmed by more
parochially Western solutions that were more agreeable to se-

nior officers and which uprooted native traditions and tried to improve upon them by starting afresh. In that sense, all the shades of gray in the world hardly mattered, for India—and by extension Asia as whole—was indeed overrun, while the qualities of the pristine place were lost. All the germs are there in Meadows Taylor's Shorapur, with irrigation, with better farming methods, with community development programs. All we need do is trace their institutionalization.

That's why we're back south of Madras, where this history begins. We're past the village of Eruvellipet and at a weir on the Cauvery River near Tiruchirapalli—Trichy for short. We're at the Grand Anicut, a weir that lies a half hour's drive downstream from town. In the hot weather it's a popular spot with Indians seeking some relief, for though the Grand Anicut rises scarcely fifteen feet from the bed of the Cauvery, it is several hundred yards long. Laid out in a crude semicircle, the weir is pierced by sluices through which water splashes into a dozen palmately radiating channels. Some are natural, but others are artificial.

The weir is mostly of masonry blocks, and plaques indicate that different sections of the work were built mostly in the late nineteenth century. But this is a case where looks are deceiving: only the anicut's erratic curvature, so foreign to Western engineering design, hints at the structure's true antiquity, which goes back to the second century A.D.

The British acquired the anicut and the delta it commands in 1801, and within three years they realized that agriculture in the delta was in grave danger because the Cauvery was getting ready to abandon its course and shift to the Coleroon River, which branches off to the left, some ten miles or so upstream from Trichy. This, they realized, would be a disaster, since the delta, with a radius of about fifty miles, was one of the most productive parts of India.

For thirty years the British temporized, chiefly by raising the level of the Grand Anicut to get as much Cauvery water as possible into the ancient canals. But this did nothing to prevent the disaster that would occur if the river changed course. That is where matters stood when a young captain named Arthur Cotton was ordered to the scene in 1827.

Cotton was then twenty-four years old, but he had already completed nearly a decade's service in India. Unlike Meadows Taylor, who was five years his junior, Cotton had been commissioned a lieutenant not in a princely service but in the Madras Engineers. His first assignment in India had been the survey of a navigation channel through the rocks and islands separating India and Ceylon. He then saw military action in Burma, where he discovered the Bible and a faith that would last him to his death.

Returning to Madras, Cotton set to work on the restoration of old irrigation tanks. I do not know if he ever read the caustic speech of Edmund Burke, who, condemning his own government, said that these tanks were "not the enterprises of your power, nor in a style of magnificence suited to the taste of your minister. These are the monuments of real kings, who were the fathers of their people." But Cotton would have agreed with every word of that, not only as it praised India's old irrigation works but as it shamed the East India Company's reluctance to rehabilitate them. Reminiscing about his work on the Grand Anicut, Cotton wrote that "in '27 I was sent to inspect it, as the people were stated to be nearly in a state of rebellion from its neglect. . . . Is it surprising the people thought us savages? I made a small estimate of £3,500 for some immediate repairs, but knowing what its fate would be, I proceeded to Madras, and arrived just in time to hear, as I expected, that the Government could not squander such sums as this upon the wild demands of an Engineer." Nothing was done for another six years, Cotton continued: "Such was the inconceivable state of things under that admirable middle-class government."

Cotton was his parents' tenth son, but he had a still younger brother named Frederick, and Frederick was also an engineer working in India. They worked together closely, and it was Frederick who was given the task in 1830 of cutting the Grand Anicut to make sluices so that more silt might drain from behind the weir. In the course of doing this work Frederick found, as he himself wrote, that "this 'Grand' anicut work was hardly more than a mass of rubbish, mud, stones, and logs of wood, the safety of which depended solely on its then plastered surface." It was an important, perhaps even a revolutionary discovery: simple inertia had been great enough to withstand sixteen hundred annual floods. Both Frederick and Arthur became believers in what Frederick would call the Madras, or cheap, school of engineering. Why invest in unnecessarily massive structures? "After all," Frederick would say, "what is good engineering but economy!"

Arthur was soon assigned to fix the river, and he decided to build a dam just below the point where the Coleroon leaves the Cauvery. He explained his idea in these words, written in 1834: "I have given such a height to the Annicut as will, so far as I am yet able to judge, exactly correspond with the Grand Annicut; that is, that when the water is even with the top of the one, it will be so also at the other." In this way, he hoped, the flow would be equalized in both channels.

Significantly, Cotton did not build a European-style dam on the Coleroon: you can go to the site today and see, under modern recent alterations, parts of the wall he built, 750 yards long, hardly more than seven feet high, and only six feet thick. True, the work rests on a foundation, but that foundation was sunk only three feet beneath the streambed, with periodic wells penetrating another three. True, too, the force of water pouring over the wall was broken by a masonry apron some twenty feet wide. Still, it was a daringly minimalist design. A similar dam was simultaneously built some seventy miles downstream on the Coleroon, where some 165,000 acres depended on irrigation waters that would otherwise be inaccessible when the Coleroon's flow was reduced.

(The granite for the Coleroon Anicut was not available locally. Where did it come from? Cotton explained that he took it "from the boundary wall of an ancient temple, standing in the jungle not far off, and long since disused." The priests approved, he said, and perhaps it is so.)

The Coleroon Anicut required adjustment over the next decade, primarily because the river threatened to shift back entirely to the course of the Cauvery, which would have been almost as bad as its abandoning the river. Hence the construction in the 1840s of another simple "bar" dam across the Cauvery: it has been replaced by a modern barrage and is marked now only by a monument. Both dams were soon given sluices so that silt could flow through as well as over them. Thereafter they functioned well, immediately protecting the irrigation of some half a million acres below the Grand Anicut and within a few years providing water for another eighty-six thousand acres.

It was a great success story, and there is still today at the Coleroon Dam an old stone monument to it. One side says simply "The Upper Coleroon anicut was built in A.D. 1836." Another side says that "the body and apron of this anicut for the irrigation of Tanjore were projected by Major A. T. Cotton and constructed by Major H. C. Cotton, A.D. 1836. N. W. Kindersley, Esq., Principal Collector of Tanjore."

Kindersley himself wrote later that there was "not an individual in the province who did not consider the upper anicut the greatest blessing that had ever been conferred upon it." Many similar pronouncements have been made since. "The permanent prosperity of Tanjore," in the words of one Bengal engineer, "are without question to be attributed in large measure, to that first bold step taken by Colonel Cotton, in the construction of the upper Coleroon Dam, under circumstances of great difficulty, with restricted means, against much opposition, and with heavy personal responsibilities."

And how fares the Cauvery Delta today? I went below the Grand Anicut to Thanjavur, the city that the British called Tanjore. Another twenty miles brought me to the town of Papanasam, with surprises like the Nehru Computer Training Center. From Papanasam, however, there was a quiet and good country road that ran south across the delta through a countryside of paddy irrigated by unlined irrigation ditches, from which water trickled into paddies through openings that were no more than breaks in the embankment, mudded closed or kicked open to meet crop requirements. This was January— always a good time to visit this sultriest part of India—and the rice was generally well along, though not yet heading. At a few lagging places transplanting was still in progress: handfuls of seedlings tied with a blade of grass.

But there is a darker side to the picture, a side that has nothing to do with water distribution or paddy production. In 1958 an enterprising journalist named Kusum Nair spent a year touring rural India. Her journal was published in 1961 as *Blossoms in the Dust,* a confusing title until you realize that she is talking about India's children. The book is not the least bit sentimental, however, and it begins with a chapter on the Cauvery Delta. In that chapter Nair makes two points. First, both landowner and cultivator are basically content: hence her chapter title "Rice-girdled Horizons." Second, local society is so highly stratified that, although land is held in ownerships usually smaller than a single acre, landowners never till their own fields but rely instead on sharecropping tenants or salaried laborers.

These observations will not be welcome to irrigation engineers, whose own horizons are usually girdled by engineering works as ends in themselves—or, at a stretch, by admiration for the green landscapes those engineering works create. Provoked, engineers will respond that it is not within their power to eradicate social inequality: one has done well enough to raise the prosperity of rich and poor alike. Perhaps it is so, but the social inequalities of the Cauvery Delta are so great that they are visible to even a casual observer, and we ought not to be blinded to them simply because no one has been able to eradicate or even to ameliorate them. They are as much a fact of life here as the canals and the verdure.

It is no accident, therefore, that out in the countryside beyond Papanasam I saw transplanting being done by men darker than the people in Papanasam. The laborers wore only breechclouts, so that in profile they appeared naked; some were entertained by radios, broadcasting over the countryside and always playing at a volume greater than the speaker's capacity. For miles south of Papanasam the road was lined with the homes of these men, which were no more than shacks. No wonder that on the way from Thanjavur there was a large Christian church; no wonder, I say, because it was from the ranks of agricultural laborers such as these that Christian converts were most easily made. The church was painted with alternating vertical bands of fuchsia and ocher, and it contained a tomb from the 1930s: "Hic jacet expectans resurrectionem Rev. Gabriel Playoust." That is what the converts, too, might have hoped for. Nowadays, there are no missionaries in India, at least no openly evangelizing ones, and in this great delta there are no forests to offer shelter, like those of the wild Godavary, to revolutionaries. There is only and terribly the status quo, represented in the delta towns by tile-roofed houses of plastered brick and steel-barred windows.

After his work on the Cauvery, Cotton turned to building India's first railway—a short line in Madras—and a church on the coast farther north, at Vizagapatnam. He made plans for developing that city's port, but he also began examining the Godavary Delta, which then lay within the Rajahmundry District. (The district no longer exists; roughly, it has been replaced by two districts, East and West Godavary.) In his characteristic voice he wrote of this surveying work to his brother Frederick: "I made a run through Rajahmundry, and could not help seeing what it wanted, which was simply everything. So magnificent a country in such a state of ruin was the greatest disgrace to a civilized Government." Here was the germ of Cotton's greatest achievement: bringing to the Godavary Delta the intense cultivation that had traditionally existed on the Cauvery.

The Godavary Delta had been devastated by a famine in 1832. One Walter Campbell, then a lieutenant stationed a hundred miles to the south at the mouth of the Krishna, has left a powerful account of that same famine, where "a strong body of police . . . [were] constantly employed in collecting the dead and throwing them into a huge pit prepared for the purpose." They could not manage to keep "the ground clear," Campbell wrote: "numbers of bodies . . . [were] left to be devoured by dogs and vultures." But the delta's problems went beyond drought and famine. Land in both the Godavary and Krishna deltas was held by big landlords, who were gradually driven into bankruptcy not only by the famine and their own profligacy but by the government's closing down of its cloth-purchasing establishments and by its neglect of the existing small irrigation works. No longer able to pay their taxes, the landlords lost their estates to the government.

What should be done with the land? The matter was first taken up in the Godavary Delta, where Henry Montgomery was appointed special commissioner for that purpose. Montgomery had formerly been the collector of Tanjore and had taken a large enough role in the irrigation works there that his name, too, appears on the Coleroon Anicut monument. Here, however, Montgomery's first task was to assign the lands in the forfeited estates to peasant cultivators.

His second task was to call for an investigation of the delta's irrigation potential. Montgomery wrote: "My own impression leads to the opinion that much may be done with the Godavari. . . . The presence . . . of Captain A. Cotton, whose acquaintance with the management of river irrigation on an extended scale has been successfully applied to the southern

districts, seems to afford an opportunity deserving of being embraced by the Government."

Cotton was pithier. He reported to the government six months later that "surely it is time to take decided steps to restore to prosperity a district which has so sunk under our management." A year later, after Cotton's initial cost estimates had been received with some alarm, Cotton stamped his foot and wrote: "If it be asked how is this great sum of money to be obtained, the answer is simply, by converting the water of the Godavery into money instead of letting it run into the sea." It is understandable that the governor-general, Lord Dalhousie, came to view Cotton as "perfectly insufferable."

Cotton's own plans for the Godavary weir evolved, but the essential and unchanging point of them was that the work should be of the Madras or cheap school of engineering. Specifically, the weir would consist of four sections separated by islands but totaling twelve thousand feet in length. "The principal part of the work," Cotton wrote, "will thus consist of loose stone, of which there is an unbounded supply. . . . This is the mode of construction originally used at the ancient native work called the Grand annicut, which has stood for so many centuries."

The Godavary weir was to rise only twelve feet above the river's premonsoon water level: in the monsoon it would be completely overtopped. Yet the foundation would reach only six feet beneath the sandy bed of the river. Cotton's main concern was, therefore, to keep the water that poured over the top of the weir from scouring under its downstream face and

---

A house of substance at Ayyampet, in the Cauvery Delta not far northeast of Thanjavur. Such wealth rests heavily on the work of Arthur Cotton, who stabilized the delta's irrigation systems at a time when they were on the verge of collapse and at a time when the government was disinclined to invest in their preservation. Yet such houses also form a grim contrast with the nearby huts of field laborers. Somehow we must find a middle path between dismissing such inequality as a fact of life and, on the other hand, demanding egalitarian leveling as an ethical imperative.

then penetrating the sand. Downstream from the curtain wall, he designed a nineteen-foot section of horizontal masonry flooring, followed by an inclined plane of clamped masonry twenty-eight feet wide and a rough stone apron about seventy-five feet wide—for a total weir breadth of 130 feet or more. Or more, I say, because Cotton wrote in 1852, "I think it will be advisable to continue to throw in 20,000 tons a year for some years to come." Indeed, over the next forty years some half million tons of rock were thrown in.

The work was authorized in 1846 and executed with a work force of about ten thousand men working between 1847 and 1852. Cotton was assisted by his brother Frederick and by Charles Orr, who a few years later would supervise construction of the Cottonian weir built across the delta of the third of the great Madras rivers, the Krishna. Apart from a medical furlough, Cotton spent the construction years here on the Godavary with his wife and daughter in a weir-side house of palm logs and thatch. His daughter, who as Lady Hope wrote a biography of Cotton, recalled "we seldom went to bed without a provision of boots or brushes to throw at snakes." And Cotton's wife? A child was born to Elizabeth Cotton here on the Godavary. The child soon died, and Elizabeth wrote with religious acceptance: "Except for periodical attacks of jungle Fever, God was very gracious to us in respect of health,—another dear little daughter was born to us in our rough house,—a sweet babe, who was her father's delight, and whose loving looks and ways, when he came in tired from his work, were always a refreshment to him. It pleased God to take her from us after about twelve months, and we buried her at Rajahmundry in a little graveyard looking down upon the river."

Cotton kept working. Lady Hope, the surviving daughter, would later write that "for days together on his long expeditions . . . [he] would live on milk and bananas." She recalls his telling her to "do something, my girl; do something. Never be idle for a single moment. Remember, Time is short, Eternity is near!" He himself, she says, "was never really happy unless he was in some manner promoting what he believed to be the furtherance of the kingdom of God in the world." And that, of

course, is how Arthur Cotton saw his work on the Godavary.
"In a country," he wrote, "where, within living memory, men
had died of famine by tens of thousands, and population has
been checked by contingent consequences of famine, we now
see a teeming population of stout, cheerful, well-proportioned
men, women and children that will compare with any in the
world for intelligence."

Few people would have argued with him, and some visitors
have been even more lavish. Some 18,000 acres had been irrigated with river water in the years before construction of the
weir; the figure rose by another 364,000 within a few years and
to 640,000 by the end of the century. A visitor from Australia
at that time concluded that "taking all things into consideration, it may be questioned if there is a more beneficent or
more profitable public work in the world." Arthur Cotton's reward for the work was to be appointed chief engineer of Madras; brother Frederick was put in charge of completing the
delta canals and operating the system.

And today? The Godavary's sanctity is second only to that
of the Ganges, but Rajahmundry at its apex is just about devoid of appeal for foreigners. Perhaps I am biased: I wound up
in a hotel with some kind of bug in the bedding. The bites,
originally on the small of my back, grew infected and spread,
and the irritation took several months to clear. Still, I remember the nearby Evangelical Lutheran boys' school, opened in
1905 and dark as any Wagnerian fantasy. I remember outside
of town and upstream some tobacco-drying barns, crudely fu-
eled with coal and wood. I remember villages where men
made cart wheels, where they splashed water on heated iron
tires that would shrink tight on a carefully shaped wooden rim.

Most of all I remember a night visit to the banks of the
Godavary in the town itself, at a place where there is a typically Indian set of bathing steps. Just upstream from those
steps there is a great railway trestle; in the British era, at least,
it was the second longest railway bridge in India. A small boat
loaded with sand took off and disappeared into the still waters
of the river. Then, thinking at first it was my imagination, I
heard a rumbling. I looked up at the old trestle and thought I

saw movement. Indeed. A train was approaching; it looked as though it might go wrong and plunge over the unguarded rails. The engine had no headlight, but clouds of cinders flew out from the firebox every few seconds and drifted down through the boxwork of the bridge. It was the first steam engine I had seen along this coast, and the bridge structure magnified the sound of the steam chests and pistons and axles. I suppose that in British times few passengers stood in open train doorways, but the train might otherwise have been crossing a gulf of decades.

The next day I drove the few miles downstream from Rajahmundry to Dowleshwaram, the site of the weir. Unfortunately the popularity of irrigation prompted the government of Madras almost immediately after the weir's completion to raise the curtain wall two feet with steel shutters; at the turn of the century the work was raised another two feet. It would have been all right, except that the apron was not enlarged proportionately. By 1960, hydraulic action had undermined the weir; engineers feared a catastrophic failure. Just upstream from the old weir, therefore, a concrete barrage has been built, and all but a few bits of Cotton's structure are now obscured.

Nearby, there is a Victorian brick building once used as housing for an officer of the public works department. (I hazard the guess that Frederick Cotton may have lived in it.) Now it is the Arthur Cotton museum. The collection includes an abundance of statues: some busts, some full-length, others equestrian. There are portraits, too, including one in which Cotton is literally beatified: white robes, a halo between his head and a dark background, his arms opened to the viewer. In the lower foreground, looking up at him, stand a mass of worshipful Indians. Lady Hope, Cotton's daughter, is memorialized, too, in her case by a crude statue in which she appears in a cross between a sari and a European dress. It is a good thing she is dead, for having spent a life filled with evangelical activity, she is shown with breasts as subtle as baseballs under a T-shirt. Still, the intention is respectful: the caption reads "Lady Hope in her teens with her pet dog. The anonymous sculptor might be one of the many million fans of Cotton."

The rest of the museum is of a more sober character, with maps and models of the weir and delta works, well done.

There is a two-lane road across the new barrage, and I crossed as far as one of the islands, then turned downstream. Eventually I got lost: I had come to too many junctions to retrace my steps. Yet it was a remarkable drive. For one thing, the canals were full of boats, just as Cotton would have wanted: despite his having built India's first railway, he was always an ardent believer in waterways. And the boats were of a sort that he himself must have seen: poled vessels, with steering oars, and often filled so high with sand, the chief commodity, that the gunwales were within an inch of being overtopped. Swamping must be rare, however, for the main canals are wide, perhaps a hundred feet typically, and straight as an engineer can make them. Periodically the water passes over drops, but the boats pass through manually operated locks.

The air was heavy and hazy, and paddies were on all sides—or if not paddies then bananas or coconuts or water buffaloes. Even the Cauvery Delta had not seemed so opulent, and certainly farmers in the Godavary Delta will tell you that their

One of the hundreds of nearly identical canal boats that ferry sand through the Godavary Delta—in this case down one of the main canals immediately below Arthur Cotton's great weir at Dowleshwaram, near Rajahmundry. Something of the scale of these works may be glimpsed from the width of this canal, which traverses countryside that, before Cotton, was almost entirely unirrigated.

delta is better—that the soil is less sandy and therefore allows greater crop diversification. I remember most of all the huge haystacks of rice straw: fully twenty-five feet high and a hundred feet long. The men building them waved like men who had just finished framing a Pennsylvania barn.

Eventually the road, without warning, intersected the main highway between Madras and Calcutta. I crossed it and headed another twenty miles into the delta. The road was paved but phenomenally rough for a district as rich as this: two hours and twenty miles later I came to Amalapuram. The town has a much better hotel than the one where I had stayed in Rajahmundry; simple, next door to a movie theater, but mercifully clean.

The canals the next morning were bathed in the heaviest dew, but sunshine struggled through the fog and created reflections of palms, coconuts, and bananas. The canals were technically in poor shape, with many concrete outlets into branch channels long ago deliberately broken to increase the water supply passing through them. Still, the delta's water supply is so abundant there is little reason to rehabilitate the system, especially since new control gates—like such structures throughout Asia—would be promptly vandalized by farmers unwilling to have anyone tell them when to take water.

Amalapuram is as cluttered as the Indian conception of cities demands, but the villages surrounding it were scrupulously clean, with palm-thatch roofs and the same kind of fresh wall mudding that Nirad Chaudhuri remembered in Kishorganj. Porches and grounds were swept immaculate, almost as if to enhance the six-foot-high clay granaries fixed to the porch floor. During the harvest festival with which my visit coincided, even the simplest huts were decorated with white and precisely geometric bands of color.

One afternoon I parked a few miles from Amalapuram just so I could walk down an unpaved side road that led through a perfectly maintained coconut grove—the grounds plowed absolutely clean to maximize soil aeration and retention of rain and irrigation water. I passed a barn housing a dozen

European-crossbred dairy animals, and I thought for a while that it must be a dairy herd for Amalapuram.

I discovered how wrong I was when I continued into a village which, at one end, had a cluster of two- and three-story houses, mostly of plastered and painted brick. All were built in the most modern architectural designs, and one boasted a satellite dish. Before I had time to think through what I was looking at, a man asked if he could help me, and so it was that I met Narayana Raju of Kodurupadu.

He, two brothers, and a surviving uncle owned four hundred acres of farmland—almost exactly a third of the village's entire area; the rest of the village's three thousand people shared the remaining thousand acres. Many of them, of course, worked for the family, and Narayana was quietly proud of the fact that he served as banker for many—lending money, sometimes without interest. It was a family tradition, he explained in fluent English. But there was a limit to community intimacy: his own son, who attended an English medium school in Amalapuram, did not play with village children. "He has no time," was Narayana's explanation, though when I pressed him he said that playing on holidays was restricted to family members.

Narayana had a barn with tractors, which he used for preparing his immense rice fields, covering more than two hundred acres. Harvesting was still done by hand, certainly a good thing for the villagers who depended upon the family for their cash income. But the opportunity to work in the rice paddies hinged upon the relative prices of paddy and coconut. For the time being, work seemed a sure thing because converting a field to coconuts requires a costly raising of the land surface to keep the coconut roots dry. If the price of paddy and coconut diverges sufficiently in coconut's favor, however, the case for conversion will grow stronger. The villagers may well be pleased that a banana disease had recently put an end to intercropping bananas and coconuts.

Narayana took canal water eleven months of the year, but when the canals were shut down for desilting he turned on his own tube well pumps. Good water lay only ten feet below the surface, he said, though there was saline water twenty feet farther down. The village pond had now been converted to a family fishpond, from which fish were taken every eight months; villagers took their water from "filter points," shallow pumps recently installed to tap the same fresh-water zone used by his irrigation pumps.

I did not ask about income, but the family's housing told the essential story. The new houses had been designed by architects in Hyderabad, Narayana said, and the satellite dish perched on one of them meant that the family no longer bothered with Indian television; they relied on Hong Kong's STAR satellite for BBC news and the American soaps they liked. Narayana himself had no outside income, though at least one of his brothers did; the uncle ran the village rice mill.

Perhaps that is why Narayana lived in the family's only old house. It had a U-shaped floorplan around a covered courtyard of several thousand square feet, tiled. The supporting pillars were of sal, a cherished Indian hardwood; the doors into the house itself were of teak intricately inlaid with rosewood; the plastering on the house was actually a coating of cement imported long ago from Britain. The house had been built a hundred and fifty years ago, Narayana said, which dates it nearly to the completion of the Godavary weir, and throughout that time the family had maintained its dominating position in Kodurupadu. When I asked Narayana for the name of the president of the village council, he laughed quietly and said "me." His whole manner was quiet to the edge of shyness—understated, cordial, and absolutely confident about the family's position.

Perhaps Narayana presents an extreme case of farmers in the Godavary Delta. When I asked him if he had had other foreign visitors, he said yes and to my surprise remembered not only that it was during the 1960s but that his visitor had been a Mr. Freeman from the Ford Foundation. The Foundation at that time was seeking out the most progressive farmers in the district, and the choice of Narayana would have been an obvious one.

Yet if Narayana is an extreme case, there are plenty of other rich farmers in the Godavary Delta. Ten miles to the other side of Amalapuram, I visited an aqueduct which takes one of the main delta canals across a branch of the Godavary. This is the Gunnavaram Aqueduct (in British times known as the Gunnaram Aqueduct), the most massive work in the delta; modified, it is still recognizable as the structure opened in 1852 to bring canal water to Gunnavaram Island.

The aqueduct consists of forty-nine arches, each forty feet long, and the most remarkable thing about it is that the whole structure was built in four months. The engineer in charge, Lieutenant F. T. Haig, got in trouble for spending 170,000 rupees on the job: only 70,000 had been allotted. Haig explained in his defense that the work required ten million bricks and that the local clay was unusual—required more fuel in its baking than expected. "I had not much time for trying experiments," he said further, explaining that he had to fire all ten million bricks in three months. He went on to say that "the coolies are grossly idle, the bricklayers worse, and the peons worse still. It is not too much to say that there was scarcely a native employed on the work who, if unwatched, would not have sat still half the day and done nothing." Eventually Haig was exonerated—indeed, he became a general in the Royal Engineers—and when the Madras government in 1896 published a semiofficial history of the Godavary works, Haig received high praise: "The aqueduct in any part of the world . . . would have been a noteworthy achievement; in an out-of-the-way part of the Madras Presidency, where machinery was almost unobtainable and most of the skilled labour required had to be trained as the work went on, it was an extraordinary feat."

I drove across the aqueduct, parked, began walking, and within ten minutes was hailed in excellent English. This time it was by a Mr. D. S. Dikshitulu, a Brahmin retired here after a career in Delhi and Bombay. We walked for a while through the village of Gunnavaram, most of whose houses were of mud brick and thatch, often laid out like an American saddleback house, with two rooms separated by an alley. The village lanes were unpaved but heavily shaded by palms, and coconuts

The Gunnavaram, or Gunnaram, Aqueduct, which brings Godavary water to Gunnavaram Island, near the Godavary's mouth. The aqueduct was built in four near-frenzied months by Lt. F. T. Haig. He lacked professionally trained assistants and he had to begin by digging, shaping, and baking the clay needed for the aqueduct's ten million bricks; the reward for his prodigious efforts was an official reprimand for running over budget.

were piled up in many front yards; the meat was for export. Here was a stall selling eggplants, tomatoes, potatoes, string beans, plantains, and other vegetables unrecognizable to me. And here were some huts on ground reserved for the poorest residents of the village.

Nearby was Mr. Dikshitulu's twenty-acre coconut garden, fenced with thorns and irrigated by a pump lifting water directly from the Godavary; near the pump he had a patch of maize, which he was growing for commercial seed. His father, he said, had bought all this land about 1930, when it was useless sand. But diesel pumps had just become available: that was the secret. And with composting and fifty years of pumping directly from the river, the soil looked as black and rich as the soil anywhere on the island.

I cannot say how much of Mr. Dikshitulu's wealth came directly from this land, but his eldest son was preparing for graduate school at Calcutta's Indian Statistical Institute, which suggests assets exceeding the income from twenty acres. The family almost certainly lacked the agricultural wealth of Narayana's, yet it was still unquestionably dominant in the village: that much was plain just from the deference with which Mr. Dikshitulu was treated. Mr. Dikshitulu hired between five and twenty-five employees—paid the men less than a dollar a day, he said; women, about fifty cents. He himself wore a snow-white shirt, a snow-white wraparound, and white sandals; a man at work in his coconut garden worked naked except for khaki shorts.

Mr. Dikshitulu lived in a house unlike any other in the village. It was a walled compound shared with several brothers, each family with a house separated from the others by what looked like a village lane. Behind iron gates, the houses were all of white-painted brick, trimmed with diamond-shaped blocks of primary colors. The roofs were hipped and either tiled or covered with heavy-gauge and darkly painted corrugated steel. They had a central portion that was flat and which drained through a hole in the ceiling into a living-room pool, which in turn was drained by a pipe to the outside. This central room was austere: a television on a table and white walls with a few framed photographs. But opening off it was a kitchen with a three-burner gas stove and with cupboards and racks filled with shining utensils; adjoining the kitchen was a prayer room ablaze with a jumble of prints perched atop a low table painted bright red and yellow. Mr. Dikshitulu was explaining to me that people here prayed to Arthur Cotton as a god when, interrupting us, his teenaged daughter appeared. My visit was completely unannounced, but she was wearing a blouse and skirt that would have been perfectly acceptable in an American high-school classroom.

All this—from the giant haystacks to the satellite dish, from the crossbred cattle to the coconut garden safely reclaimed from sand—all this, of course, is directly derived from the work of Arthur Cotton. And Rajahmundry itself is inevitably flourishing from the wealth downstream: in the main shopping street a new store had recently opened with six floors of suitings and saries. Billboards in English advertised the place far out on country roads, where passersby could read only the name of the establishment and infer its prestige from the unintelligible roman letters. The only thing Cotton could not take credit for was the social hierarchy. Rooted in antiquity, it had accommodated itself handsomely to the irrigation economy.

But Cotton did not rest with the Godavary. Before it was finished he was involved with plans to reclaim the neighboring Krishna Delta.

It's a three-hour drive from Rajahmundry to the city at the head of the Krishna Delta. This is Vijayawada, now with a million people. A new hotel had just opened when I arrived; the Krishna Residency had excellent food, comfortable rooms with air conditioning, and satellite TV; there was even an elevator, though after getting stuck in it the first day I relied on the stairs. A block away the post office had international phone lines; along the streets between the hotel and the post office, many stores were selling color televisions; outside town, a World War II airfield had daily commercial flights west to Hyderabad and north to Rajahmundry.

Vijayawada's main bazaar was so crowded in the evening that even the bicycle I had borrowed was impractical. One merchant had six-hundred-meter coils of coir rope for sale: 240 rupees, he said, which comes to about a penny a foot for rope nearly an inch thick. There were wedding chapels nearby, with electric signs identifying the nuptial partners, and there were portable public-address systems mounted on cycle rickshaws and playing music through megaphone-speakers powered by truck batteries.

Vijayawada, unfortunately, has made poor use of its riverside location: the dikes along the Krishna are lined with the worst kind of slum. But there is a good view of the delta control works, which stretch in a single uninterrupted line between the two hills confining the river. As on the Godavary—and for the same reason—there is now a modern barrage just upstream of the original weir, now used only for bathing and laundry since it was imprudently raised. But there are still old navigation locks on either side of the dam, and I saw a canal-inspection boat, the *Alexandra*, tied up at an Irrigation Department resthouse on the left bank of the river. On the grounds there was a bust of Arthur Cotton.

Amazingly, the Krishna weir was envisaged as early as 1792 by a Lieutenant Beatson. Obviously, he had seen the Grand Anicut of the Cauvery, for in recommending a low dam he wrote that "works of this nature I have seen at Seringapatam, where there are three dams across the Cauvery." The government responded to Beatson by sending an astronomer to survey the site, but the astronomer complained of his "want of proper instruments for the indispensable process (where water is concerned) of taking levels." A century later, in 1899, the government of Madras published a history of the Krishna works by George Walch, then the province's chief engineer. Walch reviewed the reports of 1792 and commented drily: "And there the matter ended, as far as can be traced, for nearly half a century."

Nothing more was done until work was under way on the Godavary Delta. Then, in 1847, a survey was undertaken by a Captain Lake, who worked in close cooperation with Arthur Cotton. Lake planned to irrigate a million acres in the Krishna Delta, and the government requested Cotton's opinion. In 1848 Cotton wrote that "I feel entirely satisfied that the objections to it are entirely imaginary, insofar as the stability of the work is concerned." The objections, of course, were the objections to yet another weir built on sand.

In the case of the Krishna, the dam was to have a crest length of 3,750 feet. It would rise fourteen feet above the summer level of the river, and would be a full 305 feet wide: a six-foot-thick curtain wall backed by a huge inclined mass of stone—the first seventy-five feet to be capped by cut stone but the remainder, as another engineer would say, "simply thrown into the river and allowed as it accumulated to assume its own natural slopes."

The work was officially sanctioned, but nothing happened. Then, in 1851, Cotton fired off another of his broadsides. George Walch in 1899 would quote the correspondence with obvious relish: Cotton, he wrote, "could no longer restrain his impatience, and on 7th January 1852 he sent to the Board of Revenue a very characteristic remonstrance." The last paragraph of Cotton's letter was this: "Whatever may now occur I thus relieve myself from responsibility of being in any way a party to the further delay of a work so long ago ordered by the Home authorities and of such incalculable importance to a part of the country liable to such awful calamities." With a twinkle Walch says: "This woke everybody up."

Construction was entrusted to Charles Orr, who simply moved down from the Godavary works. Progress was rapid, and by 1881 470,000 acres were irrigated in the delta; by 1899, the year of Cotton's death, the figure had risen to 519,000 acres. Unlike the Godavary, however, whose flow is comparatively great even in winter, the flow of the Krishna at Vijayawada falls sharply in winter, which restricts irrigation almost completely to summer crops. That is why, when I took a look at the Krishna Delta one January, most of what I saw was fallowed rice paddies. Still, the canals looked full as they conveyed water slowly to the delta's few winter-irrigated lands, near the coast.

At one place perhaps ten miles from Vijayawada I picked a ditch-bank lane at random, parked, and began walking. The lane led to a major canal, along which there was a footpath lined with houses. Although these were people without immediate frontage on a paved road, they were anything but slum dwellers. I passed a chicken coop that was thirty-feet square, with wire-screen walls and an honest tile roof; outside, a fine bull was tethered to a one-inch iron pipe, a water line. The houses themselves did not have tile roofs: they were of thatch, which extended over a wide veranda. But the walls were of mud brick, immaculately plastered with fresh mud, decorated with geometric patterns in white. They were in better shape, I thought, than the houses of my own neighbors: no flaking paint here, no discolored surfaces—just an even-hued, cinnamon-brown wall, beautiful to look at.

Goats and cattle were tethered near most of the houses, which were frequently fitted with manually operated water pumps, even if the houses were only twenty feet from the canal. Some of the houses had television antennas, and that, of course, meant power lines overhead. A full-bearded man with a pushcart on bicycle wheels was at work ironing the clothes of the housewives he passed: the iron must have weighed ten pounds and was loaded with smoldering coal. He stopped and looked up from his tidy collection of purples, yellows, greens, and blues—some neatly folded, others awaiting his attention. Good-looking children walked by on their way to catch a school bus.

Halfway to the sea I came through Vuyyuru, a town with a big sugar refinery, advertised less by smoke than by the jam of bullock carts loaded with cane. But Vuyyuru also has a Christian church and, next to it, an active church school. I took a look and was immediately surrounded by friendly students, who were then shooed away by a couple of hospitable young teachers. They explained that this was a church established by a Canadian Baptist mission in 1884. The long-time missionary here, one John Craig, wrote in 1907 an account of the mission: *Forty Years among the Telugu.* In it, Craig has a photo of the school I was looking at, physically the same though its name has been changed.

And what about the delta's elite—the people who had never converted to Christianity? Down in Machilipatnam I passed a mansion but was too shy to stop and go in. I ignored it—went on the few miles to Bandar Fort, a few miles to the east. It's as close to the coast as roads go, but it's just a clearing in the mangrove where dozens of boats make their way for unloading. The place reeked of fish, despite ice-filled baskets quickly loaded and put on diesel trucks. New boats were being built, too: wooden keels laid under hand-adzed ribs. Every shipbuilding stage could be seen, from keels and ribs to sheathing with planks and caulking with tar-soaked rope.

On the way back through Machilipatnam I mustered my nerve and stopped at the mansion I had passed an hour earlier. Two men were sitting on the porch, and I asked if one was the owner. They were businessmen, they said, here only to talk to someone else who rented the lower floor as an office. The owner, they said, lived upstairs but spoke no English. Nonetheless they called him, and it turned out that he spoke good English, held in fact a master's degree in English from a university up the coast at Vizagapatnam. He explained that the house had been built by his wife's grandfather, who had started as a lawyer but who, amassing wealth, had become a landowner. Another daughter had inherited another house down the street, but she now lived in New York City and hardly ever visited.

Like so many other former landlords, he explained that his wealth had been decimated by land reform; he now lived upstairs. Still, on the way up we passed many sacks of fertilizer, which the man's son was to use on their remaining rice fields. I sat down in the front room upstairs while he proudly brought out some ivory-inlaid boxes with British coats of arms. He had a massive highboy chest, too; it had been designed to hold Victrola records: "H.M.V.," his otherwise silent wife told me. A bed hung on chains from the rafters.

In the back, downstairs, there were other rooms rented to other people, including a government lawyer who had buried an old upholstered couch under legal files. The couch belonged to the man who owned the house, and he assured me that he would not part with it for two thousand dollars. I did not tell him that I thought the couch was worth less than that even in Europe.

The house itself had been painted only the year before, but it had not been treated with the chemicals that would retard mildew. There was no money to paint it again. We walked out to the front gate, past a heavy iron fountain, no longer working but still plainly labeled with the name of the Madras foundry where it had been cast. I tried to evade a question about the rental charges on my car, but finally confessed to his shock that it cost forty dollars a day, plus gasoline. His last words to me were directions about how to get to the house of somebody really rich.

And was this, then, Arthur Cotton's legacy: three weirs, great wealth, great inequalities? Not quite. Cotton retired to Dorking, near London; his house there still stands, though it is now a nursing home, much abused both inside and out. For many years he occupied himself with gardening experiments, with developing tricycles for adults, and with writing Arabic primers for missionaries. Always, however, there was irrigation, including correspondence with eminent people, including General Charles Gordon of Khartoum.

And always there was India. In 1873 Cotton proposed that a reservoir be created upstream on the Krishna by exploding a million pounds of gunpowder in ten mines that would create a mass of rock a quarter mile wide across the Krishna River. With such a dam, he said, a second irrigated crop would be possible in the delta: a winter crop to supplement the traditional monsoon crop of summer. Indeed. The government of Madras, however, did not take the proposal seriously: with heavy-handed ridicule, it replied by saying that the dam's outlets would have to be built before the dam was created and that "their entire destruction might be involved in its sudden precipitation on them by the agency proposed."

Such criticism only energized Cotton. He developed a plan to spend fifty million pounds sterling on canals that would not only irrigate India but would tie it together with navigation routes that Cotton was convinced would be far more economical than railways. These proposals were the subject of much attention in England, and a parliamentary committee in 1879 took Cotton to particular task for his planned Great Equalizing Reservoir on the Krishna branch known as the Tungabhadra. That proposed dam, with a crest length of eight thousand feet, was to irrigate another million acres and provide much of the water supply for a canal system literally crossing the peninsula.

Ironically, both the Krishna and Tungabhadra dams were built, although not until after the British left India. The Krishna dam is part of the Nagarjunasagar Project—NSP for short—and when it was completed it ranked as the world's largest masonry dam: more than four hundred feet tall, nearly five thousand feet long, and with a reservoir volume about a third that of Lake Mead. The Tungabhadra Dam is part of the Tungabhadra Project—TBP for short—and stands a few hundred miles upstream. As proposed by Cotton, it is a hundred feet high by eight thousand feet long.

Is *this*, then, the extent of Arthur Cotton's legacy: three deltas and ideas for yet more irrigation? And still the answer is not quite, for if Cotton were to return and visit the NSP or the TBP today he would be dismayed. Below the dams he would find hundreds of miles of distributary canals and ditches that have never seen water, thousands of acres that remain, as Indians say, "rainfed." He would see that, for some reason, water entering the main canals does not move through the system as it is supposed to; every farmer in sight would tell him that there was a "tailender" problem. I doubt that Sir Arthur Cotton ever heard that word in the deltas of the Cauvery, Godavary, and Krishna, but here on the NSP and TBP, upstream farmers take too much water and downstream farmers—the unlucky "tailenders"—get little or none.

How have things gone so wrong? The answer is complicated, but looking for it takes us to North India, where a very different approach to irrigation was developed by Arthur Cotton's great rival, Sir Proby Thomas Cautley. This was an approach that worked far less well than Cotton's, yet it nonetheless became paramount in India. We shall see why, though the answer in essence is that it broke with Indian tradition and, appealing instead to European notions of equity, promised to ration water among a great many farmers. In practice such rationing could not be enforced. Headenders took more than their fair share; tailenders got less. That's the story on big irrigation projects across Asia today—not just at Nagarjunasagar and Tungabhadra—and it derives from the Ganges Canal, Proby Cautley's great work and the first European venture in reclaiming the plains of North India from dependence on rain.

Much of this canal remains intact—and in use—and to see it I set out eastwards from Delhi one day. An unmanageably large map was draped over the passenger seat of my car as I drove on the great iron bridge that crosses the Jumna River. This is the "GT" or Grand Trunk Road of Kipling's *Kim*, and for no good reason I anticipated that it would be a high-speed highway. Not so, at least not so in early 1990. I immediately landed in a traffic jam so severe that the truck drivers were turning off their motors and gathering in threes and fours for a sociable cigarette.

I asked around and learned there was no accident: the bor-

der between Delhi and the state of Uttar Pradesh lay just
ahead. Most of the trucking firms had offices at this point to
ease the paperwork of interstate shipments, so almost every
truck wanted to stop and back into its office yard. The problem was that the Grand Trunk Road was only two lanes wide,
so once the trucks began to pile up, there was no room for
anyone to back anywhere, not without a great deal of yelling
and measuring centimeters of clearance. Not knowing how far
the jam extended, I began to wonder if this was all a terrible
mistake.

After a few hours I miraculously broke free and began scoot-
ing along to the turnoff for Meerut. I almost missed it, partly
because the people I asked could not recognize the name from
my pronunciation. (I gradually learned to accent the first sylla-
ble and include the "r" in it.) I did finally find the turnoff, and
the traffic thinned to a fine stream of bicycles. It never van-
ished altogether. There were times in the next few days when
I'd be on an unpaved track miles from asphalt. Thickets would
block my lateral view, and bends in the road would shut off
my line of sight after a hundred yards or so. I'd think I was
alone. But then a cyclist would come by, or a donkey loaded
with a few dozen bricks; perhaps I'd only hear the chopping
of brushwood.

The road to Meerut was straight, tree-lined, and well-paved;
between the shoulder and the fields I saw mud-walled stacks
of cowpats, elegantly assembled into cylindrical stacks very
different from the pup tents of Oscar Lewis's Rani Kheri. Perhaps the cylinders were six feet tall and six feet across; their
dark brown shade was handsome against the green background.

The green was largely sugarcane, and quite by accident I
was here for the start of the harvest. Everywhere I went during
the next two weeks I'd see people chewing on two-foot
stumps; often I'd see nothing until I heard a crunch and
turned to see strong teeth at work. The cane fields themselves
were impassible near-jungles, and I only saw the cutting gangs
when they emerged to carry headloads of cane up earthen
ramps for loading on bullock carts or big diesel flatbeds. The

only other field crop I noticed was wheat, six inches tall and quiet.

The irrigation works that bring the water to the wheat were in sad shape, however: the gates that were supposed to control the flow of water in the branch canals had been removed or destroyed by farmers who were free now to use as much water as they liked. Downstream, I suspected, I would find "tailenders" relying on rain or wells, and so it proved to be.

For now, however, I was headed upstream, to the headworks of the Ganges canal, and everywhere there were animals: cattle and camels, dogs and pigs, sheep and geese. There were goats, the billies grubbily contracepted with sacks over their hips. I steered around hundreds of cart-pulling bullocks, shod and clip-clopping with total indifference. The mornings were chilly, and the bullocks were covered with blankets from which a patch had been cut for their humps. Trucks and buses rushed at them front and rear, but the animals took no notice. Nor did the camels that were also walking along these roads. They were unshod and, therefore, silent, but they radiated scorn. Occasionally I saw elephants—a sad business. They walked with what looked like the stains of dried tears on their cheeks.

Meerut itself testifies to the wealth that irrigation can produce. Famous as the site of the outbreak in 1857 of the Indian Mutiny, a few months after my visit it would make the international press once again—this time for violence during the first round of voting in the electoral season that saw the assassination of Rajiv Gandhi. But what I noticed most, apart from the ferocious traffic, was a sign posted by a doctor. It said that patients didn't have to go to Delhi for a CAT scan: they could get one right here.

Along the way, in fact, I saw not a single village that didn't have at least *some* brick buildings. For that matter I don't recall seeing a village that didn't have electricity, at least poles and a couple of wires tracing their way through the main street. Markets were thriving everywhere. I know it is so because secondary highways in India think nothing of simply debouching into village lanes; the transformation from paved surface to mud occurs so fast that I often thought I had missed a turn.

Three or four bullock carts filled with cane or manure would try to squeeze by. A tractor driver would smile and motion me into the path of a bus that had no intention of stopping. Loose animals, motor scooters, pedestrians—everyone and everything was trying to thread its way through an intersection that no one through the centuries had ever thought needed supervision. Yet in towns such as these, of no more than a thousand people, I'd pass a dozen stalls with bicycles and bicycle parts. Another dozen would sell truck tires. There would be shops selling grain and shops selling cloth. There would be vegetable and sweets merchants. What impressed me most were the carts heaped with bananas. It sounds like a small thing, but every village had at least one such cart, even though bananas don't grow in this part of India. Nor were these bananas intended for India's middle classes: these were bananas in the hands of kids walking out of town into the countryside.

I wandered around Meerut in search of the old church where the Mutiny's first victims are memorialized. (The Survey of India's guide map to the town shows several churches but not St. John's: you have to ask and ask again for directions.) Only a few visitors had come recently: most of those who had signed the ledger in 1990 were Britishers or members of embassy staffs in Delhi. The nearby cemetery was more interesting than the church itself: it had the most orientalized Christian tombstones I'd ever seen, all overgrown with the scrub known in India as jungle. (Like the word *tank*, the word *jungle* is of Indian origin; coming to English, its meaning shifted.)

Late in the afternoon, as I approached Roorkee, I finally crossed the main canal, a huge work even today and the feeder, when it opened in 1854, of the biggest irrigation system in the world. Its nine hundred miles of main canal—and its many thousands more of minors—were designed to irrigate a million and a half acres. Before construction of the canal, none of them had ever received a drop of canal water.

I was worried. The World Bank was helping to pay for the reconstruction of the canal. The work was scheduled to include the construction of a new aqueduct over the Solani River, near Roorkee; the old aqueduct, built in the 1840s and containing fully eighty-five million bricks, was scheduled to be demolished. Was I too late? I could have called somebody at the Bank and asked, but the World Bank cultivates an aura of untouchability all its own, and I was more comfortable simply going and seeing for myself.

The reconstruction work was obviously moving ahead, for I crossed a new and spankingly ugly bridge of prestressed concrete. The old bridge stood nearby: gracefully arched plastered brick, neatly dated with a plaque from the 1840s.

The shoulder traffic kept increasing until I was on a town street too crowded for the car to move faster than the pedestrian flow. I was apprehensive, unsure whether cars were allowed here. Had I made a wrong turn? Suddenly I realized that I was on the canal embankment. I kept moving, crossed the canal on a bridge, and caught a glimpse upstream.

There it was: nineteen arches stretching 950 feet over the Solani River. Shorter by half than the Gunnavaram Aqueduct in the Godavary Delta, and no more than forty feet high, the Solani's claim to fame has always been its bulk, for it sometimes carries as much as twelve thousand "cusecs" or cubic feet of water per second in a channel fully 150 feet wide by 10 feet deep.

There is no shortage of information available about the aqueduct, because Proby Cautley himself wrote a full account of the Ganges Canal. Before setting out from the United States, in fact, I had rummaged around in an obscure corner of the Library of Congress. (Those were the days when that institution was still user friendly; with a little finessing, you could get a stack pass.) There, on a bottom shelf of folios, I had found Nadault de Buffon's 1843 classic *Traité théorique et pratique des irrigations*, in its day just about the only textbook of irrigation engineering. And next to it was an immense volume, one cover detached, spine badly frayed: *The Ganges Canal: Plans.* The date was 1860; the place of publication London; the author, Proby Thomas Cautley. Three big volumes of accompanying text were shelved nearby. The frontispiece of the volume of plans contained a tinted drawing of the Solani Aqueduct. Perhaps it was twelve inches by twenty-four. It showed the aqueduct in all its mass and much of its detail: decorative railings on the roadside, for example, and, at both ends of the structure, a pair of stone lions, sculpted locally by one Lieutenant George Price, 1st Fusiliers.

The aqueduct had been built so well, Cautley reported, that at the removal of the "centerings"—the wooden frameworks used in constructing the arches—the keystones sagged only about an eighth of an inch. (And the work was done so methodically that the sag of each arch had been precisely measured.) No wonder that someone at the World Bank once told me that the budgeted demolition costs were extraordinarily large simply because the work of taking the aqueduct apart would be so difficult.

And now it stood before me in the twilight: filled with water, the roadway busy with cyclists and buses. I maneuvered across the road and drove along the other side of the canal. Still unsure whether this was legal or not, I stayed with the pedestrians and bullock carts and drove slowly, slowly, across the aqueduct. No one objected, including two canal guards.

On the far side I was finally able to stop. I got out, climbed down to the base of the aqueduct, inspected the arches, noted some minor leaking and some simple timber props. I looked at the cast-iron railings. They were definitely the originals, the same ones shown in the frontispiece drawing. Then I drove a hundred yards upstream, beyond the aqueduct proper, and found the lions: flat snouted, curly maned, and well plastered with posters and graffiti. And here was the new canal, the replacement. It was still dry, and it ended just before the old aqueduct. What was happening? Later on, back in Delhi, I was told that work on the new aqueduct had been held up. People feared, according to one man at the World Bank office, "that an excellent old structure would be replaced by a crummy new one."

The headworks of the canal lay another twenty miles upstream at Hardwar, where the Ganges emerges from the Himalayan foothills: they can't be more than a few hundred yards from Hardwar's famous bathing steps—popular even in the winter, when the water is frigid. The river itself hardly exists downstream from Hardwar, for the canal takes almost all its visible flow. (Not to worry: bedflow and tributaries soon restore the river.) But the headworks are not particularly impressive: they're nothing compared with the Solani Aqueduct.

Oddly enough, the young Proby Thomas Cautley began his surveys for the Ganges Canal in 1836, the same year that Arthur Cotton built the Coleroon Anicut, and he based his plans on two earlier works, the Western Jumna Canal, on the Delhi side of that river, and the Eastern Jumna Canal, which runs through part of the plains stretching from the Jumna eastward to the Ganges. Both had been out of commission a long time when the British arrived: the Western Jumna, for example, had been built about 1350 and abandoned four hundred years later, about 1750. The British restored some four hundred and fifty miles of it by 1820. Ten years later they restored the Eastern Jumna. Proby Cautley was in charge of that canal when he began looking at the feasibility of bringing water onto the same plain, but this time from the Ganges.

Like its predecessors, the Ganges Canal was approved by the government of India as a money-making, or at least a money-saving, venture. A contemporary put it this way: "It is very certain that if the restoration and extension of these works had not promised an increase of revenue to the British Government, they would not have been undertaken." The meaning is simply that the government depended for its income on land taxes, which could not be collected in years of famine. Such a year came in 1837, when, according to Cautley, drought led "to famine in its most aggravated shape, and to misery such as is unknown in civilized Europe."

Cautley's first report on the Ganges Canal was submitted in 1840. In it he proposed a canal with a capacity of a thousand "cusecs," to use the technical term. That was just big enough, he estimated, to be a paying proposition. Within a year, however, he was told to revise his plan upwards to 6,750 cusecs—the entire visible stream during low water at Hardwar. This was an immense work, for such a canal would be about half the size of such twentieth-century American behemoths as the California Aqueduct or the All-American Canal. The work was approved, and by July 1842, Cautley wrote, his men had "lined out nearly one hundred miles, collected a large quantity of materials, and had excavation in full progress at three different points." The canal was to run 180 miles southeasterly, past Aligarh; then it would split into two roughly parallel canals, one terminating in the Ganges at Kanpur (the British spelling was Cawnpore), and the other (after dropping plans to extend it to Allahabad) terminating in the Jumna due south of Kanpur.

The government of India was fully occupied by troubles in Afghanistan—troubles that, according to Cautley, "appeared to be perpetually the rock upon which the advancement of these works was to be wrecked." And there were intrinsic difficulties: the engineers, in Cautley's words, had "to deal with the mountain torrent in all its deformity, with illimitable depths of sand, and with difficulties in procuring material such as would hardly be credited without personal experience of them."

In 1845 Cautley took a three-year medical leave: "My health," he wrote, "which after twenty-six years of Indian service had been gradually failing, determined me to proceed to Europe." In the interim the works were handed over to his assistant, W. E. Baker, and Baker's own final report, from 1848, hints at the difficulties he faced. Fearing his successors might not appreciate those difficulties, Baker observed trenchantly that "the power requisite to maintain the regular and equable motion of a vast machine, is no measure of the force required to set it going."

Cautley must have been pleased upon returning in 1848 to find the work "marked by an uninterrupted and steady advance." Perhaps it helped to have the enthusiastic support of the governor-general, Lord Hardinge. Hardinge had met Cautley in 1845 and seems to have picked up his excitement about the project: writing to his daughter-in-law in 1847, Hardinge wrote that he was "now as eager about aqueducts as bombs & shells & villainous saltpeter a year ago." As for the canal itself, Hardinge went on to say that the Ganges "is to be

brought through a sandy district of 800 miles in extent, irrigating 2000 square miles of land and producing food for a million
of people & mitigating, if not altogether preventing, the famine produced by drought."

Many years later Sir William Willcocks, builder of the first
Aswan Dam (and double-checker of Rudyard Kipling's back-
yard powerhouse in Sussex) would write of Proby Cautley that
"the word thorough was written over all his works." Something
of that quality is evident even in such a small detail as the tree
plantings that Cautley ordered: mangoes ("not grafts") were
to be placed at hundred-foot intervals on both sides of the
main canals. They were to be spaced forty feet from the inner
slope of the canal itself, and Cautley wrote that they were to
be irrigated by perforated earthen pots planted alongside and
regularly filled. Something of Cautley's broader interests can
be retrieved, too, from the project's official library a few hundred yards from the Solani Aqueduct. Alongside works on leveling and arches, the library contained Andrew Jackson Down-
ing's *Cottage Residences,* John Ruskin's *Seven Lamps of
Architecture*, and an assortment of travel books including Washington Irving's *A Tour of the Prairies*, and Herman Melville's
Typee.

The canal opened in 1854, some eighteen years after Cautley began his surveying. When Cautley left India that same
year, Dalhousie ordered a ceremonial salute at Calcutta. In
retirement in Sydenham, a few miles south of London and not
far from the eventual siting of the Crystal Palace, Cautley
wrote his account of the canal.

It was then that he got enmeshed in a dispute with Sir Arthur Cotton. He did so reluctantly, for, smiling through his
mutton-chops like Franz Schubert, Cautley was as equable as
Cotton was volatile. The dispute centered on the location of
the Ganges Canal headworks, with Cotton arguing that they
should have been built farther downstream and of the "cheap"
school. Had such a plan been followed, Cotton said, the Solani
Aqueduct could have been skipped altogether. Cautley responded gently at first but was finally provoked into saying
that Cotton was "better qualified to magnify the mistakes of

others, than to be trusted with a project of his own."

Neither man addressed the central problem of the Ganges Canal—the same problem that would emerge a century later on the Nagarjunasagar and Tungabhadra—and so many other projects: the problem of tailender shortages. Neither man in fact paid much attention to the central question of how the Ganges Canal was to operate.

Cautley had anticipated problems: that is why on his medical leave between 1845 and 1848 he made a quick visit to northern Italy to see how the canals there, then the most sophisticated in the world, were managed. Two years later he arranged to send an engineer named Richard Baird Smith on a more extended tour of Italian irrigation. Smith promptly wrote a two-volume treatise, *Italian Irrigation* (1852), which remains of great value not only for its discussion of Italian irrigation but also for its discussion of how Italian technology might be adapted to the Ganges Canal.

Richard Baird Smith took over the Ganges Canal. A man to join the likes of Meadows Taylor, Arthur Cotton, and Proby Cautley, Smith had great physical energy; on his way back from Italy he examined Cotton's three deltas and in so doing traveled fifteen hundred miles by palanquin in six weeks—surely some kind of record. (His report on those deltas, *The Cauvery, Kistnah, and Godavery . . .* [1856], remains a primary source for their history.) Much would have been heard of him in later years if he had not played a leading—some have argued *the* leading—role in breaking the siege of Delhi during the Mutiny. He received what he thought was a trivial wound to the heel, wrote to his wife in Meerut that it was hardly more than a bruise. But complications arose. A few months later he was given a sinecure, but rest did not help. He finally was sent on medical leave but died shortly after leaving Calcutta. He was forty-three. His body was put ashore and buried in Madras.

Like Meadows Taylor, Arthur Cotton, and Proby Cautley, Baird Smith had an almost religious faith in irrigation. With it, he wrote, "men who were the Ishmaelites of society fall, without force or constraint, into the ranks of the great army of industry." One hears in those words the echoes of Jeremy Bentham.

But how was the Ganges Canal to be operated? That was the critical question, and the nub of the problem was that since it had been conceived as a famine-control work it was designed to spread water thinly over a large area. That design decision had been crucially important, and it was supported by rational as well as moral justification, for some farmers might not want to pay for water—might be skeptical of its value. To recoup the canal's cost, in other words, Cautley wanted to bring water past as many farmers as possible.

But what would happen if the canal brought water past many farmers and all chose to irrigate? *That* was the all-important question. Baird Smith devised an ingenious solution. The canal, as we have seen, would divert 6,750 cusecs. Experience on the Jumna canals suggested that one cusec would irrigate 218 acres. (This was an unusually high "duty" for water: down in Madras the duty was taken to be well below a hundred acres. But the crops here were chiefly wheat and cotton, not rice. Based on Jumna experience, Smith anticipated further that about half of the land irrigated by the Ganges Canal would be planted to winter grain; the other half would be sown to summer crops divided so that a quarter of the total annually irrigated acreage would be planted to rice, a sixth to sugar and indigo, and a twelfth to cotton.)

So Baird Smith went on to multiply 218 by 6,750 to arrive at a figure of about 1.5 million acres to be irrigated by the Ganges Canal. Experience on the Jumna again suggested that most farmers would want irrigation water for only about a third of their land, partly because some of their land would be fallowed or used for summer crops that usually did not require irrigation. So Smith multiplied three by 1.5 million and concluded that the Ganges Canal could provide famine protection to the owners of almost five million acres. The great plain between the Jumna and Ganges contained about eleven million acres, so the canal in sum would eradicate famine in half the area—even more than that if one assumed that farmers without irrigation might earn money by working for those with it.

"This great tract," Smith concluded, "will become the garden of the North Western Provinces; and we shall hear no more of those devastating famines, which have hitherto swept across it."

That was the theory. But suppose farmers wanted to irrigate more than a third of their land? Suppose they wanted to grow a lot of sugarcane? Without controls, the tails of the main canals would soon be dry; so would the tails of the branches, the tails of capillary distributaries, the tails even of the village watercourses below the government outlets. Cautley had looked for solutions to this problem during his visit to Italy; so had Baird Smith. Both men knew that continuous monitoring of the canals was impossible. It would be doubly impossible to watch how farmers divided water among themselves below the outlets. A contemporary put it this way: "To attempt to regulate all village water-courses, numbering (as these do) several thousands, we regard as impracticable." Trying to do so, moreover, "would place an enormous degree of power in the hands of a corrupt, because under-paid establishment."

So it was that Baird Smith proposed the following procedure. First, determine how much water would be required below each outlet. Then make sturdy outlets with a fixed discharge sufficient to meet the land's requirement. (Here, in particular, one sees the Italian influence, for Smith had seen such devices there.) Finally, enter into twenty-year supply contracts to supply water at its true value. "True value" was difficult to determine, but Cautley insisted that "to know, in fact, the true value of the property that we hold for distribution . . . [is] the great desiderata." And in a way that a modern economist would applaud, Smith encouraged a local market for irrigation water. Farmers, he anticipated, would sell their rights to one another and thereby disclose the true local value of irrigation water, which in turn would be used in setting lease terms. The great virtues of Smith's system, he wrote in conclusion, were that it required almost no policing and would lead to the economical use of water.

During the canal's first season, the summer of 1855, Smith wrote optimistically that annual contracts had been issued to a total of forty-eight villages. The average contract called for the release of less than one cusec. That was hardly a drop of the canal's initial flow of three thousand cusecs, but Smith was not discouraged. Down in the Etawah District, the collector wrote that his farmers "as a rule believe that irrigation neither improves the quality nor increases the quantity of the produce." But this was a transitory state, Smith argued: farmers closer to the existing Eastern Jumna Canal knew better, and he detected an "induced effect, so to speak, exercised by the Eastern Jumna Canal districts on others near them, which is stimulating to irrigation."

In the following winter 107 villages applied for a total of ninety cusecs, and by the summer 1,134 villages were irrigating about fifty thousand acres. Using his own one-in-three rule, Smith calculated that the owners of about 150,000 acres were, therefore, already protected from famine.

The Mutiny flared the next year; Smith went to Delhi and never returned. His system was soon abandoned. Why? The reasons were discussed most clearly in the report of the Indian Irrigation Commission of 1901–1903. The commission's president was Sir Colin Scott-Moncrieff, who after twenty years of working on the Ganges Canal went to Egypt as head of a team sent to modernize that country's irrigation system. Something of Scott-Moncrieff's character may be inferred from a letter he wrote during his early years in India to Charles Gordon, whom he sought to join in the Sudan. "I am no sportsman," Scott-Moncrieff wrote, "and know nothing of horses, but don't mind a ride of one hundred miles. I have always been used to hard work." Returning to India to serve on the commission, Scott-Moncrieff produced what remains the most valuable survey of Indian irrigation.

It was probably Scott-Moncrieff who was responsible for the irrigation commission's statement that the Italian modules did not work on the Ganges Canal because the distributaries did not operate at a constant supply level. Moreover, in what I assume are also his words, "the cultivators on the Ganges Canal were not used to irrigation, and looked on the module with considerable suspicion. . . . The system was [therefore] abandoned, and it has never since been restored." Abandoned, too, were the long-term leases, wisely in Scott-Moncrieff's view, because the canal was being continually modified and "it would have been fatal to have stereotyped for a long period of years the existing conditions of each irrigation outlet." As for the crop-water requirements that Baird Smith had wanted to investigate, nothing had been done in the interval of fifty years. The commission report states that the farmers have "no idea of the quantity of water required for the irrigation of an acre." Worse yet, neither does the irrigation staff, though the knowledge remains "extremely desirable."

But if Smith's ideas foundered, what was the alternative? The answer is that the Ganges Canal began to operate just as the Jumna canals had always operated: by charging—and these are Cautley's words—for the "surface of land irrigated, without reference to the amount of water taken, but *with* reference to the species of crop." It was a poor system, Cautley wrote, "but bad as it is, it has been much easier to recognize its imperfections, than to remedy them."

What imperfections? For one thing the system implied the costly measurement of irrigated acreages each season. Second, it encouraged farmers in the summer season to delay signing up for irrigation water until they were sure that the monsoon would fail: as one observer wrote, "Every cloud in the sky is watched . . . in the hope of being able to dispense altogether with canal water." Third, it gave farmers no incentive to conserve water. Fourth, it was a system that almost encouraged cheating. Smith grew angry enough to write that "stealing water should be stamped as a felonious act, quite as much as stealing money."

But how to cope? In 1873 an engineer in Cawnpore said simply that "the stronger parties generally take more than their share." He did not use the term "tail-end shortage," but that is what he was describing. Moreover, as Smith knew, the subordinate staff was corrupt. There was nothing secret about this, although the irrigation department didn't advertise the fact. In times of shortage, the outlets were put on a rotation known as a tatil, under which farmers at each outlet were allowed to take water only at certain times. That was the theory; the practice was that powerful farmers bribed their way to extra water.

Colin Scott-Moncrieff had encountered this situation as a young man. In a letter to an aunt in 1859, he wrote that "seeing that the Government subordinates don't practise bribery and oppression, etc., and that all get fair justice in the water-supply, it is often depressing enough to see how a native revels in bribery and forgery, lying and double lying, as if his creed was, 'Thou *shalt* bring false witness.' " Twenty-odd years later he wrote, in a more temperate and official capacity, that "measurements have been dishonestly performed, lands have been unfairly assessed, water has been given out of turn."

And what was the result? On one hand the irrigation department had an incentive to encourage the development of sugarcane, which would require water year after year without fail—and which would use so much water that the canal's effectiveness as a preventer of famine would decline. On the other hand, the ability of powerful or head-end farmers to get an inequitable share of canal water compounded the problem of tail-end shortages. Consider an example. A superintending engineer is speaking to the irrigation commission about the system as it had operated in the 1880s: "Water was consumed with much waste in the upper reaches of channels; but little got down to the middle reaches; and scarcely any, or none at all, flowed to the tail, where the outlets were starved." Here is another engineer, giving an example of conditions on one distributary in 1877: "The distributary is 18 miles long and in the first 6 miles there was in 1877 an enormous area irrigated; from mile 6 to mile 13 a part was irrigated; from mile 13 to mile 18 absolutely none."

The problem of equitable apportionment was not insuperable, even in practice. William Willcocks, for example, who began his career on the Ganges Canal before he went on to build the first Aswan Dam, recollects in his memoirs how

the monsoon rains of 1877 failed along the Ganges Canal, and we had the greatest difficulty in insuring the irrigated crops against

drought. The principal part of our duty was patrolling the distributaries and seeing that the rotations were properly enforced. My
wife took the keenest interest in the work, and through the
whole of the hot weather did her share of the inspection just as
though she were a canal official. She rode down one distributary
recording facts in her note-book, while I rode down another, or
we rode on different banks of the same canal. We met at mid-day
at some inspection house. On one occasion she had a sunstroke,
but I was able to get ice by train and pack it round her head.
After a day's rest she continued her work.

These efforts sound promising—as if the solution were simply
diligent inspection and enforcement—but Willcocks's unin-
tentional punch line is this: "We were encouraged by seeing
the splendid appearance of our irrigated fields in the midst of
the general desolation." In short, compliance was the exception, not the rule, and it was destined to remain so, because
reforming the irrigation bureaucracy has never appealed to
government, either before or after independence.

The British ameliorated the shortages on the Ganges Canal
in two ways. First, they increased the canal's water supply during the 1870s by adding a second diversion point from the
Ganges: this was the so-called Lower Ganges Canal, which not
only had its own command but which intersected and topped-
up the lower half of the Ganges Canal. Ever since, the original
canal upstream of the intersection has been known as the Upper Ganges Canal. Arthur Cotton must have been pleased—
must have taken it as vindication of his old argument that the
diversion should have been where this new canal's intake actually was.

The new supply helped, but demand was so great that water
remained short: one study suggests that a cusec used at the
top of the canal irrigated less than half the land irrigated by a
cusec downstream. Or, to take another case, upstream Meerut
District was able to spread a cusec over 265 acres, but downstream Bulandshahr spread it over 396 acres.

The second thing the British did to reduce shortages was
to reconstruct, mostly during the 1890s, the distributaries to
operate biweekly, rather than continually. The result was that

tatils were abolished. With them, the prime source of corruption disappeared, for it is a much simpler thing to turn off an entire distributary than to see that outlets along its course take water according to schedule.

Some examples may clarify the point. The chief engineer of the United Provinces told the irrigation commission of 1901 that in 1887 he had been stationed in Etawah District and had completely redesigned the distribution system there. The "number of outlets," he said, "was reduced from 7,500 to 4,500 and an immensity of waste prevented." At the same time, he continues, "tatils were abolished and the power of the petty officials in levying blackmail was minimized." The payoff was dramatic: irrigation in the canal's Etawah division rose from 170,000 to 230,000 acres without any increase in the water supply. The same work was begun in Bulandshahr District in 1892: "In one year 1,700 outlets were cut out of a total of 5,700 and tatils abolished," while winter irrigation with the same water supply rose from 134,000 to 180,000 acres. "Tatils used to be so strict in this division that murders were frequent," the engineer concludes, "and petty canal officials amassed large sums by illegal methods."

Another engineer, with a different perspective, testified that he had worked on the Ganges canals between 1881 and 1893, then had gone elsewhere for seven years. When he returned, "the most notable and far-reaching change was the abolition of internal tatils on distributary systems. When I left it was exceptional for any distributary of any size to run except with internal tatils of outlets; in other words, the capacity of the distributary was not equal to the total outlet discharge. On my return I found this system abolished. Distributaries had been remodelled . . . and the system of alternate running of distributaries had replaced the old tatils."

So much water was saved by this reconstruction that it was possible to build new branch canals. This was all to the good of famine prevention, but Scott-Moncrieff was surprised to learn that much of the water saved went to increase the acreage irrigated by farmers who had been irrigating for decades: there was simply too much political pressure to resist these fortunate headenders. Scott-Moncrieff asked one district collector the following question: "People say the irrigated lands are not half as well protected as they used to be. Is there anything in it?" The collector replied yes, "the demand for water is enormous." How enormous? "In Meerut and elsewhere we are told that 70 or 80 percent of the land is now watered every year."

The inequity bothered Scott-Moncrieff. In the famine year of 1878 he had been in South India, in Bangalore, from where he wrote of "a scene of lamentation and mourning and woe. . . . We went to church, and I remember when the familiar 'Be joyful in the Lord, all ye lands,' was chanted. I felt, What nonsense this is! How could we be joyful?" A friend adds that Scott-Moncrieff came to Bombay and collapsed: "He was not delirious, but told me he was *haunted* by awful sights—little children like skeletons gazing at him with wistful, pleading eyes as if he should help them. 'And I can do nothing,' he exclaimed."

As president of the irrigation commission a generation later, Scott-Moncrieff brought that compassionate perspective to bear. "Water," he said, "is so priceless that I should be jealous of giving more where there was enough already." He asked one engineer in particular: "Do not you think it would be better, with whatever water you saved, instead of going in to the same old villages if you might extend the area of irrigation?" The engineer replied: "I think it is too late in the day to consider that now; it should have been considered sooner." Scott-Moncrieff persisted: "But this increase has occurred within the last seven years; it is not of very long standing." The engineer said: "It would lead to very great trouble if it were at all tampered with now." So it was not tampered with, and the problem of inequity was let be for the remainder of the British Raj.

And today? To find the answer, I traveled down past Aligarh to the point where the canal splits into the Kanpur and Etawah lines. The division works are essentially as Cautley left them, with a stone plaque dated 1852, but I saw only slack water in the canal—no movement. And I went down to villages below that point and asked farmers who spoke English if they received canal water; the answer was not at all. They irrigated, but with groundwater they lifted with the aid of pumps. The canal water, I believe, was being diverted upstream. I cannot prove it, because data on the actual performance of the system remain amazingly rare—even rarer, I think, than they were a century ago. And the reason is plain enough: no irrigation department stands to gain by documenting its own deficiencies, and in the case of the still-underpaid Indian irrigation bureaucracy there is much to be gained by letting things remain as they are.

In this connection I spent a frustrating hour with the director of an irrigation-management research center at Okhla, on the outskirts of Delhi. I was asking about disparities, inequities of water delivery, and the director's initial strategy was to assure me that the Ganges canals worked as they were supposed to work. He brought out a leaflet showing the operating times and design discharges of each channel. Deviations? He said he knew of outlets that had not seen water in five years, but on average farmers at heads and tails were getting within 15 percent of the same quantity of water. I doubted this, but without facts I could not dispute his point. He, with the means of building a mountain of data, had no reason to do so.

Still, when I left his office one of his staff members invited me to his office; almost clandestinely he told me about a small study he had been conducting on the Agra Canal, which starts at Okhla with a fine late-nineteenth-century channel, these days filled up with frighteningly fetid Delhi sewage. He told me about a study he had made of a minor canal that branches off near the tail of the Agra main. The minor channel, he said, was supposed to carry twenty-two cusecs but actually carried fifteen, thanks to excessive withdrawals upstream. Worse, the minor canal was supposed to supply thirty-five outlets, each one irrigating the lands of perhaps a dozen farmers. In fact, he said, only a dozen outlets got water on schedule; the two dozen tail-end outlets got water at night or not at all. I asked about the Ganges canals, but he said he did not know; there had been no studies.

Some days later I was talking in Delhi with Dr. Ikbal Singh, an agricultural economist at the Pusa Institute, which is India's national agricultural research organization. He himself was from a village near Meerut, and the minor canal serving his village had received no water at all during the last five years. The situation was deteriorating, he said, because demand for water was continuing to rise at the same time as farmers no longer feared punishment for violating the canal-operating rules. The result? Previously, he said, farmers in his village had relied on wells for supplemental irrigation; now those wells were their sole source of irrigation water. The "15 percent deviation" I had heard at Okhla he dismissed as nonsense.

Now we can understand what happened in the projects that Arthur Cotton had advocated but which were not built until long after his death. As early as 1901, during debates on the merits of building a dam at Nagarjunasagar, the acting chief engineer for Madras argued that "the stored water should be utilized in the upper taluks [district subdivisions] and not in the delta proper." The engineer went on to say that in principle "I consider it is better to increase the area of irrigation than to try double cropping."

This was a departure from the Madras school, from Arthur Cotton. It was an echo of Proby Cautley, a plea for equity. And when Nagarjunasagar was finally built, its water was indeed assigned in the name of equity to the nearby plains, not to the delta. The planners went further and rationed the water with a "localization" plan. On the right-bank canal, for example, head-end farmers, who generally cultivated light upland soils, would be told to irrigate crops that required little water; tail-end farmers, who farmed heavy soils closer to the Krishna River, would be allowed to grow rice. It was perfectly logical because rice paddies on light soil waste water. But why would head-end farmers worry about waste? The government of India lacked the means to impose discipline, at least on more than a pilot-scale level. And so by 1980 about 1.2 million acres were nominally irrigated on the NSP, but only half that land actually got water. What land was irrigated? Head-end land. What was grown? Rice.

The same thing happened on the Tungabhadra Project, that descendant of Arthur Cotton's Great Equalizing Reservoir. Water began to flow through irrigation canals in 1953, but thirty years later only two-thirds of the 600,000 acres to be irrigated on the left bank actually got any water. Why? Localization plans called for 60,000 acres of rice, but project farmers ignored the plans and grew rice on a quarter million acres.

Who was to stop them? These are huge projects, after all. The left-bank NSP alone has fifteen thousand miles of branch canals and distributaries, and landholdings are so small that twenty or more farmers clamor for the water released at each hundred-acre outlet. The irrigation officers themselves? They are underpaid, easy to bribe. There have been reports explaining how these engineers buy their jobs, how they recoup the cost through demanding payments. But corruption reaches to the top, according to the reports, and so nothing is done.

What can be done? A member of Parliament stood up in 1952 and said that his constituents believed that "with independence they would be saved." He meant, of course, saved by irrigation. It's the same today: time and again, the logical and humane wish to provide a little water to a great many farmers has swept away the demonstrated fact that water cannot be spread thinly, at least not in a country where the poor do not resist the rich.

It is not just an Indian story. By the late nineteenth century the British were already concentrating their irrigation-development efforts in the Punjab, where chunk after chunk of semiarid plain was settled by colonists cultivating land newly irrigated by huge canals. The Punjab was split in 1947, of course, and twenty-five million irrigated acres shifted to Pakistan. There, as in India, aid agencies are now rebuilding the old British systems; still, there is no real prospect of an end to tail-end shortages. After all, these are political problems more than social ones, and farmers can always find a way to circumvent engineering.

Time and again it has happened across Asia: perhaps the visiting expert installs special floating gates, developed in France and much ballyhooed by many French engineers.

Then he finds that the farmers prop up the gates so that water flows freely. I recall a project I once visited near Chainat, a hundred miles north of Bangkok. The control gates on the branch canals had simply been removed by local farmers. I asked a group of engineers when this had happened, and they replied matter-of-factly that it had happened the day the gates had been installed. Or I think of Sudan and Africa's largest irrigation scheme, the Gezira, where folk wisdom knows that those same gates make excellent baking pans. You can hunt all day for one and have no luck until you visit a lady's kitchen.

And let me stress again the North Indian connection. Who is responsible for the irrigated plains north of Bangkok? Choose one person and it will be Sir Thomas Ward, an old Punjab hand whom the Thais hired in 1913 straight from India. And who conceived the Gezira Scheme? Name one person and it will probably be Sir William Garstin, who was one of the handful of engineers whom Sir Colin Scott-Moncrieff brought to Egypt from North India. I do not say it is incestuous: I have too much respect for the integrity of these men to make jokes like that. I do say that the connection is very clear and very strong. And the consequences go beyond low irrigation efficiency: they go to the kind of world these projects create.

I think of the east side of our own San Joaquin Valley and of a place where a new irrigation canal—all white cement, neatly poured—runs parallel and close to a nineteenth-century canal that, unlined and heavily overgrown, meanders on a near-contour. Engineers will deplore this old ditch: it loses water to percolation and transpiration, and its rough edge impedes the flow of water. Yet the one looks natural; the other does not. The one could be the subject of a painting; the other will only be photographed. The one is beautiful; the other, as Joan Didion once remarked about the generators at Hoover Dam, is autonomous. It rebuffs—is insulted by—any human being who seeks to establish rapport with it. It has, as my Muskogee friend would say, no spirit.

Arthur Cotton's projects had spirit, were grafted onto the indigenous style of irrigation development. But Arthur Cotton is now a historical curiosity; Proby Cautley is the man with the influence. And you can see the results all over Asia today.

I think of Sri Lanka, once British though never administratively part of the British Indian empire. The highlands around Kandy are elaborately terraced and irrigated with ancient and indigenous canal systems. Yet superimposed upon them—and the pride of the nation, one would sometimes think—are huge new storage dams and concrete canals built to bring water through a capillary distribution system to newly irrigated plains. Perhaps these new systems will work better than those of India, though there is plenty of evidence of headender dominance in Sri Lanka. But where will a publicist turn for pictures? To the old terraces, of course, not to the fine products of modern engineering.

Or I think of Bali and of deep ravines intricately terraced for rice. The traditional diversion works were simple—just rocks and logs—but the ditches were carefully maintained; sometimes the structures even included tunnels through ridges of relatively soft volcanic ash. Everything was village-made, down to the bamboo logs laid horizontally across the head of each branch canal. Notches cut in the log made sure that the volume of water in each branch was proportional to the amount of paddy land it served.

But water was "wasted" in these systems, wasn't completely captured at the diversion; if captured, it was lost to seepage. And so about half of the island's thirteen hundred such irrigation systems were "improved" by the Asian Development Bank about a decade ago. Improved with steel and concrete. I visited one of the projects. The villagers were unhappy. They could no longer control the flow of water and were no longer willing to maintain a system that the government had insisted on building in the first place. I remember one quick tour of the massive concrete headworks of one of these new structures: a farmer had put an offering of a tiny lump of rice on a leaf and left it on a concrete railing. The young engineers showing me the dam were embarrassed. They were looking through the eyes of men from another culture who had been dead for centuries, men whom they had never even heard of.

FARMING

AS MUCH AS THE TRANSFORMATION OF THE
Asian landscape owes to irrigation engineers, they have not
worked alone. Their work, rather, has provided the basis for
new farming methods which have also contributed to the
transformation of the countryside. How long has this been going on? We saw it as far back as Meadows Taylor experiment-
ing with American cotton in Shorapur, but a better example—
one more fully integrated with the modernization of Indian
agriculture—comes from Etawah, the district whose collector
in the 1850s we heard warning that farmers in his district were
dubious about the benefits of irrigation.

That collector was Allan Octavian Hume. Hume's name is
well known among educated Indians, because after a long and
obstreperous career in the government of India Hume had the
audacity to almost single-handedly establish the Indian National Congress, which became the major institution in the
fight for national independence. Like Meadows Taylor in
Shorapur, Hume is still remembered in Etawah, too—remembered so well, in fact, that if you pronounce his name incor-
rectly you will be swiftly corrected. "Home" is the correct pronunciation.

Hume laid out in Etawah a neatly gridded commercial district that is still known as Humeganj—pronounced, of course,

"Homeganj." That, too, helps keep his name alive, at least in Etawah. And he· built, partly with his own money, a high school here. It is still in operation, now as a junior college, and it seems as though everyone in town knows that the building is laid out with a floor plan resembling the letter H. This, they will tell you, is an indication of Hume's imperial ego, though the form is so unobtrusive that I at least would never have noticed it if people didn't point it out.

Hume was appointed collector of Etawah in 1856. He was only twenty-six years old then—had joined the Royal Navy at thirteen, come to India at twenty. Almost as soon as he arrived in Etawah the Mutiny broke out. He tried unsuccessfully to retain control of the district but finally fled the seventy miles to Agra and its fort. A lawyer whom I met in Etawah—a Mr. Chaturvedi—knew all about the episode and made it sound as if Hume ran like a rabbit. A fair judgment? No, but a good indicator of the thin skin so common among Indians.

Hume returned to Etawah as soon as he safely could, and a few years later he made his comments about irrigation skeptics. They were in a remarkable letter to the Manchester Cotton Supply Association. Remarkable because in that same letter Hume went on to say that "if really good seed were furnished them numbers would be *glad* to buy it on a small scale at first and if it succeeded on a large scale afterwards. The fact is that as far as my experience goes, Hindoos like Englishmen, are perfectly ready to take any good advice or adopt any good plan, if you only demonstrate to them practically that *it pays*."

The advice sounds merely sensible, but for its time it was revolutionary. It's the beginning, in fact, of the transformation of Indian agriculture, for it implies that Indian farming can change rapidly with the right technology, effectively demonstrated. There you have the Green Revolution in its essence: a fully developed understanding of the crucial role of new technology combined with methods to get it adopted.

Compare Hume with the agricultural-development program suggested by the governor of Madras in 1863. An experiment station had been set up at Saidapet, a neighborhood now swallowed up by the growth of metropolitan Madras. The station, according to the recollection of someone who worked there, imported "a steam plough, a variety of smaller ploughs, harrows, cultivators, seed-drills, horse-hoes, threshing machines, winnowers . . . [and] chaff-cutters." But there had been no study of local agriculture, no attempt to find out what local farmers knew or wanted—or what innovations might be profitable. England's best was simply brought out and put out, to rust unused. The Saidapet station was abandoned as a failure, reinforcing the old idea that Indian agriculture was mired in conservatism.

Perhaps I am unfair. The British, after all, did establish several botanical gardens that were responsible for several commercially successful crop introductions. Calcutta came first, in 1787; another garden was established in 1817 in Saharanpur, near what would become the head of the Ganges Canal; a third was started at Bangalore in 1819. Important botanical collections were begun at these places, and with them were laid the foundations for the first Indian floras. The gardens also helped introduce many domesticated plants to India, among them potatoes, tobacco, pineapples, and strawberries—and things that one is likely to imagine were in India all along, such as guavas and papayas, cinnamon and nutmeg.

The Agricultural and Horticultural Society of India was established in Calcutta in 1820, and by 1830 it was importing corn and new varieties of cotton and sugarcane; a few years later, when the society had all of five hundred members, new varieties of wheat were introduced from Australia. Meanwhile tea had been found in Assam, and the British had encouraged the development of a local industry. On the other side of the Peninsula a dozen American cotton growers had come to Bombay at the government's request. It was from them, I assume, that Meadows Taylor secured the improved cotton seed he introduced at Shorapur.

Hume understood that the broad advancement of Indian agriculture required more than crop introductions; it required the British to learn as much from the Indians as Indians learned from the British. Unfortunately, the subsequent history of India's—and Asia's—agricultural development can be read as the story of Hume's insight sinking in, only to be rejected.

Hume was eventually promoted from Etawah to the position of commissioner of customs for the government of India. That job brought him to Simla, where until 1947 that government resided most of the year, a mile high in the Himalayan foothills north of Delhi. The Viceroy's Lodge, used today as the home of the Indian Institute for Advanced Studies, had not yet been built—that would come in the 1880s—but Simla was already an elite place, part of India yet apart from it.

Hume built a house there, which he called Rothney Castle. He spent fifteen thousand pounds sterling on it, enough to make it one of Simla's most impressive private buildings. In it he indulged his passion for ornithology; he built up a network of associates who sent him literally tens of thousands of bird specimens. The birds can be seen today in startlingly fine condition at Tring, a town north of London where the British Museum maintains its ornithological department. The museum still owns some eighty thousand of Hume's "skins," lightly stuffed with cotton and placed in stacks of large drawers; there are thousands of eggs, too—altogether almost three hundred "type specimens," the ultimate taxonomic reference points for their species.

But agriculture? Hume's hopes were raised by the appointment as viceroy in 1868 of Richard Bourke, Lord Mayo. Mayo himself had been a farmer, and he wrote on arriving in India that "the time is come when we ought to start something like an agricultural department in the Government of India. . . . Agriculture, on which every one here depends, is almost entirely neglected by the government. . . . We believe it to be susceptible of almost indefinite improvement." The "we" may well have been Mayo and Hume, for it was Mayo's intention to put Hume at the head of the new department.

What did Hume hope to do? He began by stressing how much Indian farmers already knew about their soils and climate, about plowing, about crop requirements, and about weeding. ("Their wheat-fields would, in this respect," he said, "shame ninety-nine hundredths of those in Europe.") Still, Hume argued, Indian agriculture had not changed for thousands of years; yields were not two-thirds of what they might be.

"First and foremost unquestionably stands the increased provision of manure . . . the crying want of Indian agriculture." That was Hume's starting point, and he proposed to develop fuelwood plantations "in *every* village in the drier portions of the country" and thereby provide a substitute heating and cooking fuel so that manure could be returned to the land. Such plantations, he continues, were "a thing that is entirely in accord with the traditions of the country—a thing that the people would understand, appreciate, and, with a little judicious pressure, cooperate in."

Second on his list came an attack on rural indebtedness, chiefly by forbidding the use of land as security, a practice the British themselves had introduced. Hume denounced it as another of "the cruel blunders into which our narrow-minded, though wholly benevolent, desire to reproduce England in India has led us." Third, Hume wanted government-run banks, at least until cooperative banks could be established.

Beyond these things, he noted, there were "innumerable other minor matters" for the department: they included the provision of seeds, the reclamation of salty soils, and plant breeding—a point on which he was astute enough to warn against selection merely for grain size: it was essential, he understood, to choose varieties suited to local physical and cultural conditions. He finished his list with a call for agricultural machinery, especially wind pumps, which he thought promising in a country where "gigantic wind-power (second only to the equally unutilised sun-run power) is running to waste, utterly uncared for over the whole empire."

How were these things to be done? Some years later Hume explained that Mayo had intended to create a director-general of agriculture with a small staff of experts and a minimal office.

There was to be as little writing and as much actual work as possible. Directors of Agriculture were to be appointed in each province, also to be aided by experts. They were to work partly through the direct agency of [demonstration] farms and agricultural schools, and partly through the revenue officials of all grades down to the village accountants. . . . The Director-General was to be moving about generally whilst the crops were on the ground . . . [and was to] make himself fully acquainted with local wants and wishes, . . . watch closely all the schemes and experiments carried out by the Provincial Directors . . . , procure for them, if they wished it, chiefly through the Agricultural Societies of Europe and America, any information, seeds, cattle, sheep, models of implements &c, that they required . . . , keep all fully informed . . . [and] lay down the broad lines of the general policy in regard to agricultural matters that the Government should pursue.

It was pure Hume: study local conditions, introduce possible improvements, and help spread them through the country.

All in vain. Lord Mayo supported Hume's program wholeheartedly, but Mayo, the viceroy, was opposed by his own council: a typical comment from one member was that the "present is not a favourable juncture for the creation of the new department." Mayo was stung and replied that he had to "dissent from the statement that the proposal is in any degree premature. My astonishment is that it was not made 20 years ago." Angrily, he went on to say that he would "make the proposal to the Secretary of State, and leave the responsibility of defeating a safe, easy, and cheap administrative reform to those who think it their duty to oppose it."

The result was a compromise. Mayo and Hume got a department of revenue, agriculture, and commerce, but the secretary of state for India would not even allow agriculture to be listed first. Mayo was soon assassinated by a convict on the Andaman Islands (he was the only viceroy ever to be assassinated), and though Hume stayed on as departmental secretary for nine years, no scientific staff was appointed. Hume's limited time for agricultural work was restricted to the compilation of statistics.

In 1879 Hume was abruptly and mysteriously dismissed, apparently for speaking his mind too plainly. He requested a reason for the dismissal, got none, and went on to publish in

1879 a bitingly critical pamphlet called "Agricultural Reform in India." In it he unwittingly revealed the very frankness that had probably cost him his job: he began, for example, with the comment that "this paper, written many months ago, had been long in type, when the Government emphasised many of the remarks that it contains by abolishing altogether the Department of Agriculture."

Demoted, Hume spent the next three years back down on the plains at Allahabad, the capital of the United Provinces. Then, in 1882, he retired and returned to his house in Simla. The notes he had gathered for an enormous book on his bird collections had meanwhile been stolen. They were never recovered, and Hume had not the heart to begin again. The birds went to Britain: a collection so large and important that the British Museum sent a man to India to supervise their packing and shipment.

In sympathy with nationalist aspirations, Hume went on to create the Indian National Congress. Perhaps that explains why in Simla even today it's easy to get directions to Rothney Castle. When I saw it the place was in a wretched lurch—half the abandoned mansion (with fresh and grotesque *trompe l'oeil* murals) and half an incomplete and apparently abandoned luxury hotel. As for himself, Hume returned to England in 1891. Ever the amateur scientist, he established the South London Botanic Institute. But agricultural reform was not abandoned; it simply went into hibernation. (In an astronomical conceit Hume once wrote of this matter that "the orbit is not calculable, but a certain periodicity has been observed, and every ten or fifteen years the idea has emerged into the blaze of public opinion.")

The very year after his sacking in 1879, a famine prompted the creation of a new government position: secretary of agriculture pure and simple—no revenue, no commerce. Provincial directors were appointed, too—as early as in 1875 for the United Provinces, but in 1880 for the Punjab and in 1884 for Bombay; Madras settled for an agricultural expert, appointed in 1882. Little seems to have been accomplished at any of these levels. Then, in 1889 and not long before Hume packed up and left India for good, the secretary of state for India sent out to India one Augustus Voelcker to undertake a survey of Indian agriculture. Voelcker was the consulting chemist to the Royal Agricultural Society. (Confusingly, he was also the son of a German immigrant who held the same position and had the same name.) Voelcker spent a bit over a year in India—slightly more than half that time traveling.

There is no mention of Hume in Voelcker's lengthy report, but the two were in Simla simultaneously for several months, and there is certainly a heavy dose of Hume's outlook in the Voelcker report. Unlike Hume's pamphlet, the Voelcker report received official attention and is often cited even today as a landmark in Indian agricultural history.

Like Hume, Voelcker was impressed by the peasants he saw: so much so that he began with the premise that "in many parts there is little or nothing that can be improved" in their farming practice. Many critics of Voelcker, seeing this statement, have concluded that Voelcker's book was a counsel of despair, an apology for indefinitely postponing a program of agricultural improvement. Not so.

Voelcker, for example, was in full agreement with Hume on the importance of maintaining soil fertility by returning manure to the land: along with water, he writes, manure constitutes one of "the cultivator's chief wants, and must, like the latter, be taken up by Government, otherwise the soil will not be able to provide for the increasing millions of the people." Voelcker's solution to the fuel problem was the same as Hume's: the establishment of forest plantations grown as fuel and fodder reserves, especially along canal banks and railways and as hedgerows. As for new implements, Voelcker echoed Hume and said that they must "be the outcome of a study of native requirements." Perhaps Voelcker's most significant *disagreement* with Hume was on the subject of agricultural education: he supported it. Hume, in contrast, argued that such schools should wait until research had produced something for the teachers to teach.

Matters stood still until 1899, which proved to be another famine year—and the year in which George Nathaniel Curzon was appointed viceroy. In 1905, on his departure from India, Curzon would look back and say, "What have we been doing for agriculture? Our real reform has been to endeavour for the first time to apply science on a large scale to the study and practice of Indian agriculture." This is not just utilitarian rhetoric: it is a fair appraisal. Curzon began in 1901 by elevating the Bombay director of agriculture to the new position of inspector-general of agriculture. Curzon also undertook the expansion of provincial research, linked to districts by experiment as well as demonstration farms. In 1901 he appointed an imperial mycologist and an imperial entomologist; two years later he appointed an imperial agriculturalist and an imperial economic botanist.

Some of the earliest results of this new interest in agriculture came from the provincial stations. They included the extremely important crossbreeding of thin native sugarcanes (such as those near the Tagore house at Silaidaha) with the thick or "noble" canes first introduced to India from Mauritius in 1827. This work was done between 1912 and 1919 under the direction of a South African named Charles Barber, and it was done at Coimbatore in southern Madras because only in the south was the climate warm enough for the thick cane to set seed. The intention all along, in other words, was to improve the canes grown in the Ganges Valley, and this is exactly what Barber did. After the complementary development at Kanpur by the chemist George Clarke of a cultivation method involving green manure and castor cake, cane yields in the Ganges Valley roughly tripled.

Meanwhile the imperial scientists assembled at Pusa, a village about fifty miles north of Patna and now in Bihar, though then in Bengal. It was a site that had belonged to the government for a long time, but Curzon had big plans for it. He had just had a visit from Henry Phipps, an associate of Andrew Carnegie and a major philanthropist in Pennsylvania. Phipps had come to India for the ceremony acknowledging Edward's accession to the throne. What had brought him? I do not know, but Curzon's wife was an American socialite, and I suspect she had something to do with it. (She had been living at Dupont

Circle in Washington, D.C., when she met the young Curzon; the two were married in the fine church that stands across Lafayette Square from the White House.) Phipps gave Curzon an unrestricted grant of a hundred thousand dollars, and with it Curzon decided to build at Pusa an agricultural research station for all of India. An immense building went up—two massive stories, solid brick, with domes and porticoes enough for a national parliament.

Much basic scientific work was done over the next three decades at Pusa, but the station's remoteness was a perpetual aggravation, and many people were quietly pleased when an earthquake in 1934 severely damaged the building. Rather than repairing it, the station was relocated to the western edge of New Delhi, where it survives, now expanded into a huge campuslike complex. Like all such institutions, however, the character of Pusa survived the earthquake and the move: what one sees on the Delhi campus today is the direct descendant of the institution Curzon created.

What kind of institution was it? The simple answer is that it was much like the national agricultural-research organizations emerging during the same period in Britain and the United States: bureaucratic, highly specialized, and with a strong bias in favor of the life sciences, rather than either the social sciences or some synthesis of the life and social sciences. Was this a good thing? The conventional answer is a firm yes. One thinks, for example, of India's dependence on grain imports during the 1950s and of the dire predictions made in those years about the looming threat of famine. Yet it is common knowledge that the disaster never came: it was averted by the introduction of high-yielding varieties of wheat and rice, signaled by India's request that Norman Borlaug come to India from Mexico. That was 1963; two years later the government ordered 250 tons of seed from Mexico.

But India did not rely for long on imported seed; it was soon growing its own and breeding a great many locally adapted varieties of high-yielding seed. By 1990 India's wheat production had increased 500 percent from its level in 1960. Higher yields came more slowly with rice, but by the 1990s India's

rice production had more than doubled from the level of the
1960s. (In 1960 India produced more than twice as much rice
as wheat, but the two grains are now about neck and neck.)

It is difficult to attack such a record; to do so one must look
at the long-term implications of the new technologies. Yet one
need not go out on a limb of one's own here: one need look
no farther than Albert Howard, the one-time director and
probably the most eminent of the scientists appointed to the
early Pusa staff.

Howard had come to India in 1905 after working in Barba-
dos on arrowroot and in Kent on hops; in India he turned to
wheat, and by the 1920s some two million acres of India were
sown with the so-called Pusa wheats that he and his wife and
colleague Gabrielle developed. Some of the wheats were of
Australian origin, having been brought to India in 1897; others
were true Mendelian crossbreeds of Indian and Australian
wheats. (Ironically, one of the straight Australian varieties,
Pusa 4, was apparently introduced to Australia, where it
promptly won a prize.)

The Howards were more than plant breeders, however:
they were exponents of the grandest kind of holistic research,
and it was this that would eventually set them at odds with
the research community within which they worked. Howard
once wrote that he had luckily "escaped the fate of the majority of agricultural investigators—the life of a laboratory hermit
devoted to the service of an obsolete research organization."
Beginning with their work in shaping their experimental plots
at Pusa for better drainage, he and Gabrielle became interested in the importance of soil aeration, in the nature of soil
fertility, and in the relationship of soil fertility to plant and
human health. After retiring from Pusa, they moved to the
town of Indore in the Central Provinces, where they developed a composting method that they called the Indore Process
and which they continued to develop in England—Albert
alone after Gabrielle's death. In humus, they believed, lay the
secret of good farming.

And here is where the Howards got into trouble. India's
chemical-fertilizer industry had consisted in Howard's time of

one company in Madras that made fertilizer for tea and coffee planters. How much has changed since then! In 1952 Frank Parker, a Du Pont veteran, arrived in India as the American ambassador's foreign-aid advisor. At Parker's urging India was soon conducting an immense program demonstrating the benefit of chemical fertilizers. In 1961, two years after Parker's departure, the Fertilizer Corporation of India was created; it built immense factories. During the 1960s India's production (and consumption) of fertilizer tripled. It tripled again during the 1970s—and again during the 1980s. The government's own semiofficial history of agriculture in India says that "in the entire history of international co-operation since Independence, no foreign expert has served India with such dedication and sincerity as Frank W. Parker."

Perhaps it is so: certainly the yields that pulled India up from near famine during the late 1950s could not have been achieved without fertilizer. And so it is almost an embarrassment to recall Albert Howard's saying in the 1930s that the introduction to India of inorganic fertilizers would be "a disaster of the first magnitude." Howard knew he was swimming against the tide; his last book appeared in 1943 as *An Agricultural Testament.* There Howard wrote that "the agricultural practices of the Orient have passed the supreme test—they are almost as permanent as . . . the primeval forest . . . , the prairie, or . . . the ocean." He asked why this should be so, and his answer was that India's farmers planted many crops and balanced them with livestock.

Howard contrasted this kind of farming with "the NPK mentality [that] dominates farming alike in the experimental stations and the country-side" of England. With this modern farming, he continued, "the principle followed [is] based on a complete misconception of plant nutrition. It is superficial and fundamentally unsound. It takes no account of the life of the soil, including the mycorrhizal association—the living fungous bridge which connects soil and sap. Artificial manures lead inevitably to artificial nutrition, artificial food, artificial animals, and finally to artificial men and women."

"In the years to come," he continued, "chemical manures

will be considered as one of the greatest follies of the industrial epoch." They were already bringing us endless outbreaks of pests and diseases. "Insects and fungi," Howard wrote, "are not the real cause of plant diseases but only attack unsuitable varieties or crops imperfectly grown." The diseases that agricultural scientists were struggling to combat, in short, were the result of "the breakdown of a complex biological system, which includes the soil in its relation to the plant and the animal."

Howard's second wife, Louise, took pains to stress that Howard was not "slavishly subordinate to a kind of Nature worship. He was a very bold and courageous innovator." That is true, but even before his retirement from Pusa, Howard was at war with the research community around him, and the final words of the *Testament* leave little room for compromise. Howard writes that "in allowing science to be used to wring the last ounce from the soil by new varieties of crops, cheaper and more stimulating manures, deeper and more thorough cultivating machines, hens which lay themselves to death, and cows which perish in an ocean of milk, something more than a want of judgement on the part of the organization is involved. Agricultural research has been misused to make the farmer, not a better producer of food, but a more expert bandit. He has been taught how to profiteer at the expense of posterity."

Clearly, Albert Howard was as outspoken and tactless as Arthur Cotton or Allan Octavian Hume. And not just in print. Consider his reaction to the 1928 Royal Commission on Agriculture in India. The only commission of its kind ever to survey Indian agriculture, this commission was under the presidency of a future viceroy, Victor John Hope, Lord Linlithgow. The commission worked for about a year and a half, traveled eighteen thousand miles, spent about a hundred thousand pounds sterling, and produced a massive report deploring the lack of cooperation between Pusa and the provincial research stations. Part of the problem was Pusa's isolation: the commission wrote that "we cannot but regard it as a matter for regret that the site actually selected was one six miles from a railway station, in an out-of-the-way district to which access from most parts of India can only be obtained by a river crossing, and from all parts by a somewhat tedious railway journey."

But there was another reason for Pusa's declining status. In 1919 the Indian constitution had been modified to make agriculture a provincial rather than a central subject. Pusa was now having trouble attracting good staff. The commission's chief recommendation, therefore, was the creation of an imperial council for agricultural research, "a new organization to which Pusa and the provincial research institutions would stand in exactly the same relation"—namely as organizations seeking council funding for their research.

The council was duly created, and Albert Howard could not have been more virulent in his opposition. In public he said that "if the Research Council had been created for the purpose of wasting public money and hampering the progress of rural India no more perfect instrument could have been devised." What was his objection? After all, most modern agricultural research is funded in exactly this way. The problem, in Howard's view, was that such a council was likely to move in the direction of ever-greater specialization and teamwork. Again one is tempted to ask what's wrong, but Gabrielle Howard had written as early as 1905 that "the plant knows no division of science. . . . Therefore men with good insight in all will be most likely to make real advances." India needed not an army of technicians, the Howards believed, but men with the vision of a Darwin. In a not-so-veiled slap at Pusa, Howard went on to say that the council was "attempting to perpetuate a research organization that was obsolete before the Council was born."

Howard's outburst had been provoked by a report published in 1939 by Sir E. John Russell, the eminent director of the Rothamsted Experimental Station at Harpenden, north of London. Russell had been asked to report on the progress made by the council, and he had concluded that the "great problem in Indian agriculture is not so much to acquire new knowledge as to bridge this gap between peasant practices and experiment station achievements." It sounds very modern— almost a ritual call for agricultural extension—but Howard would have none of it. Russell's report, he said at a public meeting, was based on a single "lightning tour," and its author knew nothing of Indian agriculture. How, therefore, could he judge what India needed? One hears the echo of Allan Octavian Hume.

As for his own appraisal of the council's work, Howard said bitterly that "good farming seems to have disappeared from the programme of agricultural work subsidized by the Government of India." Was Howard right? I don't know. It depends on how much confidence you have in modern agricultural technology. What is perfectly clear is that Howard's views, like Hume's, have been pushed aside.

I went down to Pusa, mostly because I was curious about what was left of the old building. It's still out of the way. You start at Patna, which lies on the Ganges midway between Benares and Calcutta and which conforms more closely to the nightmare image of Calcutta than does Calcutta itself: the city is full of pavement sleepers who rise at dawn to wander among decaying old buildings. Not far away from those same sleepers is a famous granary built by the British in 1786; beehive-shaped, almost a hundred feet high, it was intended to be filled from the top and emptied from the bottom. In fact it was never filled—though when I saw it, curiously enough, it *was* being used in a small way as a food warehouse, with sacks of grain carried in at the bottom.

The drive to Pusa begins with a very long viaduct across the Ganges and then drops down to a barely two-laned road that, unsigned, keeps forking. This part of India is the original habitat of the grass from which sugarcane comes; by no coincidence it is also the part of India where thatching is most nearly ubiquitous—thatching made from that grass. Some people will see in this thatch a sign of Bihar's abiding poverty; others, a sensible reluctance to switch to metal sheets that bake in the summer. But even in Bihar things change. Fish is no longer a rare treat, for example: I was told of a wedding party at which the servants refused to wait for a delayed fish course that once they would have waited all night to enjoy. And at a tea-stop along the road to Pusa I walked past a hut hardly big enough for an American bed. A man sat on a string cot next to a built-in clay stove, and he listened to a battery-powered boom box.

I had a driver with me that day, and eventually we came to Pusa Road, the railroad station a few miles from Pusa proper. Albert Howard had hated the isolation of Pusa—found the compound mentality stultifying and said he could have got twice as much done in a more accessible location. There were no experts in sight this day: the station's single open platform was nearly deserted.

We edged through a crowded market and continued a few miles to the Bihar Agricultural University, a big place with many new buildings. I stopped at the gate and asked for directions to the old Pusa Institute. "It's gone." I had hoped that the old earthquake-damaged building might have been restored and put to some other use. Not so.

A monsoon cloudburst broke as I parked on the site of Henry Phipps's gift. I walked into the adjoining and totally uninspired generic-modern building that houses the Bihar Sugarcane Research Institute. Almost immediately I was captured and drawn into the office of the director, Dr. K. C. Jha, who, after a few moments' conversation to determine my interest, called for Dr. V. S. Bhide.

It was true, Dr. Bhide said: the earthquake-damaged building had been utterly demolished and its site reassigned to the state government for sugarcane research. Now the Sugarcane Research Institute itself had fallen on hard times. The Bihar Agricultural University had been created in 1971. Most of the institute's land had been assigned to it. Even the institute itself came under university direction. "Bigger fish eat smaller ones," Dr. Jha explained.

The rain had let up, and Dr. Bhide took me on a tour of the grounds. We passed an impenetrably overgrown British cemetery and some fourteen old residential bungalows. Most were huge and had been cut up into apartments; others were abandoned, including one known only as Number One. This was the biggest but most distant of the bungalows; in the old days it had been assigned to the institute's director. For some years that would have made it Albert and Gabrielle Howard's home.

Now it was officially designated as an inspection bungalow for visitors from the Pusa Institute in Delhi, which still retained some research plots here. The bungalow grounds were in rough shape, and Dr. Bhide said that the occasional visitors preferred to stay elsewhere; I recall he mentioned something about snakes.

Dr. Bhide and Dr. Jha together told me that 360 locations had been examined in the course of choosing Pusa as the site for Curzon's institute. After they finished praising the extraordinary fertility and agriculturally benign climate of Bihar, however, I couldn't help asking a question. Why was Bihar so backward? On the drive up, I said, I had been surprised to see only one tractor; had seen very little water in the rice paddies; had seen much idle land in short grass. Both men smiled demurringly, but they made it clear that the problem lay not with nature but with the wreckage of Bihar's political system. Everything could be done here, they said, but Bihar needed land reform and field consolidation. Both were dead letters on the statute books. It needed irrigation, too, but this again required political will. Farmers were so demoralized under current conditions that they worked no more than five hours a day.

It was pleasanter to talk about the institute's work, its focus on finding cane varieties that were productive without irrigation—not an impossible assignment, considering the local ancestry of cane. We did so, then I thanked them and left.

And what about the nearby Bihar Agricultural University? There are dozens of these institutions in India today; the first was created in Uttar Pradesh in 1960. All have been modeled, thanks to the American consultants who helped to create them, on that American innovation, the college of agriculture. They are weak in the humanities; tolerably strong in the social sciences, particularly economics; and strong—sometimes very strong—in the hard sciences, especially those bearing on agriculture.

As teaching institutions, of course, the agricultural universities deviate greatly from the American model, because few sons of Indian farmers can afford to go to university, and almost none of the few who can afford university have any intention of farming themselves. Even the students who do have a village or small-town background—and there are many of them—are determined to use their university degrees as insurance *against* a life on the land. Most join government agricultural services, private companies selling to or buying from farmers, or research institutions such as the universities themselves. From the perspective of Allan Hume or Albert Howard, it is a tragic situation, because the graduates of such schools will hardly care about the problems Indian farmers face. The innovations produced at such schools will reflect the interests of the research community, not the needs of India's farmers. It's back to ground-zero.

And that brings us to a certain Presbyterian missionary, a man named Sam Higginbottom, who in 1911 proudly opened the Allahabad Agricultural Institute. He had modeled it directly on Ohio State University, from which he had just returned, degree in hand. Here is the germ of India's agricultural universities, for Higginbottom quickly gave up his hopes of training farmers: like the students at the Bihar Agricultural University, none of his students wanted to be farmers. Higginbottom hoped at least to train his graduates to listen to the farmers he hoped they would serve, but he had little success. Listen to his testimony given in 1928 to the Royal Commission on Agriculture: "That is our greatest trouble, we know so little about village life, and if that were not the case we would not be having this Commission sitting here to-day and making inquiries into these matters."

Ironically, Higginbottom himself was not a farmer: he had been born in Manchester, where his father's career declined from middle-class comfort to driving a horse-drawn cab. Higginbottom tells us in an autobiography published in 1949 that his elder brother managed to get to the United States to study at the school created by the famous evangelist Dwight Moody and that he himself followed and went on to Princeton University.

By then, Higginbottom says, he had decided on a career as a missionary, but it was only a chance meeting with a missionary back from India that brought him to India at all, let alone to Allahabad. Arriving in Calcutta in 1903 and expecting to start evangelizing in the countryside, he was assigned instead to teach economics at Allahabad's Ewing Christian College. The campus still exists, close to the park where, in 1858, the Allahabad Proclamation was read to announce Victoria's assumption of direct rule in India. The college's brick buildings are intact, but the tower clock stopped a long time ago, and the many gothic windows of the classroom building are broken, revealing chairs covered in dust. Down at the Proclamation Park, Victoria's famous words have been obliterated from the monument that once carried them.

Presumably things were in better shape during the six years when Higginbottom taught at the college, but those years weren't happy ones for him. He himself had taken only one course in economics, and his students were parroting answers, rather than seeing any relevance of the material to their own lives. Higginbottom began pushing them to the field and in particular to a nearby prison whose warden had set up a model farm that—chiefly because of organic fertilizer methodically trenched into the soil—was far more productive than the lands outside the prison grounds.

Higginbottom later wrote that he remembered Dwight Moody's asking "of what use it was to get a hungry man converted." And so, Higginbottom says, he gradually came to believe that he should give up not only economics but evangelizing as well: he could help India most by improving Indian agriculture. In 1909, on his first furlough home, he and his wife asked themselves if they should "go on living our lives as our lives had been lived. . . . We arrived at the conclusion that, before I could really help India, I must make a much more serious study of agriculture. . . . It was a drastic decision. I was thirty-five years old."

Higginbottom enrolled at Ohio State and within two years completed a bachelor's degree in agriculture. Not only that: he lectured incessantly about his plans for the institute and raised money a dollar at a time, with occasional thousand-dollar contributions from people such as a McCormick heiress. He went back to India with thirty thousand dollars, especially necessary because his superiors were willing to support the institute only if it cost the mission nothing. Fund raising became a never-ending struggle for Higginbottom, and he gave literally thousands of speeches in the cause.

Returning to India in 1911, Higginbottom took charge of 265 acres of eroded and weedy land across the river from the Ewing college. He went to work improving the land, chiefly by damming gullies and killing weeds by deep plowing during the hot weather. In years to come he would retain rainfall on the land with contour-hugging furrows. He would introduce American dairy bulls, too, and silage pits, which were unknown in India. The farmers called him the "crazy man," he writes: "they were sure I was mad when I dug great deep holes into the earth and put good green fodder into them."

A rare glimpse of Higginbottom's character emerges at this point in his autobiography, for he writes of a visiting expert who had never seen silage before but who asserted categorically that it was worse than feeding manure. Higginbottom said nothing at first, only brought out some cows and let them choose between fresh fodder and his silage. The cows chose the silage, and Higginbottom said: "Doctor, in many things I respect your opinion, but on the subject of silage, I prefer the opinion of the cows."

Higginbottom probably knew that an agricultural college had been opened at the Saidapet experiment station in Madras as early as 1876; a college near Poona had begun teaching agriculture in 1879—had begun issuing diplomas in agriculture in 1890 and in 1905 had become the Poona Agricultural College. But both these schools catered to the production of revenue officials, not scientifically trained farmers.

The Royal Commission on Agriculture knew it, too: writing of these colleges and of others that had later been established at Coimbatore, Nagpur, Lyallpur, Cawnpore, and Mandalay, the commission said that all were "regarded as avenues to employment in the agricultural departments." The agricultural advisor to the government of India added his own view that "a very large number of students" at the Nagpur college, where he had once worked, "were men who did not belong to any agricultural class; they did not really want to go back to the land."

Higginbottom hoped to escape this trap. Appearing in 1928 before the Royal Commission on Agriculture, where his testimony is far more revealing than his autobiography, he said that "when I began this work I was looking forward to a college in agriculture which would give training to a young man in India equal to what he would get in Europe or America." What he found, of course, was what the agricultural universities find today: a strong interest in getting a degree but no interest in farming. Worse, the institute had no academic affiliation and so attracted few students: only 101 students graduated between 1912 and 1923—on average ten a year. Later, the institute did win an academic affiliation to the University of Allahabad, and in 1934 it awarded its first Bachelor of Science in Agriculture. Enrollment began to rise, but fewer than one in ten of the graduates actually farmed, and of the eighty early graduates whose careers Higginbottom could trace for the Royal Commission, only six were farming their own land. More than sixty worked for government agencies, most commonly as teachers or as officers in revenue or agriculture departments.

Higginbottom was asked by the commission if he would "not regard it as a feather in your own cap if a larger proportion of the students who pass through your institution went in for farming?" He said yes, of course, but pointed out in his defense that even in the United States the early graduates of agricultural programs became teachers. "I think India will have to repeat that experience." Perhaps he was right, but three generations on, nothing has changed, and the gulf between farmer and researcher is as great as ever.

And how fares Sam Higginbottom's institute today? I had no idea what to expect but crossed the Jumna, turned under the railway bridge, and headed upstream. The Ewing Christian College stood across the river now, and here, alongside the left-hand side of the road, were the same men's dormitories pictured in Higginbottom's autobiography: two-story, brick, severely plain. Here, on the right, was what in Higginbottom's time had been the science building. It was a more elegant building, also two stories and of brick but with gracefully arcaded verandas. The lower floor was now faculty offices, locked but identified as used by the faculty of a "special course," its nature unidentified. Upstairs was a dormitory, the rooms unoccupied but obviously inhabited.

Behind the old science building and overlooking the Jumna stood a group of bungalows. One had a sign saying "Dr. H. Shepherd, Officiating Principal." I knocked and was welcomed in, though I was obviously disturbing the family's leisure. Dr. Shepherd was an Indian Christian; he introduced me to his wife and daughter, gave me something to drink, and graciously told me that the institute had a faculty of ninety and a student body with about two hundred students in each undergraduate year. It was a big jump from Higginbottom's later years, when the institute had fourteen faculty and admitted hardly more than twenty students annually. Now, Shepherd said, there were graduate programs leading all the way to doctoral degrees. About half the institute's students were Christians—many from the South, where Christians are particularly numerous.

The school's literature, samples of which he handed me, still described the institute as "A Christian Institution of Rural Life" and declared that it was managed cooperatively by a board including representatives of the United Presbyterian and Lutheran churches of the United States. But Dr. Shepherd said that foreign contributions had almost disappeared and that the institute, determined to maintain its Christian character, had cut itself off from more than minimal government support. It had been a painful decision but one that allowed the institute to provide agricultural education to Christian students who might otherwise be admitted nowhere else.

Dr. Shepherd took me over to Sam Higginbottom's old silage pits—twenty feet deep, twenty feet across, and still sound and in use next to handsomely whitewashed brick dairy barns. The head of the department of animal husbandry came over and told me sadly that the institute's dairy program had collapsed when the foreign bulls on which it relied died of old age. The institute had been unable to afford replacements.

I was lectured briefly on the institute's experience with silage: it worked fine but had not been adopted locally because farmers wouldn't cooperate with one another on cooperative pits. The words rang a bell, and later on I found out why: Higginbottom writes in his autobiography that the villagers had rejected his idea of cooperative silos into which villagers could bank measured quantities of fodder and later withdraw silage. The idea would not work, they had said: "Half of the village would be murdered and the other half in gaol for committing the murders."

The institute's new director, Dr. Rajendra Lal, came around and proved most eager to talk. He had just returned after five years in Manhattan, Kansas, where he had earned a doctorate in soil science. Now, he said, he was trying to get American productivity out of his Indian staff. He had already stirred such resentment that guards had been posted around his house.

Dr. Lal took me past the institute's department of agricultural engineering—the first in Asia, he said proudly. We passed an old steel-plate water tank, with box-girder legs, a spherical base, a cylindrical body, and a conical cap: straight out of the Midwest. He said it was the only one of its kind he had ever seen in India, and I agreed—could not remember having seen one anywhere else in the country. The institute's farm was fallow, because the monsoon was late and there was some mechanical problem with the irrigation pump. Research? The institute had once bred a famous white guava, but there was no money left for research.

We went back to Dr. Lal's bungalow, the same one the Higginbottoms had used. The building was unchanged, though the garden was poorly tended. We went inside, where Dr. Lal explained that his parents, both Indians, had worked with a Protestant mission in Etah District, between Agra and Etawah. Like his parents, he too had "had a call" and would stay in India from now on. Still, he wanted me to meet his eight-year-old son, who was having problems. After all, the boy had spent his third through seventh years in Kansas. Now he was back in India, and he didn't like it.

The son came in, and his first words were "how is the U.S.?" His next were "don't you find India dirty?" and "do you like Indian food? I don't." I thought of Hari Kumar in Paul Scott's Raj quartet: the English-educated Indian forced to return to India and to forget the person he has been. Here was a boy who wanted hamburgers and pizza, jeans and computer games. I asked his father whether it was better to seize the opportunities that occasionally came along or to do everything possible to help the boy forget. Dr. Lal said he didn't know. I ineptly asked if there was anything I could send that the boy wanted. The answer was no.

Outside Dr. Lal's office a large signboard listed the institute's principals chronologically, with Sam Higginbottom from 1910 to 1945 and with fifteen successors in the not quite fifty years since. Clearly this was still the Higginbottom Institute, and, just as clearly, it was not teaching Indian farmers how to improve their farming methods. That's why I jumped when I learned almost by accident that the "special course," which I had seen the sign for, was a short-course in practical farming. Was the Higginbottom dream alive after all? Was there a hope of bridging the gap between researcher and producer? Was there something here that would have excited Allan Octavian Hume and Albert Howard?

Dr. Lal spoke of the course with a reticence that I understood only when I found out that it was run not by Indians but by the World Council of Churches, with support from many organizations, including the Presbyterian Hunger Program of the United States. Indeed it was the only place on campus where there were still foreign missionaries: Japanese, German, and Australian. They were just about the last of their kind in India, because the government of India now requires missionaries to have work visas that it will not issue.

I did not meet the German, but I did meet the Australian, Dennis Muldoon. He had been at the institute with his wife Elizabeth and their three very blond daughters for nine years. They had just returned from a furlough home; Elizabeth talked about her inevitable bout of supermarket madness. Dennis had readjusted quickly; he was setting off that night

on a third-class railway journey to Madras. When I left him he
said "God bless." The words felt surprisingly good.

The next morning I met the "special course" leader, a Japanese agronomist named Dr. Kazuho Makino. He had been
working as a missionary in India for twenty-one years, and
though his business card identified him as a "fraternal worker,"
there was no fraternal slack about him: I got on the back of his
Honda motorcycle and we zoomed around the campus while
he tried to keep his students working. Working at what? The
special course admitted ten students for a ten-month course
stressing field and vegetable crops. The name Albert Howard
didn't appear in the course literature, but the curriculum included compost pits and green manure, as well as practical
work with dairy cows and poultry and lectures in related topics
such as entomology, plant pathology, and economics.

The upstairs dormitory of the old science building was used
by the students in the special course. Some of them were at
work digging up trees for transplanting; others were puddling
a rice paddy manually—six young men pulling the plow that
was guided by a young woman. All had been admitted to the
course on the assumption that they were "dedicated to serve
people at the grass roots level" and were "able and willing to
participate in daily manual labor," but now they wanted to
know only if the mud was sufficiently stirred. Dr. Makino told
them it wasn't. I have never seen Indian university students
knee-deep in mud, but the sight raised a question: how many
young Indian farmers would need a lesson in puddling? The
explanation was that these students were not farmers at all;
they were workers in private development agencies from vari-
ous parts of India. That was why they knew nothing about
puddling.

It was all to the good, of course, that they should have such
practical experience—far better to work in the mud than to
hear a lecture on puddling. Perhaps someday they would even
show farmers that they knew what puddling was about, which
is more than graduates of the agricultural universities would
do. The pity was that they would have no ties to the country's
research establishment—would have none of the professional

status needed to make that establishment listen to what they learned from India's farmers. The link to Hume and Howard was there, but attenuated to the vanishing point, and the consequences were that India's agriculture was going to look more and more American, not like something homegrown.

VILLAGES

EARLY IN 1993 I VISITED ASHILL, A SMALL VILLAGE in Norfolk, England. It is very quiet, with perhaps a thousand people and with no building more prominent than a modest stone church. As soon as I entered the churchyard, I found what I was looking for, the tombstone of Frank Lugard Brayne. It's a simple stone, with Brayne's name, his dates—born 1882, died 1952—and his decorations: a Military Cross from World War I and companionships in the orders of the Star of India and the Indian Empire. At the bottom there was a verse from Luke 22: "I am among you as he that serveth." Frank Brayne served during the 1920s as the deputy commissioner (the Punjabi equivalent of collector) in the Gurgaon District, which lies immediately south of Delhi. There, he single-handedly conceived of and executed what became famous as the "Gurgaon Experiment." He publicized his work through several books on what he called "village uplift," all published by Oxford University Press. The Royal Commission on Agriculture in India praised his work highly, and I suspect that Brayne generated more attention and publicity for his district than any other district administrator in the history of British India.

Appearing before that commission, Brayne gave some background. Since 1920, he said, he had worked "in one of the poorest districts in the Punjab, I have been there for six years,

I have visited thousands of villages, I have got 1,200 villages, I suppose I have been into every village once and many villages several times; I spend the whole of the cold weather and a good deal of the hot weather in the villages themselves, so that I have a very close acquaintance with the actual cultivators." On the basis of this experience, he continued, he was convinced that "we are beginning [at] the wrong end with agriculture before uplift."

"Uplift"? Brayne said that he "would insist with all my power that no improvement of agriculture is of any use whatever without uplift. An uplift campaign must precede and accompany all efforts at improvement of agriculture. Improvement in agriculture cannot precede an improvement in the standard of living and no improvement in the standard of living is possible without breaking the hard brake of custom which grips the rural area. The people do not know how to spend the money they have got, so what is the use of giving them more money till they have learnt this lesson? They live in the most unnecessary squalor, misery, suffering, degradation and disease." Improving agriculture was easy: a matter of "better seed, better implements, and more manure." The hard part was "to jerk the villager out of his old groove, convince him that improvement is possible, and kill his fatalism by demonstrating that both climate, disease, and pests can be successfully fought."

How? Brayne and his wife Iris therefore set up schools. For boys, there was a school of rural economy, where "the dignity of labour is the first and greatest lesson to be taught" and where the curriculum included not only agricultural methods but sanitation and public health, stock breeding and forestry. For girls? Brayne told the commission that the "heart and center of the uplift campaign ... [is] the elevation of women. India is the most backward of all countries because it regards women as hardly human." In 1926 classes were conducted under his wife's direction for some eight hundred fifty girls studying childcare, first-aid, village sanitation, and domestic skills like sewing, knitting, and cooking.

For the district's adults, Brayne explained that he set out to "deluge the area with every form of propaganda and publicity that we could devise or adopt or afford." He distributed thousands of pamphlets and hired some thirty young Indians as "village guides." (He dismissed the graduates of the Punjab Agricultural College in Lyallpur—now Faisalabad in Pakistan—by saying that they "cannot hitch a pair of bullocks.") The guides were young men, he said, "who look at village life as one big whole and can advise him [the villager] generally about the many problems of his life."

And what were those problems? Like Allan Hume and Augustus Voelcker and Albert Howard, Brayne selected soil fertility as the starting point: "It is utterly useless and worse than useless," he said, "introducing better machinery, better seeds and better farming until we can stop the people ruining their land and impoverishing and degrading themselves by the making and burning of dung cakes." His solution was to have villagers dig pits into which all their wastes—animal, vegetable, human—would be dumped, then later excavated as fertilizer. It was a procedure that not only improved soil fertility, of course, but helped make villages cleaner.

The Gurgaon Experiment had a livestock component too. "At Gurgaon," Brayne told the commission, "we have got 600 stud bulls; I believe we have the biggest breeding establishment in the world." Gradually, Brayne hoped, he could upgrade the quality of the bullocks essential to India's farmers, but a lack of serum meant that "we have got every known epidemic raging." Moreover, Brayne's requests for improved bulls from the Government Livestock Farm at Hissar, a town two districts to the northwest, had been reduced "in order to enable Hissar to fritter away its bulls in twos and threes all over the Province." (One hears a hint of exhaustion, and Brayne, in fact, was very tired. In written testimony he accused the government of seeing the local district officer as "a convenient beast of burden to be loaded with routine and drudgery.")

But Brayne persisted. There had been no iron plows in the district in 1920; Brayne urged farmers to buy them, and by 1926 there were 1,337. In 1920 Gurgaon farmers used leather buckets to lift water from wells; by 1926 the district had six hundred Persian wheels, which Brayne recommended. In 1920 the district grew only traditional varieties of wheat; by 1926 there were fifteen thousand acres of a Pusa variety wheat. What was Brayne proudest of? Nothing as grandiose as a new mentality, an end to fatalism: Brayne was proudest of the hundreds of deep pits that the villagers had dug for all their organic wastes. They were the one thing, he was convinced, that would survive him.

They didn't. I know, because I've looked. It's not much of a trip: leaving Delhi's airport, you pass a highway sign pointing left to Delhi and—in equally large letters—right to Gurgaon. I've often wondered what arriving tourists think when they see that name. Nothing, I presume.

Because Gurgaon District is so close to Delhi, its northern half is dotted with housing subdivisions, country clubs, motels, and factories. (Automobiles are made at the biggest of these factories: Indian-made Suzukis, in a plant employing thirty thousand people.) On the district's south side, however, Gurgaon is still a primitive place. There is an explanation for this, for the southern part of Gurgaon is dominated ethnically by the Meo, a Muslim group that has been a challenge to government officers for a long time; as early as 1879, a report spoke of them as "comparatively lazy and superlatively unthrifty." In sum, the northern half of Gurgaon District is generations ahead of Brayne—in a way it is even ahead of Ashill where Brayne lies buried—but the southern half is still waiting for him to come.

Looking for some relic of Brayne's work, I found a remarkable antiquarian book dealer in the main market of Gurgaon town who knew of Brayne. (Antiquarian book dealers are rare in India, and Vijay Kumar Jain specializes in government documents—a niche rare anywhere and one occupied to my knowledge by no one else in India.) Jain said that his father personally remembered Brayne; nobody else did, and there were no memorials. Later, I found half an exception, on John Hall Road. The funny thing is that there has never been anyone named John Hall. The road takes its name instead from the John Hall, which is the colloquial name of the meeting hall used by the government employees of Gurgaon. The hall stands directly across from Brayne's old residence, still fronted with potted plants in a long driveway and still occupied by the Gurgaon deputy commissioner. But on the hall there is a plaque stating that the building was dedicated in 1925 to the memory of John Goble Brayne, the second son of Mr. F. L. Brayne. No age is given for what I take to have been a boy. Brayne had told the commission that "a magnificent hall is being erected at Gurgaon by public subscription as the centre of all our many activities," but he had made no mention of a son.

Official authorities, well represented by the commission, thought that Brayne's work was outstanding. Malcolm Hailey, an eminent governor of the United Provinces, contributed an introduction to one of Brayne's books, *The Reconstruction of Rural India*. Never before, Hailey wrote, had the British "deliberately attempted to effect that change in the psychology of the peasant, and in his social and personal habits, without which it is impossible materially to improve his conditions of life." Why had it not been tried before? Hailey's answer was that "not many of us, to tell the final truth, have had the missionary spirit necessary for the enterprise."

But if Brayne was so successful, why is so little left of his work? The answer is not that India has gone beyond compost pits, Hissar bulls, and Persian wheels. It is that the experiment collapsed as soon as Brayne left Gurgaon. The Royal Commission on Agriculture feared precisely this result: "The moment you disappear from the Gurgaon district, what will happen to the wholesale propaganda which you are carrying on?" Brayne had been optimistic in reply: "I think my successor will continue it."

No so. We know what happened when Brayne left Gurgaon because of an account given in *Rusticus Loquitur*, a book written by Malcolm Lyall Darling. Darling, who brought E. M. Forster to India and supervised the work of George Orwell at the BBC, was a career civil servant who toured Punjabi villages on horseback and published the results. It happens that he came through Gurgaon seven months after Brayne's departure.

"Now, seven months later," Darling wrote, "all is changed, and the most optimistic estimate is that amongst the peasants themselves not more than one-third of the activity remains." The Gurgaon villagers find the improved bulls too heavy, the improved plow too expensive, and the Persian wheel unsuited to spots where the groundwater is deep or the water table subject to rapid fluctuations. And Brayne's darling, the compost pits? There is no one to empty them, Darling writes: there are not enough sweepers to do the work, and farmers will not accept Brayne's idea that villagers should clean their own. Besides, if all the organic matter is turned into compost, there will be no cooking fuel, and it does the villagers little good to grow more food if they cannot cook it.

Where did Brayne go wrong? The answer, Darling says, was in his dictatorial methods. Everything Brayne accomplished, Darling quotes one observer as saying, was done "by order and through fear." Is it so? From a distance of sixty years it is difficult to say for sure, but Brayne himself told the commission that "so long as they prefer rings to mosquito nets . . . , I do not think it is much use helping them with agriculture." And so, convinced that the Indian practice of putting capital into jewelry was wasteful, Brayne insisted that any man having business with him remove his earrings before coming into his presence.

It sounds less like an attack on village fatalism than it does another arbitrary demand of another feudal lord. And Brayne did unfortunately tell the commission, "I suppose some sort of a Mussolini influence is necessary to awaken the people." Granted, this was 1928, but even in 1928 there were people who disagreed with Brayne's approach. Malcolm Darling, for one, considered Brayne's emphasis on propaganda to be absolutely wrong, as wrong perhaps as the nonsense about earrings. The reliance on propaganda, Darling wrote, "is the chief cause of the ephemeral character of . . . [the experiment's] success." Darling goes on to distinguish between "the teacher . . . [who] tries to make people think things out for themselves [and] the propagandist . . . [who] saves them the trouble of thinking at all. . . . Of teaching," he concluded, "we cannot have too much; but of propaganda we can hardly have too little."

Over the next thirty-five years India searched in vain for a more empathetic approach to uplift. The lineage of experiments began with the YMCA, which in 1915 began a program of what it called "rural reconstruction." The name was coined by one K. T. Paul, and it is significant, because it implies continuity as well as change—a graft, not uprooting and starting over from scratch.

The YMCA work was based at Martandam, a village not far south of Trivandrum in what is now Tamil Nadu. Here a Cornell University graduate named Spencer Hatch developed a comprehensive program specializing in education and spare-time industries such as beekeeping and poultry production and marketing. In Hatch's words the program set out to be "the people's own"; its goal was to train them "to help themselves upwards on all sides of life."

Hatch set up a School of Rural Reconstruction to train workers farther afield, and in 1932 he himself went briefly to Baroda in Gujarat. Baroda, which is now a city renamed Vadodara, was then the center of a princely state, and the prince wanted to establish his own program of rural reconstruction. He entrusted the work to V. T. Krishnamachari, who, after Independence, would serve as Jawaharlal Nehru's right-hand man on the all-important Planning Commission. (One may infer from this connection that "uplift" would, in the years ahead, be strongly supported at the highest levels of India's government.) In terms reminiscent of Brayne at Gurgaon, Krishnamachari wrote of the Baroda program that "no lasting improvement can be achieved in the conditions of rural life unless all sides of it are attacked at the same time." With Hatch's help, Baroda established four-member teams to work in agriculture, animal husbandry, cooperation, and engineering. The teams toured the state, offering help to the cooperatives widely established there.

In 1937 the government of the United Provinces undertook its own program of rural development. A new department was created, and rural development officers were appointed to stir "a desire in the villagers for improvement." Their assignment—and it will sound familiar by now—was to "change their whole outlook on life . . . , help the village people realize that their salvation lies in their own hands." The work was supposed to include the establishment of manure pits, improved livestock, and better agricultural implements, but little was done because the province's Congress Party government resigned in 1939, and civil servants that did *not* resign in sympathy were shunned.

A few years later, in 1945, yet another venture was tried: the India Village Service. It was launched in the United Provinces' Aligarh District by American Methodist and Presbyterian missions, and the work was directed by the missionary William Wiser. (He and his wife Charlotte are best known today for *Behind Mud Walls*, a study of Karimganj, a village near Mainpuri; first published in 1930, it went through many editions in the United States and is still in print in India.)

The India Village Service was small: in 1950 the corps of what the service called "teachers" consisted, in all, of eight people—all Indian, half men, half women. All were college graduates. Each was given a bicycle and a cluster of villages. The familiar objectives were to help villagers help themselves in seven domains: health, sanitation, homemaking, agriculture, recreation, industry, and general education. The unfamiliar method was to win the villagers' confidence, to learn their "felt needs"—how deep go the roots of development jargon!—and, in response, to provide accurate technical information. Wiser wrote that the teachers were expected to work "in the spirit of *humility, sympathy, understanding, appreciation and love.*" It's Gandhian as much as it is Christian, of course, and it's a very long way from Frank Brayne.

Of these three post-Gurgaon experiments I have no first-hand knowledge, but India soon embarked on a vast national experiment in community development, and with this I do have some personal acquaintance because the work began in Etawah of all places, the old home of Allan Octavian Hume.

There was a time during the 1950s, in fact, when visiting scholars interested in India's rural development were told to avoid Etawah. It was a showplace, they were told, no longer

representative of Indian conditions. U.S. Ambassador Chester
Bowles had been a visitor. So had Paul Hoffman, president of
the Ford Foundation. So, literally with a red carpet, had Elea-
nor Roosevelt. I do not know how many other famous visitors
came to Etawah, but the list was long enough that Albert
Mayer, the American city planner in charge of the project from
1948 to 1952, feared that the work would be undermined by
all the attention: the villagers in the neighborhood, he wrote,
were complaining that the project staff had no interest in anything except showing off to bigwigs.

What was going on?

The highway to Etawah from Agra crosses the Jumna—the
Taj Mahal is visible in the distance downstream. It stays
within a few miles of the west bank of that river for many
miles, but you never see the Jumna again, only sandy, scrub-
covered hills that drop down toward the river. "The police
don't go here," one man told me, alluding to bandits. Perhaps
it is so, but there are roads that branch off the highway and
cross the Jumna downstream from Agra. I took one of them
and in daylight at least the countryside seemed perfectly safe,
with occasional fields of sorghum wherever there was a bit of
flat land. Over the rougher spots donkeys carried loads of fuelwood to weighing and shipping yards. The only disturbing fact
was that the poor Jumna—a hundred and fifty miles downstream from Delhi—was still literally black with untreated
sewage.

On the left-hand side of the highway and stretching away
toward the distant Ganges, the chief winter crop was mustard,
four feet tall in January's full bloom. It stretched field to field,
so that from a distance dozens of fields merged, bounded only
by the sky and groves of mangoes or acacia. (I gave a ride
through part of this mustard sea to two gentlemen who were
working on the upcoming census of India. They commented
on the beauty of the countryside, felt it as much as I did.) Of
sugarcane there was little, because of Ganges canal water there
was almost none, even though we passed plenty of Proby
Cautley's fine old branch canals.

For lack of canal water, farmers used wells. Occasionally we passed crank-type cavity wells, abandoned but not as old as they looked: one such well, for example, bore the inscription "Mr. Hiralal Lala, 1945: Public Works Department." The farmers had switched to tube wells. Those for domestic use were operated by hand, but those for the fields were driven by diesel pumps or electricity. (Each fuel has its pros and cons: electricity supplies often fail in India, but on the eve of Desert Storm there were long lines of farmers sitting on jerricans and waiting for diesel fuel at the local gas stations. There was panic buying all across India in those days.) I saw only one Persian wheel, the sort of thing Frank Brayne had recommended in Gurgaon: the bullock walked round and round, attended by a boy.

No sooner had I arrived in Etawah than a reporter for the local newspaper materialized and asked for an interview. I was amazed at the attention but dodged him and asked instead if he knew about the Etawah Pilot Project. I drew a blank. I tried the personal touch: "Albert Mayer?" Another blank.

I settled for directions to the collectorate, the district's administrative center. It was on the edge of town and was surrounded by large old bungalows—very un-Indian with their spacious grounds. The collectorate itself was a compound with scattered buildings around which dozens of lawyers congregated. They sat on chairs before tables shaded by metal or bamboo awnings, and they wore black coats and judicial white collars. Patiently, they waited for customers. (I think of Brayne, who, asked if the villagers of Gurgaon were fond of litigation, replied: "It is their chief hobby.")

I walked around until a peremptory voice called out: "What do you want?" I turned and saw a lawyer, collar in place, Hindu sect mark on his forehead. I asked where the district's development office was. "Not here," was his reply. I said I was interested in the "pilot project." Again a blank. "Albert Mayer?" Nothing. Then a "come." We walked over to one of the courtrooms, where a small crowd gathered. I took out my tiny camera, but it was waved away from the sacred precinct. I tried my mantras: "Pilot Project?" "Albert Mayer?" Nothing.

I headed back to the city hall, in the center of town. The

old Anglican church near the city hall was now an indoor badminton court, and a Muslim civil servant on the Etawah City
Board told me that such desecration was "shameful." I was
surprised that he felt so strongly about it, especially when he
made it plain that he wanted me to write his words down; he
watched as I did so. Why? I am sure it was his way of com-
menting on the strained relations between Uttar Pradesh's
Muslim and Hindu communities. When I asked as tactfully as
I could about the difficulties faced by Muslims here in Etawah, he fell back on body language. A teenaged boy who
walked around the town with me early one morning was more
explicit: things were dangerous. His father was a senior engineer in Lucknow, the state capital; but for all his advantages
as the son of such a father, the boy was still worried.

But how was it possible that nobody knew of Albert Mayer's
work? Long before coming to Etawah I had read of how Mayer
had come to India during World War II as a colonel building
military airfields. He had been introduced to Jawaharlal Nehru, then chief minister of the government of the United Provinces. Americans being Americans, Mayer told Nehru what he
would do if *he* was about to take charge of India. Mayer said
he would set up a group of pilot projects and try to find the
best way to rebuild India—literally tearing down the half-
million villages of the country and starting over, brick by brick.
Mayer would provide better housing, better roads, sewage dis-
posal, water supply, mosquito control, irrigation, dispensaries
and hospitals, schools, and community houses and warehouses.

It has never been satisfactorily explained, so far as I can tell,
why Nehru a few months later wrote to Mayer in New York
and asked him to try his hand. Certainly Nehru was eager to
transform rural India: as late as 1957 Nehru would say, "I am
not really enamoured of the Indian village, as it is. I want it to
change completely, gradually no doubt, but completely." And
equally certainly, Nehru could hardly call upon the British to
help him in that task.

Mayer soon met with Arthur Mosher, an agricultural economist with a doctorate from the University of Chicago. Mosher

had spent the last fifteen years teaching at the Allahabad Agricultural Institute; now, with Higginbottom retired in Florida, Mosher was principal. Mosher seems to have persuaded Mayer of the impracticality of his (and Nehru's) plans to rebuild the country: India couldn't afford it. What was the alternative? Mosher would later write: "I pulled out a ten-page project which I had been working on and gave a copy to Al. At that time I couldn't get the money. The approach was extension oriented, but where Allahabad, with its small tenuous extension staff put emphasis solely on education, Etawah stressed the input side and the need to insure supply lines." India would now import another American idea: Sam Higginbottom had tried to establish an Indian equivalent of the land-grant agricultural university; Mayer would try to establish the Indian equivalent of cooperative extension.

In the States, extension had evolved during the fight early in the century against the boll weevil. It was the great accomplishment of Seamon Knapp, for whom the U.S. Department of Agriculture named the Knapp Arch, which ties together the two main USDA buildings on the mall in Washington, D.C. Ironically, Knapp's work was just taking shape during the years when Sam Higginbottom was enrolled at Ohio State; Higginbottom just missed the curve, so to speak—had been at school a shade too soon to pick up the extension idea. By the time of the Royal Commission on Agriculture in 1928 he was all in favor of it—testified that in Canada and the American South extension had "revolutionised rural life."

Now, with Mosher and Mayer, extension would be introduced in India. As early as 1946 Mayer wrote to Nehru that "over here our Department of Agriculture has evolved a very successful system of 'county agents' who not only give instructions, but who continuously circulate among the people, answer questions, take personal interest, and have gained the confidence and friendship of the cultivator." This was a task beyond the range of a city planner, so Mayer brought into his work an agricultural extensionist named Horace Holmes, originally from Tennessee and the New York State Extension System, but latterly from China.

How would the system work in India? The answer, in a nutshell, was like an India Village Service with money. There would be no arrogant "guides" here, no propagandistic hand: Mayer knew all about Brayne. Mayer's extension agents were known in Hindi as "village servants," although the official English translation was the more respectable "village-level worker."

Mayer himself set the tone. A senior assistant would later write of the day Mayer's pickup truck broke down, stranding Mayer and one of his men. "At long last, one of the villagers arranged two ponies. . . . One of the owners of the ponies accompanied them to bring back the ponies. After Mr. Mayer had a ride for about a mile and half, he got down and insisted that the owner of the pony should ride." Mayer, this same assistant continued, "on the average . . . worked for 18 to 20 hours a day. He ate very little when he was in the villages—a few oranges, a water melon or any other fruit he could find. His Indian colleagues did not have to make any arrangements for him."

Work got underway in 1948 with 64 villages; the number rose to 97 in a year. Another 125 were added in 1951. Mayer spread the village-level workers thickly, with one man for three or four villages. Rather than dictating to the people they served, the agents were expected to determine the most pressing need in each village, work with the villagers to solve it, then build on that relationship to undertake a wide array of cooperative projects that would ultimately lead the villagers to work without direction.

Only advice was given free: there were no grants-in-aid here, no programs of aided self-help. But the Etawah Pilot Project was soon able to point to dramatic successes. Wheat production tripled after the introduction of a new variety. Villagers balked at composting, so a rotational green manure was introduced instead. With it, of necessity, a moldboard plow was introduced: more than a thousand were in use by 1950, and they continued to be used even after the green manure was abandoned during the 1950s in favor of the chemical fertilizers that India was just beginning to use. Roads were built by the villagers, and malarial ponds were drained. A "rural youth organization" was set up along the lines of American 4-H clubs. Work even began on Mayer's original scheme of village construction: subsidized brick was supplied through a cooperative kiln.

Meanwhile, more village-level workers were being trained. Holmes told one class of trainees that "you will be called upon to work as probably you have never worked before. You will be asked and expected to do nothing that those men supervising you do not do, but you will be expected to do everything they do. There is nothing of benefit to the farmer that you and I will hesitate to do because we might feel that it is beneath our dignity to perform menial tasks."

In 1952 the Etawah Pilot Project was visited by Paul Hoffman, president of the Ford Foundation, which was then setting up an office in India. Hoffman was impressed; so was an American agricultural extensionist accompanying him, Douglas Ensminger, who would run the foundation's office for nineteen years. They were so impressed, in fact, that they agreed to pour more than five million dollars into building schools to train more village-level workers. At the same time the Allahabad Agricultural Institute got a grant for more than a million dollars to help develop its own agricultural-extension program.

Even more important than the Ford connection was the visit Etawah received in 1951 from Chester Bowles, the new American ambassador in Delhi. A former advertising executive, Bowles had never before set foot in India, but within a month he was in Etawah and ready to make a major commitment to the project's enlargement.

How did it happen so fast? Both Hoffman and Bowles were primed because of one man, Yen Yang-ch'u, known in the United States as Y. C. James Yen. Working as education secretary for the Chinese national committee of the YMCA, Yen had introduced Spencer Hatch's "rural reconstruction" work to Hubei Province in the late 1920s. Yen went on during the 1940s to become a member of the Chinese Joint Commission on Rural Reconstruction. With degrees from Yale and Princeton, he had an easy time impressing Americans, including Hoffman, who before joining the Ford Foundation had served as the first administrator of the Economic Cooperation Administration, the United States' post–World War II foreign-aid organization. Yen knew Bowles, too: Bowles acknowledges as much in the first of the two memoirs he wrote on his years in India.

That is why the American commitments to Etawah came so fast. "When we first visited Etawah," Bowles wrote, "the work was being carried out in ninety-seven villages with some sixty thousand inhabitants. Village workers had been carefully trained, first to win the confidence of the villagers and then to introduce in each village new methods of fertilizing, better seeds, public health measures, primary education and literacy courses. . . . As I listened to the hard-working, dedicated instructors in the village worker school and watched workers in the fields and villages, it seemed that this was the key to the future of India and Asia. Here was an administrative framework through which modern scientific knowledge could be put to work for the benefit of the hundreds of millions of people who have so long lived in poverty. That night I went to work with pencil and paper. How many village workers would it take to cover every village in India? How many public health specialists would be needed? How many agricultural engineers, soil conservation experts, irrigation specialists?"

On Thanksgiving Day, 1951, Bowles met with Nehru and offered $54 million in U.S. aid to begin expanding the Etawah work. The men agreed to spend the money over three years on approximately fifty projects, each with three hundred villages. With wildly unrealistic expectations, the planning document actually specified that each village in the program should be provided with adequate drinking water, with agricultural extension and veterinary services, with drainage facilities where needed, with irrigation for half its land, and with substantial grazing and forest reserves. Moreover, each group of twenty-five villages was to be clustered in a market unit, and each five market units would be grouped in a "block" whose central settlement would have accommodations for a thousand families, electricity and telephone services, an agricultural school, a plant nursery, a small hospital, and small-scale industries.

It was much too much, much too soon, but carried away with his own enthusiasm, Bowles wrote that "it is not difficult to foresee the day when the agricultural phase of Community Development will everywhere lead into this second phase of building, when teams of millions of people, young and old, will give a few hours a day to their village and country, after their own work is finished. . . . I can visualize a wave of construction which can sweep through 500,000 villages and change the face of the whole subcontinent."

Fifteen pilot extension areas were approved in 1951. Each covered a hundred villages, and each was under the control of an extension director with a staff agricultural officer, three agricultural technicians, and about a dozen village-level workers. (Other technical areas, such as education, would rely on cooperation from existing branches of government.) At the top of the hierarchy was a Community Development Administration, reporting directly to Krishnamachari and Nehru in the Planning Commission.

The administrator was Sachindra Kumar Dey, a former employee of the General Electric Company and a man eager to get out of Mayer's shadow. The relationship between the two was not good: Mayer's own book about Etawah does not mention Dey; and though Dey wrote a book in which he *does* mention Mayer, he does so in only one paragraph, where he manages consistently to misspell Mayer's name. Mayer gradually withdrew.

In 1952 the government recommended the establishment of fifty-five community-development blocks, each with 330 villages; a year later a second tier of less intensively supported national-extension-system blocks was proposed, each with about a hundred villages and sixty thousand people. In 1955 the government decided to divide the whole country into development blocks; almost half would be favored as the more intensively subsidized community-development blocks. Ten years later, in 1965, the entire country was covered by community-development blocks.

But how had the pilot project fared meanwhile? Bowles in 1954 wrote that "so far experience indicates that long before the end of the three years of subsidized work, profound improvements can be achieved in each village." Dey, the administrator, was even more effusive. Speaking on All-India Radio, he said: "India slumbers in her villages..., yet there was a time when our villages hummed with the music of working men and women.... [Now, with the program,] roads began to be built: schools, community centres, hospitals came up overnight. Demonstration farms, breeding and artificial insemination centres, fruit and vegetable gardens and nurseries began to spring up. New village wells, reconditioning of old ones, paving of village lanes and drains assumed the form of a new mass movement.... Community Development promises to grow into a global mission . . . to show the way out of the psychosis of fear and hatred which rules the destiny of man today."

Yet here I was wandering around Etawah, and no one knew what I was talking about when I mentioned the words "pilot project" and Albert Mayer. Finally I was directed to Mr. R. S. Agarwal, who ran a bookstore-cum-publishing house. And in his shop, at last, I met someone who knew. "They came to me," Mr. Agarwal said. "They had no money for stationery. I said I would give them whatever they needed on credit." But what had they done, I asked? "They didn't work here," said Mr. Agarwal. I slumped. "They worked down in Lakhna and Maheva."

True enough. Feeling stupid, I got back in my car, drove past Victoria Hall (originally built for civic meetings but now used as another badminton court), and went down to Lakhna, perhaps ten miles away and close to the badland fringes of the Jumna.

I drove slowly through the single-lane unpaved main street and was surprised at the obvious poverty of the place. It certainly didn't look like a showplace. I stopped to ask if anyone knew anything about a pilot project. I tried a doctor, a goldsmith, a book dealer. Everyone looked at me blankly.

I went on to Maheva, another five or ten miles. Here is where Mayer lived on his annual visits—lived at first in a temple, the only accommodation he could find. I got out of my car and tried again: "pilot project." Blank looks. "Albert Mayer?" Nothing. Then someone offered the words "first block." "Yes," I cried: "yes." I was quickly led to the Maheva Block Development Office.

None of this stumbling would have occurred, of course, if I had come to Maheva in an official capacity. But I hate the handcuffs of chauffeurs and official meetings, and here in Maheva, where I needed a little official meeting, I got one on the spot. Tables were set up in the unpaved but shaded courtyard of the office, the simplest kind of building—literally a block: one floor, perhaps twenty feet by forty. Milk tea was handed out in little clay cups that were tossed aside and shattered when empty. People smiled, and there was only a slight murmur of discomfort when I asked how long it had been since the last visitor. "Ten years," someone quietly replied.

The gentleman in charge—he turned out to be the assistant block development officer—pulled out a notebook and read off the hallowed phrase: "Pilot Development Project, September 15, 1948." I floundered for a question, and in response he told me that there were now nearly 40,000 families and 155,000 people in the block. (That's up from 20,000 familes and 100,000 people in 1960). There were also almost 80,000 acres, of which three-quarters were arable and half irrigated. The average holding, in short, was two acres. In 1960 it had been twice that.

A small, thin man came quietly into the courtyard and shook hands. People on all sides deferred to him, yet he didn't look like any civil servant I had ever seen in India. Was it the bulky-knit sweater? The stubble? From the way people deferred to him, I assumed he was the block development officer, but he just didn't look the part. Finally I asked him point blank if he was "the BDO." Everyone laughed. He smiled quietly and said no, he was just a farmer old enough to remember Albert Mayer. He corrected my pronunciation to a Germanic "Meyer."

We walked along a neatly paved brick lane to the temple where Mayer had once lived. The temple had been built in 1912 by a landowner; now the side rooms were given over to

Ayurvedic and Sanskrit colleges. "Mr. Albert," the priest said, pointing to a cell on the left. It was entered from the veranda that rimmed the temple's paved courtyard. "That was his room."

Outside, there was a temple garden covering perhaps an acre, and adjoining it there was a workshop where, long abandoned, there stood a rusty horse-drawn forage cutter—a lot like a big hedge trimmer. A sign said "Pilot Implement Company," but there were no other implements that I could see, and I was steered to a building now used for handloom spinning. It was the original block office, bigger than the new building and with two floors. It was severely plain, however, and a half-dozen women sat on the floor inside; each cranked a small spinning machine. Finally we came round to the only unusual building I saw in Maheva. It was perfectly circular, like a brick snare drum fifty feet in diameter. This, I was told, was a warehouse built in the project's early days, and it was circular because it was built on the foundations of an older building—an indigo warehouse from the nineteenth century, before synthetic dyes killed indigo.

Living in a room adjoining this warehouse was an elderly man named Yogendra Singh Tripathi: tall, thin, dark, white-haired, with blue pajamas and a brown shawl over his shoulders. He was living here, he said, because his own house down near the river was unsafe: bandits. I had been warned that Mr. Tripathi and his son were ardent supporters of the Hindu nationalists who were so worrying Indian Muslims. And Mr. Tripathi didn't mince words. The Israelis, he said, knew better than anyone else the true character of Muslims: great as India was, she was threatened by the Muslim determination to dominate all other peoples. His nationalism spilled over to the Etawah Pilot Project, for he remembered not only Albert Mayer but Horace Holmes. He grew enthusiastic as he recalled, plain as day, Holmes standing up and telling the assembled farmers: "India is yours."

Many people in Maheva had connections to the Pilot Project. One afternoon I met two young men. One of them was Manaj Kumar Shukla, who explained that he was an unemployed civil engineer. Mayer had worked most closely with an elderly farmer of that name; sure enough, it was this young man's grandfather. Manaj told me that his grandfather had been dead for many years; his several hundred acres had been taken by land reform, and his big old house had been turned over by the family to holy men.

But why had the Pilot Project faded into distant memory? Why hadn't it left behind the kind of cooperative organization that Mayer had intended and which Bowles and Dey had seen radiating across India?

The Pilot Implement Company had obviously fallen flat. Near the circular warehouse there was an abandoned pea cannery—another failure, despite initial success. It turned out that Mr. Vyas—the man with the bulky sweater and the stubble—had managed it for a while. What was he doing now? He was, he said, just a farmer. But there was an appreciative murmur in the group at those words. I asked how much land he owned, and he quietly said a hundred acres—fifty times the block average. Everyone listened respectfully while he explained to me that mustard grown for oil was very profitable but that other crops, including wheat, were not. Later on, one of the officers mentioned to me quietly that Mr. Vyas was "a farmer, not in service, so he is very wise."

Mr. Vyas heartily approved of community development. But then he *would* approve of it, wouldn't he? I mean that Maheva was visited in 1958 by Kusum Nair, the journalist who was touring India to write *Blossoms in the Dust*. With deliberate irony, her Maheva chapter is titled "A Decade of Development," and it begins with the story from the *Ramayana* of how nectar fell from heaven, revivifying some of the dead but leaving others untouched. "This is how it is with 'development,' " one of the farmers told Nair: "Even though it is designed for every one and offered equally to all only some benefit from it." That "some," of course, included people such as Mr. Vyas. And what was the nectar? Block development officers in Uttar Pradesh have what is called "distribution authority." That's the official phrase, and it refers to the control of seed, fertilizer, and pesticide from the many warehouses in each block. The materials are not given freely but are sold at subsidized prices. Access is everything.

I asked Mr. Vyas if he found his village servant useful. He was silent. I tried again. "Do the BDO's stay here long?" "No," said Mr. Vyas. Why? The group had shrunk to an informal four or five, and everyone chuckled, Mr. Vyas included. The BDOs were transferred, someone explained, "for political reasons." With deliberate naiveté I asked for clarification and got another chuckle: the transfers occurred whenever the BDOs tried to resist requests from powerful people for improved seed, perhaps, or a pesticide. Mr. Vyas said nothing. A minute later we were back at my car. Mr. Vyas posed for my camera and assured me that I would always be welcome in Maheva.

So the Etawah Pilot Project had been co-opted, made into a farm-supply store for the rich. But it had happened with plenty of warning. Early on, Mayer realized that many people wanted to join his staff simply because it was a branch of government—a way of escaping village life. "We must fight against the possibility," he wrote, "that a bureaucratic and mercenary spirit may invade us." His own assistants were fighting for a larger project staff, simply in order to match the staffing and therefore the prestige of other government departments. And out in the field? In 1952, even as the national program was gearing up, Mayer wrote that the village servants in Etawah merely contacted "a few individuals of the middle or upper middle class. . . . [They confine] their work to this class." And one of Mayer's staff people observed that some villagers were complaining that their village servants now "seem to work with mercenary motives, and not as missionaries as they used to. I agree that our last selections of Village Level Workers have not been good."

S. K. Dey, the community development administrator who took over the program in 1952, realized that everything depended on the village-level worker, who had to be "the first-aid man in all fields of rural development—fields such as agriculture, animal husbandry, public health, village industries, co-operation . . . , and rural engineering. He is a multi-purpose man trained over a period of eighteen months in special institutions set up exclusively for the purpose." But it was never so. Another of the people involved early in the national program recalls that "our colleagues looked at us as fools. They used to say, you are gazetted, yet you are working in the villages, why?" And another man remembers that by the time the program went national "you forgot the farmer, you forgot the villager, you did what you were told. You gave the result on that which was expected because the first need was to please the higher-ups and somehow show the result. The programs were only on paper and the whole thing became a big game."

Astonishingly, Nehru himself identified the program's Achilles heel at the very outset. It happens that Chester Bowles returned to India during the 1960s for a second stint as ambassador, and in a memoir covering those later years he adds a crucial detail that he had omitted from the earlier account. Only in this second book do we learn that Nehru had been unenthusiastic when Bowles had proposed taking community development national. Nehru, Bowles tells us then, had replied that "it was impractical in India on a large scale since the educated young people were unlikely to respond. Etawah, he thought, was a special case."

True. But why, then, had Nehru capitulated? Bowles explains that he told Nehru that he "was surprised that a man with Nehru's commitment both to democratic economic progress and to young people should react so negatively, and I said so." This was cold war hardball, disguised none too subtly; it was a test of Nehru's commitment to the United States. Nehru went along, and the result was the predictable collapse of the idealism felt by the early village-level workers. As Horace Holmes told an interviewer some years later, "There was tremendous pressure on the U.S. side to use up the monies and to get more."

Perhaps Bowles speaks more freely in his second memoir because by then the whole strategy of agricultural development in India had shifted away from community development to the straightforward stimulation of agricultural production. An "intensive agricultural development program" had been launched with some fifteen million dollars of Ford Foundation money. It aimed to provide a package of improved seeds and fertilizers and pesticides to those districts able to adopt them quickly. (It was this "package program" that brought to the Godavary Delta the Mr. Freeman whom Narayana Raju remembered.) Bowles supported the new program, but the results were poor, partly because of the seemingly inevitable political pressure to dilute the program through expansion and partly because staff were rotated too quickly to accomplish much of anything. Yet the program's timing was impeccable, for its last years coincided with the introduction of high-yielding varieties and some of the most spectacular production increases the world has ever seen.

And community development? Until Nehru's death in 1964, the Community Development Ministry lingered on. Dey was still in charge, dealing now with Nehru's successor, Lal Bahadur Shastri. Shastri told him that he knew that "Jawaharlalji had unquestioned faith in these institutions. I must confess that I do not have the same faith in the ability of the common people to guide and regulate themselves for many decades to come."

Shastri didn't want to move hastily, and the move to axe the ministry was postponed until Indira Gandhi's time. She had no such hesitation. Dey writes that he was transferred without warning to the Ministry of Mines and Metals: "When out of consternation I virtually woke ... [Mrs. Gandhi] up at her house, she was visibly embarrassed. With regrets she insisted, I must continue as she felt convinced I could impart life even to stones." Dey goes on to describe the agriculture minister of that time as "a great protagonist of centralisation and of everything being controlled from Delhi." This was the influential C. Subramaniam, who on his own initiative had imported from Mexico the new wheat seed for the Green Revolution. It was Subramaniam who saw to it, finally, that the Ministry of Community Development was merged into his own Ministry of Food and Agriculture. With the merger, Dey continues, Subramaniam "had what his mind and heart had been after." The block system remained, but it was nothing more than the input-supply system I could see for myself in Etawah.

And that is the story of community development in its Indian phase. I will look at it again later, in Bangladesh and Pakistan today; here, let me add only two anecdotes.

Back in the days of its Ford Foundation support, the Allahabad Agriculture Institute had provided extension services to a village called Serangapur. I paid a visit and found that the extension office in the village was now a public school run by the institute. Extension services were still provided, however, by a young and energetic institute staffer named Robinson Robin.

We visited the school together. Younger boys and girls sat on the floor of the bare school rooms, but desks were provided for the teenage students, who were all girls. Their parents would not send them to the public high schools of Allahabad, which are residential and, therefore, expensive.

The whitewashed walls of the classrooms used by these older girls had simple anatomical diagrams and a world map; the girls, hair braided and turned up in loops, wore neat white blouses and pink jumpers. They were studying civics, "democracy" it happened. A girl defined it for me as a land with many people. Perhaps the difficulty was in language, but there was no problem when I asked how many watched television nightly. Half raised their hands. What did they watch? Not the news but the soap opera that came after it. And what was the soap? It was apartment life in big-city India, and it was introduced by a whole string of advertisements. One night I made a list of the ads: in uninterrupted order for cola, toothpaste, Band-Aids, chewing gum, drain cleaners, mango candy, shoe polish, and something called "candy chocolate." I know about rising expectations—at least have heard the phrase. But I still wonder about the impact such advertisements have on the millions of Indian villagers who see them.

Close to the Serangapur school Robinson and I met a villager standing in front of his house on the unpaved main village lane. The facade was perhaps fifty feet long on each of its four sides, and on its front face clerestory windows were cut in a wall rising behind a lower street-front room. Pantiles covered the whole roof.

The house was so impressive that I asked if I could enter, and we came through the narrow doorway, which led into a low and narrow front room running the whole length of the facade. The walls were of partly mudded-over brick, and the ceiling exposed the roof tiles through a wooden supporting frame. Other than bits of green fodder on the floor, there was nothing in the room. It was, I realized, the family barn, where the man kept his one water buffalo.

The barn led through a central doorway into a higher room, more neatly mudded and with a two-tone treatment on the walls—light above, dark below. But this room, too, though clean, was almost empty, except for a clothes line and a clay vessel as big as a water heater and filled with grain. Unlike the barn, this room was subdivided: a fourth of it at one end was walled off from the rest. The power was off and I could see nothing, but a flash camera eventually revealed a bedroom with a traditional string bed, covered with neatly folded bedding. The room was tiny and had no other furniture except a padlocked metal trunk. Clothes hung from hooks on the walls; so did a few calendars with flamboyant religious motifs and, above them and near the exposed beams, four family photos in a crooked frame.

The empty room outside the bedroom opened into an un-paved courtyard perhaps forty feet square. A well was in one corner and a very modest brick planter in the middle; rooms opened on the side to my right, but they, too, were so dark that I could see nothing. A camera flash revealed, weeks later, that the mud walls of the room were extraordinarily clean but that the room contained almost nothing except a couple of storage vessels and a few metal dishes and implements. Almost nothing, that is, except two women and a girl, whom I had not seen in the darkness.

During the 1960s, the village lands had been consolidated: rearranged in single pieces so each owner got back approximately the same amount and quality of land he owned previously, though now arranged so that he didn't have to spend hours walking from one parcel to another. The general experience in Serangapur had been that the larger owners did better than the smaller ones; the smaller ones at least were the ones who expressed dissatisfaction. The larger owners were now able to install pumps and irrigate their land, but the smaller owners did not have enough land to support such an investment. The man whose house I was visiting, for example, bought irrigation water from a neighbor with enough land to justify a pump.

Robinson and I went out to the fields and saw some of those pumps, at least one of them handled in a sophisticated way, with concrete-lined distribution channels and siphons under cart tracks. We met up with a farmer—careworn but only in his early forties, I judged. He was growing a field of vegetables. He had been having problems with some kind of insect, but Robinson had helped him fix the problem—I presume with a pesticide. Did he follow Robinson's advice for rice, too?

It was a leading question, because extension agents in India had for a long time advocated the so-called line planting of rice (often called the "Japanese method," chiefly in order to give it some foreign éclat). But this farmer, like Indian farmers generally, have stuck with random transplanting. The farmer explained that Robinson had indeed told him to do line planting because it made weeding easier. But, he continued, the people he hired to do his transplanting didn't like line planting and charged an impossibly high premium for it—some four times the charge for random transplanting. I looked at Robinson and chided him about not listening to the farmers. But he insisted on going by the book: the farmer could make the necessary calculations and decide whether or not line planting made sense.

At least Robinson was honest. I say this because I asked about the local village-level worker, who was supposedly doing the same work that Robinson was doing. The farmer grew indignant at his very mention. Why? Robinson smiled and told a story about his own dealings with this man. The villagers had wanted some service, Robinson had helped them obtain it, and the village-level worker had come to him to complain

angrily. Complain? Yes: Robinson, he said, had cost him two
thousand rupees. That was the bribe he demanded for the
service the farmers wanted, and now he'd never get it.

So much for the debased relic of Albert Mayer's experiment.

And now for a quick ghost story. I was in Etawah town and
talking with the district's chief development officer. He was
young, handsome, and intelligent, a member of the elite Indian Administrative Service. He had never heard of Albert
Mayer or Frank Brayne—I asked—but he told me that I might
be interested in a universal-literacy program he was running.
Village women were the chief target. The program was most
interesting, he said, because the teachers were all volunteers.
Really? Well, politicians had been asked to participate, but
they had quickly dropped out. Local teachers, on the other
hand, were volunteering their spare time. Volunteering? Well,
yes, although their willingness to participate was noted on
their annual evaluations.

And what kind of result was the program getting? Things
were coming along satisfactorily. The chief obstacle was the
resistance of upper-caste women who declined to mix with
lower castes. I asked how he handled the situation, and he
smiled. "I take them by the hand and pull them into the
group." No doubt it helped that he himself was a Brahmin,
but I almost asked if he told men coming into his presence to
remove their earrings.

THE HEARTLAND

ARROGANCE PERMEATES THE HISTORY OF RURAL
development. Not just community development, with its
Frank Braynes and all his intellectual descendants. It is
equally at the root of the failure of huge irrigation schemes to
provide water for tailenders, and it is the fundamental reason
as well behind agricultural researchers who know nothing—
and want to know nothing—about farmers. I remember a senior irrigation officer in Morocco who was jostled by a circle of
farmers. They were upset because they were receiving no water. Angrily, he shouted them down—cowed them in an amazingly few seconds. Then he drove off, deliberately spinning
his wheels to spray the men with gravel and dust.

An alternative has been known for a long time. For example,
these are the words of Tagore: "Come inside India, accept all
her good and her evil; if there be deformity, then try and cure
it from within, but see it with your own eyes, understand it,
think over it, turn your face towards it, become one with it."
But becoming "one with it" is precisely what foreign experts
have been unable or unwilling to do. Maybe Sir Arthur Cotton
is an exception, but I can name no others. That's why Frank
Brayne's epitaph about "he that serveth" is as false as it is true.

But these are the concerns of a development historian or
critic, and much as they are part and parcel of my efforts to

understand the culture of development, viewed strictly they are peripheral to my theme. For three long chapters I have been wending my way through this history not for its own sake but because I wanted to understand how the culture of development took root, how it grew, how it came to preempt or monopolize our thinking about the changes we wish to see in rural Asia. I have been seeking to understand the culture of development as a kind of blindness that has left us oblivious to the effects development is having on the beauty of the Asian countryside.

I have tried to say something about the quality of that countryside as I have wandered from place to place in these discussions, but I want now to quit history, put my three historical strands together, and look at the contemporary Asian landscape as it has been shaped by irrigation engineers, agronomists, and community developers. I want to show how profoundly that landscape is changing both at the core, by which I mean the prime lands most attractive to industrial agriculture, and at the periphery, by which I mean the remoter areas where one might expect to see abandonment. I want to show how much we are losing.

That's why I left Delhi very early one Sunday morning. I wanted to take a look at Haryana, which is part of the old Punjab and which, along with the state of Punjab itself, is famous as the home of India's most progressive farmers. Of course you can't escape history in India, and heading north through the old city, I passed St. James Church, which was built by James Skinner, a man of mixed Irish and Indian descent. He had created the famous private regiment called Skinner's Horse. It had played a major role in suppressing the Mutiny.

On the northern fringe of the city, I came to another Mutiny memorial: an almost totally forgotten mound with a modest red sandstone obelisk. It commemorated the Gordon Highlanders who fell, according to the memorial's inscription, "while charging the mutineers' guns" on the eighth of June, 1857, and "to whose gallantry the victory of that day was due." The inscription did not say how many bodies lay in the mound below, but the hillock was small enough that I would never have noticed it at all if I hadn't already been stopped.

I had been driving along when I noticed a half-dozen enormous sheet-metal roofs mounted on poles and surrounded by unpaved parking lots. Literally hundreds of trucks swarmed around the sheds. I parked, threaded my way through some noxious puddles and found myself in the almost impossibly crowded Delhi wholesale fruit market.

The shed with the most activity handled nothing but apples. The fruit was not of a quality to excite much enthusiasm on the part of someone from the temperate latitudes, but buyers and sellers were busy anyway, shaking hands under a handkerchief where hidden finger taps hid the price from crowding competitors. This was not merely the apple market for Delhi: it was the national apple market, and the destination of each lot of apples could be approximately inferred from the size of the truck into which each lot was loaded: small trucks for Delhi, big ones for more distant destinations. One grower, just in from Kashmir, said the trip down had been risky. He was never sure, he said, when he would be stopped and, if lucky, only robbed. Three days and a thousand miles later, his apples would be a lot mushier than they already were, despite being repacked in straw for their onward journey.

I wasn't going as far as Kashmir. I wasn't even going as far as the politically unsettled Punjab. I was only going to Karnal, a district in Haryana. Haryana was created only in 1966. Twenty years had by then passed since the international partition of the Punjab between India and Pakistan; now the Indian chunk was split into a Sikh-dominated fragment, which retained the name Punjab, and a Hindu-dominated fragment that took the name Haryana, an allusion perhaps to the historic Aryans.

There has been no looking back: the state highways are cluttered with signs about "moving forward" and "new horizons." But history is hard to avoid even in Haryana, and the Grand Trunk Road north from Delhi goes through Panipat, famous for ancient battles and still possessing, if you get away from the highway, some old walls and gates. I ignored them and continued to Karnal, on the very banks of the Western Jumna Canal.

The canal itself looked for all the world like a study in perspective, with a wide placid expanse of green water receding, straight as a die, to the vanishing point. The canal had scarcely been touched since the late nineteenth century, and the gates controlling the minor canals were museums of antiquated gearing. I walked down one of the branch canals, which was in desperately poor shape, but it led only to an abandoned grain mill that was almost identical to the grain mills I had once seen in Pakistan's Northwest Frontier Province. Proby Cautley and Baird Smith wrote about building such mills and renting them out, and I wondered—wonder still—whether the mills are of a British design that diffused to the mountains, or whether the British copied what they found already in use. This particular mill contained a gang of seven millstones, each perhaps twenty inches in diameter. They were lined against a wall and separated by slabs, like urinals in a men's lavatory.

I walked down another branch canal and to my surprise found myself in a sea of paddy irrigated by ditches so uncontrolled that downstream tail-end shortages were inevitable. Even here the farmers had supplemental wells, however, and looking down the open ones I judged that the water table was perhaps twenty feet below the surface.

I say that rice was a surprise, and I mean that my atlas to the 1909 *Imperial Gazetteer of India* shows rice covering only a small percentage of Karnal's cropped area; the 1925 *Crop Atlas of India* says the same. The 1978 *Agricultural Atlas of India* says that the land around Karnal is mostly poor or with such limitations that it is good only for grazing or forestry; somewhat paradoxically, another map in the same atlas suggests that it is cultivated in millet and barley, which implies, to me, that irrigation can overcome natural limitations.

These maps tell me what I'd expect: rice, after all, is a crop I do not associate with Indian districts as hot and dry as Delhi: in such places I expect wheat in winter and mustard or cotton in summer. Of course, I should know better: on the way through Meerut to the Solani Aqueduct I had seen sugarcane growing happily. But then why should the maps show no rice on this side of the Jumna?

The explanation waited on the western outskirt of Karnal, at the Central Soil Salinity Research Institute. I dropped in there and met Dr. R. K. Gupta, who like every other researcher I've ever met in India was most courteously willing to explain his work to a total stranger. The soil around Karnal, he said, had for generations been seriously affected by at least partly natural salt accumulations. Sodium chloride was the least of the problems, for it could be flushed away, but alkali— chiefly calcium carbonate—had been a real impediment. Most of the district until recently had been cultivated only once a year, with salt-tolerant winter millets—or winter wheat on the few patches of good soil.

Established in 1969, the institute had quickly devised a program of leveling, bunding, flooding, leaching, and—critical for the alkali—applying gypsum: six tons to the acre. Most of the cost of reclaiming private lands had been borne by the government. And now the formerly fallow fields of summer grew rice. Why rice? Partly because the reclamation process had prepared it for flood cultivation, partly because rice is relatively tolerant of salt, and—neat timing—partly because high-yielding rice varieties had become well established in the late 1960s, just as the institute was getting started.

The problem now, Dr. Gupta explained, was controlling the water table. Between 1974 and 1989 it had fallen locally from about fifteen to about twenty-five feet; eventually a time would come when the water would be too deep for farmers to pump economically. Dr. Gupta was already exploring the idea of deliberate power cuts to reduce ground water depletion, but it seemed plain that farmers would find ways of circumventing those cuts, perhaps by protests, perhaps by converting to diesel. There was another possibility, too. The local farmers were apparently willing for now to comply with a rule that they could not take more than a third of their water from the canal. If pumping were really jeopardized, however, the headenders would surely take more.

I drove west from Karnal to Kaul. Along the way there were

plenty of paddies being puddled by tractors pulling gangs of discs: no particular surprise, because the road up from Delhi had brought me past lots of tractors, mostly operated by hard-driving Sikhs in dusty turbans. I saw rice being hauled to threshing floors in wagons pulled by tractors. No surprise there, either; such things exist everywhere in India.

Then, next to a field being harvested by women, I saw a field being harvested by a combine—a combine no different from those used in California's Sacramento Valley, a combine fitted with a pick-up reel with spring teeth. A tractor ran alongside and pulled a wagon to receive the grain. It was unbelievable: the only visible difference between this combine and those in the United States was the brand name: Swaraj 8100.

Swaraj, or "self-rule," was the word used by Gandhi when he called for independence. What would that apostle of hand labor have thought of this Indian-manufactured monster?

The combine operator spoke no English, but the next day I went to an equipment dealer in Karnal who did. His name was Mr. D. N. Arora, and he worked at the local farmer-service center of the Haryana Agro-Industries Corporation. Karnal, Mr. Arora said, had the most progressive rice growers in India: many were triple cropping rice or were growing two crops of rice and one of wheat annually. There were more than five thousand tractors in the district—mostly in the thirty horse-power range—and land was now worth ten thousand dollars an acre.

Mr. Arora went on to explain that the first combine in Karnal District had been sold in 1970. Now there were a hundred combines in the district, and they harvested fully half of the rice as well as nearly all the winter-wheat crop. Did that mean that a hundred farmers owned half the cropland? No: half the combines depended entirely on custom work. (Strange, but back in 1907 the imperial agriculturalist at Pusa had written an article in which he anticipated just such custom harvesting. He called it "the peripatetic system" and imagined that it would rely on steam-powered "thrashers" made of teak. Wrong on details, he was still definitely on the right track.)

The district's problems? Mr. Arora said that, so far as his

own business went, the corporation was no longer even stocking combines. Not that there was something wrong with them: the problem was simply that the market was saturated. A few years back, there had only been fifty combines in Karnal, and the machines had worked forty to fifty days a year; now, with a hundred, they worked for less than a month.

More broadly, Mr. Arora shared Dr. Gupta's concern about water supplies. And he mentioned something else—said he worried about shrinking farms, the old and nearly ineradicable tradition of subdividing at his death every man's land among his children. Strange to hear such fears in Haryana! Shortly after independence, the East Punjab Holdings Act ordered the compulsory consolidation of farms throughout the state. Not only that, all the old land lines were altogether eliminated, replaced by three-thousand-acre squares laid out by the Survey of India and then subdivided into one-acre rectangles, each 220 by 198 feet. The program was slow to get moving: the work was not finished until about 1960. But it *was* done, and you can see the results from the air: the Punjab and its calved-off Haryana are the only states in India where the field layout is a grid more precise than the one we imposed on our own Midwest.

Consolidation encouraged the installation of tube wells; the perfectly rectangular fields were meanwhile splendid for machinery such as combines. But now, Mr. Arora suggested, the good that had been done was threatened. The consolidation program had passed the generation mark. The rectangular fields persisted, but family holdings were again being subdivided. Holdings might once again be reduced below economic levels—might gradually become an obstacle for both tube wells and machinery. Brothers might farm cooperatively, of course, but they might not.

I asked Mr. Arora if he was worried about the impact of machinery on labor. He wasn't. He explained that the old one-crop calendar had never supported a large population. With the conversion to double cropping, landowners had been forced to import seasonal labor from places like Bihar. (It turns out that those same laborers, whom at Pusa I had heard described as demoralized and unproductive, work famously hard in Haryana.) The Bihari laborers, in short, could go home if machinery replaced them.

But what would they do back there? And what about the impact of such displacement in parts of Haryana without labor shortages? Were the displaced laborers to find city jobs? Were they to rely on the clout of a local politician who might bring a factory to them?

Such things happen: I think of a hypodermic syringe factory at Jind, fifty miles southwest of Karnal. I passed that factory on my way from Karnal to Hissar, once a famine-prone district. Now, down among the branching tails of the Western Jumna and Bhakra canals, Hissar is green. Still, tails are tails, and I saw no rice here: instead, I saw wheat; on an earlier trip, in summer, there had been mustard and cotton.

It had been sultry and wet that time, even though Hissar lies on the edge of the Great Indian Desert. Now, in the rain, I could see why farmers paid so much attention to protecting their dung cakes—and not only with the pup tents I knew from Rani Kheri or the mud-walled cylinders I had seen near

A classic element of the common landscape of North India and a utilitarian solution to the problem of protecting fuel and fodder, this structure is a masterpiece of twig-and-thatch construction. The design varies from place to place; this is the form common to Rohtak, between Delhi and Hissar.

Meerut. Here the cakes were kept under handsome thatch domes, layered like an onion and neatly trimmed. When the cakes were needed, the thatch domes were broken open on one side.

I had stopped for the night at Rohtak. Through the window of my room I saw a small lake fringed with palms and weeping greenery: more tribute to the Western Jumna. Next to the lake there was a small zoo, with sagging cyclone fencing around a tiger in tall, wet grass; there were three Himalayan black bears, one in a fouled cage on wheels. Back on the highway a billboard advertised "superstrong" Godfather beer, and back in my room the air conditioner had been stuck in the wall with about three inches of unfilled airspace on three sides—plenty of room for mosquitoes, despite my stuffing the gap with drapes.

I went into the Rohtak market that night and stepped between the puddles. The rain continued, and the streets of Rohtak the next morning were nearly impassable: dead-flat streets under about ten inches of water. I didn't know where the potholes were, and so when possible I stayed in the wake of big trucks.

Fortunately the highway to Hissar was high and dry, and I was there by noon. To the north of town, I knew from a map, I would find the famous Government Livestock Farm. It had been established in 1809 to breed camels, but almost immediately it had shifted to breeding the Hissar or Hariana breed of cattle for which it became famous. These were fine animals, the same that Frank Brayne prescribed—the animals that Gurgaon farmers found too big and expensive.

To the west of town lay the Haryana Agricultural University. Not as old as the Livestock Farm, it was set up first as the Indian Punjab's veterinary college after 1947, when the original Punjab veterinary college wound up on the Pakistani side of the international-partition line. In 1962 Punjab established an agricultural university in Ludhiana, but Ludhiana wound up on the Sikh side of the second partition of the Punjab, the one in 1966. And so, in 1970, the veterinary college in Hissar was redesignated as the Haryana Agricultural University. It grew rapidly.

It was a Sunday when I arrived, and Hissar was very quiet. Quite by accident I came upon an immense bungalow perched on the sheer side of a hill. It was remarkable: there aren't many hills in this part of India. I asked and was surprised to learn that it was the Livestock Farm's headquarters. The building was doubled by reflection in a monsoon pool at the base of the slope, and a guard shooed me away when I approached. When I persisted, he became threatening. I am grateful, because the following day during office hours I discovered that the building was also the home of the farm's director.

I drove out to the farm itself, which had once consisted of some forty thousand acres of dry countryside, a "reserved forest" stocked primarily with native grasses. The animals had lived rough—been led out to the pastures in groups of a hundred by cowherds who knew the grounds intimately. Only in poor years did the farm turn to irrigated fodder: by 1900 there were some twenty-five hundred acres of clover and alfalfa and millets irrigated by the Western Jumna Canal. By 1960 the figure had risen to four thousand, about a tenth of the Farm.

The logic for relying on rough grazing was sound: in the words of the inspector-general of the Civil Veterinary Department in 1905, "It is useless to select a . . . soft animal, requiring good feeding, if the conditions of the tract demand a small, active, hardy animal that can easily exist on poor feeding." But the farm I saw now seemed to be divided almost entirely into irrigated pastures; moreover, it had lost much of its land to neighboring institutions, including two that had been established twenty years before by Australians and which were now trying to adapt sheep and Jersey and Holstein cows to Indian conditions. The dairy barns were of Australian standard—stanchions and all—and on the sheep farm I saw a half-dozen wet sheep dogs in pens. I am not particularly fond of dogs, but their eager barking was upsetting. It seemed that these animals thought that their master had remembered them and come to take them home.

On the way back to Hissar I passed a highway bus on whose back panel someone had painted "and miles to go before I sleep." Who had made the connection to Robert Frost?

The campus of Haryana Agricultural University, like every other Indian university, was impressive from a distance; up close, the big buildings were in need of maintenance they would probably never get. Still, the graffiti quotient was low, the lawns were green, and the library's periodical room was well stocked with criminally expensive foreign journals.

The journal that made the greatest impression on me was a domestic one: *Haryana Farming*. Here was a twenty-four-page monthly, published by the university in both Hindi and English editions. I looked at articles about sunflower seed production, potato disease control, the use of common trees, honey, weather, and food. In each issue, there was also a "what to do this month" section. For the latest issue on the shelf, which was June, the column began with paddy and spoke of puddling and transplanting. For chemical control of weeds, it said to apply "Machete EC or Saturn EC or Delchlore EC at the rate of 3 litres/ha to be mixed in 150 kg of dry sand and apply uniformly within 2 to 3 days of transplanting in standing water." There were instructions about millet, a major crop in Haryana: something called HHB-45 was particularly recommended, along with five other varieties. There were instructions for corn: "line 75 cm apart and use 17 kg seed/ha." There were instructions for peanuts, cotton, and a dozen other crops.

A long way from Sam Higginbottom—and an impressive magazine for a state seeking to modernize its agriculture. Perhaps the journal was of limited value to farmers (only seven thousand copies were printed in Hindi and only a few hundred in English), but Haryana certainly knew how to follow the American model. Indeed, *Haryana Farming* was an American clone down to its back cover, which for June carried an ad for Foratox-10 ("guarantees freedom from pests").

The university's experimental farm was quiet on this Sunday, and nothing caught my eye except a storage yard with stacked sacks of wheat seed ready to go: "known pedigree;

treated with poison." On the far side of the farm, however, I came out at a village called Lodas, where a farmer in shorts and a T-shirt was walking behind a camel pulling a simple cultivator through a cotton field. The field was green, but the technology wasn't sophisticated. Nor were many of the isolated farmsteads I saw farther out in the fields: homes of earthen blocks, dark within, cows tied before a heap of straw, a tree for shade.

Modernization apparently had not swept uniformly through Haryana, not even here near the university, the technological epicenter. So where was the Green Revolution in Hissar?

The first signs of it were back in Hissar town itself, where I passed a tractor-repair shop with a Gandhian homily in letters two feet high: "productive labor is prayer." There was a line of shops selling motor vehicles: Bajaj motor scooters ("value for money, for years . . . you just can't beat a Bajaj"), Mahindra "jeeps and commercial vehicles," and Supreme tractors.

Then, on the town's outskirts, I stopped at a sign that read "A Healthier Tomorrow: Tariq Poultries." A hand-drawn poster on the office door showed a chicken and two chicks under the words "Sun Rises With Me." Next to it there was a long brick building, really a roof supported by brick columns and walled with wire screens. Inside there were a few hundred white chickens, mostly young but some laying. They were cooled by electric fans, though in winter they would be warmed by mats hung on the exterior screens. I poked around for a few minutes, then a handsome young man came up on a motorcycle.

He was the owner, and his name was Arjun. A 1990 graduate of the university in veterinary science, he said that he presently had a thousand Cobb chickens. They had been air freighted to him from Pune. He explained that he was in the business not of selling birds but of selling fertilized eggs to local farmers producing eggs and meat for the huge Delhi market. I was impressed.

The bird house, he went on quietly, was lit sixteen hours a day in order to insure that each chicken laid 160 chicks over its seventy-two-week life cycle. The birds' feed, he continued from memory, was produced by a Lipton subsidiary and consisted of 56 percent maize, 8 percent peanut cake, 10 percent de-oiled rice bran, 8 percent soybean, and other constituents that he enumerated faster than I could write. He mixed the chicken droppings with sawdust and used them as fuel, but he also had a generator set, chiefly to run the incubators when the power supply was cut.

I assumed that things were going well, but when I asked what his major problem was Arjun smiled sadly and instantly replied: "Marketing." Thanks to price manipulation by a few giant producers, things were so bad that he was contemplating getting out of the fertilized-egg business altogether and joining with his brother in Delhi to try to produce eggs for the hotel trade there.

I saw Arjun again the next winter, when I came in from Karnal and Jind. It was a sad meeting: he had given up his hotel-supply plan as impractical. He seemed more tired than I remembered from our last meeting, less optimistic. Our conversation drifted off to politics, which seemed to be tearing the country apart. Quietly he said that "politics in this country are a cheap business."

Arjun's great-grandfather owned thousands of acres near Daulatpur, an hour's drive to the north. Such holdings no longer existed, but one of Arjun's uncles had been vice-chancellor at the university, and another uncle farmed three hundred acres that he sowed with tractor-drawn seed drills and which he treated with tractor-drawn sprayers. Arjun's own father, who farmed a mere hundred and fifty irrigated acres, could be found, Arjun explained, if I simply went to a certain village near Daulatpur and asked for "Major Sahib."

Asking proved unnecessary: there was only one house that fit the bill—a one-story house, modern and well maintained. I knocked and found that I was interrupting a farm-management meeting. A halt was called, and Arjun's father came into the sitting room.

His chief crops, he explained, were cotton and millet. They were grown by sharecroppers, each of whom cultivated six or seven acres and each of whom kept two-thirds of what he grew. For his own third of the crop, Arjun's father was responsible for plowing—which he did with a tractor—for providing seed, and for providing irrigation water for the cotton. The water came chiefly from the great Bhakra Canal, which brings water south from the Sutlej River. Down this far in the command, however, the canal ran short in summer; Arjun's father then turned on his half-dozen tube wells. The tenants did the weeding and harvesting, but threshing was done mechanically, by a machine he provided.

Interestingly, Arjun's father was not cultivating a remnant of his grandfather's estate. On the contrary, he had inherited only twenty-two acres and had bought the rest in 1976, after retiring from the army. It had not been an investment from career savings; rather, he had paid for the land by custom plowing for his neighbors. Clearly, he was as much an entrepreneur as his son, but he was still dependent on his military pension: farming, he said, was "not economical at any scale."

The conversation was coming round to the same point it had reached with Mr. Arora, the farm-equipment salesman in Karnal. On the one hand Arjun's father was not in favor of land reform: "Dishing out land," he said, was the same as "dishing out the poverty." The villagers for the time being were lucky, he continued, because increased irrigation supplies and better seeds had increased the amount of farm labor the village used. That would suffice for this generation, but what lay beyond? How would the next generation live? I asked him, and he asked me back.

His own sons had told him they were prepared "to do anything but not agriculture." And this despite his insistence that they attend local elementary schools and stay in Haryana for their higher education. He had allowed "nothing fancy" in the way of their schooling, yet they still wanted out of farming. I thought of the forty-five veterinary science graduates in Arjun's class. He had been the only one to go into production; all the others had gone no closer to farming than government jobs or positions with agricultural-service companies. It was Sam Higginbottom all over again.

I finally got around to the Government Livestock Farm during working hours. I met there two other graduates from the university, one from the class of 1974, the other from the class of 1984. How many of their classmates had gone into production? The answer in both cases was none, although fully half the students had come from farm backgrounds.

And the consequences? The director of the farm told me that some years ago the farm had decided to "deemphasize" the Hissar breed that had made the farm's reputation. Why? Because Indian farmers no longer needed draft animals, he said: they had tractors. It wasn't so: one had only to go off the Government Livestock Farm in any direction to see as much. Yet the farm had shifted to developing two breeds of small dairy cattle: the brown Sahiwal and the white Thaparkar. Semen for these breeds was sold, but the supply was limited, as were markets. No surprise, I thought, for the farm was breeding animals suited to irrigated pastures.

Discouraged, I returned to the university to talk about community development and agricultural extension. Early in the 1970s the World Bank had decided that the time was right to try again with agricultural extension in India. This time the program would be the bank's own Train and Visit, or T&V, system. The bank swore by the merits of this approach, in which extensionists met fortnightly not only with farmers but with their own teachers. T&V extension had been introduced to India on some irrigation projects in 1975; a decade later it went national, with each state adopting it with slight variations. But rot had set in fast: as early as 1980 I heard jokes on South Indian irrigation projects about T&V standing for "train and vanish" or, better still, "talk and vanish." Had things fared better in forward-looking Haryana?

I met Dr. R. K. Sharma, a professor and former head of the university's extension department. He explained that in the Haryana version of extension the village-level workers of the Ministry of Food and Agriculture had been shunted off to non-agricultural assignments: extension was now the exclusive duty of agricultural development officers. These men were all university graduates, and they were responsible for four or five villages—say a thousand families. They were backed up by subject-matter specialists with whom they met regularly.

Does it sound promising? Certainly it sounds a good deal like a more focused version of Etawah, but Dr. Sharma made no effort to disguise his own disillusionment. A decade after its creation, he said, this new generation of extension agents had already succumbed to lethargy. Why? Low pay, low mobility, low recognition, lack of authority: the reasons tripped from his tongue as though he had recited them a thousand times. What was the result? The men worked only in accessible villages and only with the few farmers with whom they had become friendly. It *was* Etawah all over again.

It didn't matter. That was the surprising view of Pardeep Singh Shehrawat, a young assistant professor who joined us. He was preparing to go to the United States to start work on a doctorate in agricultural extension. Oddly, he was wearing a suit and tie, but Dr. Sharma asked if I'd like to accompany Pardeep right now to his own village, Kharar Alipur. Why not?

On the way, Pardeep explained what he had meant: the farmers of Haryana needed seeds and fertilizer and pesticides; thanks to demonstration farms and word of mouth, they did not need extension officers. If that was so, it raised a question about why Pardeep was bothering with a career in extension. I didn't bother asking, for I thought the answer—a sinecure with prestige—was obvious and timeworn.

Kharar Alipur turned out to be about twelve miles from Hissar. On the way, Pardeep explained that it was a very big village, a place of fully ten thousand people. Like Rani Kheri, it was a Jat village, and Pardeep himself came from a farming family. Indeed, only about five hundred villagers had jobs or income from outside the village. He was one of them, but he continued with his father to cultivate ten acres, divided in winter between wheat for subsistence and mustard for sale. The land was irrigated partly from the Western Jumna, partly by tube well. And how useful was his own agricultural development officer? Pardeep said he did not know the man's name and that big as the village was—and accessible by paved road—the man had not been there for two or three months. Pardeep spoke matter-of-factly, as if it were a commonplace.

I should have inferred much about Pardeep's status simply from the fact that he not only wore a suit but drove his own car; it was a wedding gift, he explained, from his wife's parents. We stopped at first at his father's house, of which I saw little except magnificent gates, and then went on to his own. He had been married less than a year, but already he and his wife owned not only the car but a motorcycle, a refrigerator, two gas cookers, two wells for domestic water, and electric fans—not only for themselves but for the water buffaloes they kept for milk in a spare house nearby.

I soon realized that Pardeep had returned to Kharar Alipur this noon for a reason: a political speech was to be given in the town square by a former minister of the government. The speech gave me an hour or so to wander through the town, which was nearly deserted for the occasion. There was a post office, and there were banks; there were dispensaries for people and animals; there was a public telephone, an office for the electrical department, one for the village council—even one for the agricultural development officer. Amazingly, the village had no police station. It was hard to believe, but Pardeep later insisted that the reason was simply that the town was free of crime. The nearest police station was six miles away.

Pardeep's status was made even clearer as soon as the speechmaking was over, for the ex-minister was ushered straight to Pardeep's father's house. As some sort of trophy I was plumped on the couch next to him, which proved mildly awkward for both of us, since he was that rare phenomenon, an Indian politician who cannot speak English. Still, he was in a good mood: he came from the People's Party, which was slated to win the upcoming election in Haryana because of its support for farm subsidies. We all drank glasses of warm buffalo milk—they at a gulp, me sipping interminably to avoid gagging. Then Mr. Jayaprakash was off to his next speech.

Pardeep's wife was pregnant, but squatting over her cooker she made a fine lunch. All three of us then returned to Hissar—he to his office, she to her obstetrician. Pardeep asked for information about American graduate schools; his wife asked for a fashion magazine so she could plan her wardrobe. I

A tap supplying domestic water to Khaluwas, a village south of Hissar town, in Haryana. No doubt this pumped system is judged by the villagers to be a great improvement over the old wells, but the contrast between tap and pots almost suggests that, given a choice, human beings will take ugliness over beauty. Shall we frame that more cautiously? In the name of progress, we manage to surround ourselves with so much ugliness that we forget we have a choice.

thanked them and decided to try the road that takes off from Hissar into the countryside at south by southwest.

Within half a dozen miles I was facing a ridge of dunes, an outlier of the Great Indian Desert that stretches off to the south forever. Close to the foot of the dunes I came to Khaluwas, a village on a low sandy hill. I circled the hill, past farmers weeding cotton fields with pairs of white oxen—all the animals muzzled with rope nettings. Domestic water taps had been installed at the base of the hill; women were gathered in small groups with brass or clay pots that they filled and carried uphill to houses the color of the surrounding plain. There would be no ministerial corteges here, nobody in suit and tie, nobody planning an overseas wardrobe.

I parked at the base of the hill and walked up the main street, which was strangely abandoned. Khaluwas was no Rani Kheri: its adults could not be commuters to Hissar. Why, then, were the courtyards so quiet, the street so deserted? I walked quietly along the unpaved street and craned my neck around compound walls of mud brick the same light color as the street dust. I could see cattle eating fodder from mudded-brick tubs built into the compound walls, but no people.

At the top of the hill there was a temple, vaguely Islamic in character even though the decoration was clearly Hindu. There were a few buildings of fired brick, a few very simple shops, and people sitting in doorways. Still, there were no vehicles. Now, however, I began to attract attention, and within a few minutes I was joking and taking pictures and mincing my way through another glass of hot sweet buffalo milk.

Eventually someone appeared who spoke a bit of English: Kishori Lal Sharma, holder of an M.A. in economics from Kurekshetra University. Kishori was unemployed but didn't seem particularly unhappy about it. In fact he wasn't doing too badly. We walked to his family's hilltop compound, and people along the way deferred to him as "pandit." His family's compound was surrounded by a fired-brick wall perhaps twelve feet high; an arched gateway revealed, straight ahead, a heavy cast-iron fodder chopper.

We went to his private room, whose floors and walls and ceiling were bare except for a fan and a light. The windows were unscreened but barred: no malaria here, Kishori said—hardly any mosquitoes. There were two single beds with hard sleeping mats, a couch, two cane chairs, two built-in cupboards, and a television in a cupboard with a rolling shutter.

Khaluwas, I now learned, was a Bhishnoi village. The name was new to me. There were other castes in it: sheep- and goat-herders for one; for another, tanners who worked as general laborers. But the Bhishnoi were dominant, and they were that most curious of things, Hindu Sufis. The men in Kishori's room were proud to show me the painting they wore as an amulet round their necks: it showed Jambheswar Maharaj, the sect's founder. They were happy to explain the sect's twenty-nine rules, though I caught only the ones prohibiting sexual relations during menstruation and, most strikingly, preventing the cutting down of live trees.

The Bhishnois, it turns out, come from Rajasthan, the desert state where a prohibition against chopping live trees makes a lot of sense; they had come here and established the village of Khaluwas some three centuries ago. The unusual temple was, of course, a Bhishnoi temple, used for the sect's Sufi rites, in which a spiritual master guides the approach to God. It was a cult of ascetics, I was told, and apolitical. Ascetic perhaps, but rich—much richer than it looked. And in this richness lay the key to the village's abandonment.

The ground water here was brackish, and until 1960 there had been no canal: the farmers of Khaluwas had depended on rain to grow millet in the summer and some beans in winter. Then a branch of the Western Jumna was pushed through. At first the canal was useless, because it was unlined and so much water was lost to seepage that supplies were hopelessly insecure. Then, a decade later, the canal had been lined. Khaluwas was luckily located at the head of its own branch canal, the Deosar Feeder.

The farmers were told to take irrigation water for a third of their land; the rest of the water was for people farther down the canal. No chance. I saw a farmer with his tractor parked at the canal bank at a time when the water was low—and intended for downstream villages. The power offtake on the tractor was driving a pump that lifted canal water into a ditch that should have been dry. The farmer and I could not speak to each other, but his guilty smile made clear that he knew exactly what he was doing.

And that was only half the reason the farmers of Khaluwas were rich. The other half is that landholdings in Khaluwas were large, and that's because the farmers before irrigation had needed big holdings to survive. Many people now irrigated over thirty acres, and *that* meant they were too busy farming to waste time living in the village. Those compounds I had thought curiously empty in fact *were* empty—demoted to barns. Of Khaluwas's 350 families, the richest hundred had literally moved out. They were now living on their neatly consolidated farms, many of them with small citrus groves around their houses and many not only with tractors but cars.

Here, as in Karnal District, we can see the kind of landscape slowly emerging across North India's plains and, for that matter, on the other prime lands of Asia. The pristine landscape, with villages rising above seas of mustard and clumps of mango, is being replaced by a landscape from the American Midwest, a landscape of square fields, machines instead of animals, and dispersed settlement. It is true that much of the year these plains have always been paradigms of heat and dust, but they have also had their gentler moments, and the memory of those moments and of the villages sprinkled across the plains has gone with Indians wherever they have migrated—Trinidad, Durban, so many other places. But what will be left of Khaluwas in a few decades? A ghost village? An archaeological dig? A place where visitors stop and see a plaque on a post set in dust that was once brick? As I write, the sun rises above the equally flat landscape of central Oklahoma, and I think of all the ghost towns that lie between me and that red ball.

One might ask that land-use planners provide a shopping list of incentives to maintain village integrity; one might, reduced to simpler things, ask only that landscape architects take a look at power-line routings, or that trees be given some degree of protection by law, as they are in Bhishnoi custom. Yet it will not happen anytime soon in busy Asia. I think of roads outside Xi'an, that old Chinese capital of the Ch'in Dynasty. The tourist buses head each day to the tomb of the terra-cotta warriors, and they pass fields that have lately been rectified, squared up in the name of efficiency; power lines run in every direction across the landscape, a line of poles here, another there. These, too, are prime lands: they lie at the edge of the great North China Plain. No one—not even me—will ask that we stop the pursuit of greater production: the press carries headlines reporting Asia's need to double rice production and lamenting the West's complacency about food security. But who will even ask that we ameliorate the impact of modernization on these plains? Who will ask that we keep an eye out for ways to minimize the impact of what we do? The silence is very great.

The next morning I took a quick look around a park in downtown Hissar and discovered that behind a clump of bushes there was a red sandstone monument nearly obscured now but still legible. It had been erected long ago to honor the "victims of 1857," including the collector of Hissar, one John Wedderburn, age 32, his wife Alice, 23, and their infant son John, six months. Small world! John Wedderburn was the older brother of William Wedderburn, who in 1913 published a biography of Allan Octavian Hume.

And if that's not ghost enough, consider this. I headed back to Delhi through Hansi, a town twenty miles east of Hissar. There I passed a very large but nearly ruined gate, a brick structure with wrought-iron gates perhaps fifteen feet high. The gates were pretty much frozen half-open; behind, there was some open ground: grass with scattered trees. An unpaved lane curved into what was apparently some kind of estate.

I parked and walked inside. A few hundred yards down the lane there was a one-story building with an arcaded veranda and a rooftop kiosk clad in corrugated iron. Two stone lions sat in front of the building like sphinxes. A man appeared and told me to wait.

Then—in a bathrobe, for it was early—a tall and vigorous man of perhaps sixty appeared. He had a characteristically British face, craggy, long, with a prominent nose and deep wrinkles. He extended a hand and introduced himself: "James Skinner." He must have seen my jaw drop. Yes, he said, a direct descendant; the church in Delhi had been built by his great-great-grandfather, who had also built this house. Before the Mutiny it had been the regimental mess; now it was simply Skinner Mansion.

We went inside. There was a portable pulpit, used by the first James Skinner to sermonize. High on the wall there was an oil portrait of John Lawrence, the brother of the Henry Lawrence who had "tried to do his duty." John Lawrence had been in his own right a famous governor of the Punjab and, after the Mutiny, viceroy of India. Many people have thought his face cruel, but to me it is a fine face, with eyes that have seen things no man should ever see. (That same expression appears with even greater force in the portrait that hangs in London's National Portrait Gallery; surrounded by illustrious men of the empire, John Lawrence stands out there, effortlessly and beyond question the most powerful man in the room.)

Lower on the walls of Skinner Mansion were paintings and photographs of the Skinner family, including a large photograph, much water damaged, of the James Skinner I was talking to. It showed him as a boy of perhaps three, dressed in a plaid cape with a dashing crown of a hat. The boy stood on a fine dining-room chair, whose back he held in front of himself for support.

"Call me Jim," he had said—a remarkable thing to hear from an Indian. But then James Skinner wasn't quite Indian. He explained that the family's estates had been confiscated. Not literally: it was just that the family had been forced to sell its lands for a pittance during the 1960s, when land-reform legislation made it obvious that the land would otherwise be taken. Real Indians might find ways to circumvent the laws, but not a family of mixed ancestry: for the Skinners the law would be enforced to the letter. And so thousands of acres in the family for generations had shrunk to this, the few acres of the mansion.

Skinner lived here with one of his three sisters. He had five brothers, he said: scattered from Australia to Britain. One lived in Houston. He himself had lived in the States for a while—taken a degree in agronomy at Kansas. But James Skinner hadn't been out of India since his return in 1961. With rupee devaluations, he explained, he wasn't going anywhere.

·· 8 ··

THE PERIPHERY

ONE ALMOST GETS WHIPLASHED BETWEEN THE centuries: the old, the new; the fading, the modern. And yet I would not have us lose sight of the point I wish to make. In the Hissar canals and their tail-end shortages we see the legacy of the Ganges canals. In the pampered cattle of the Government Livestock Farm we see the agricultural-research-station mentality bequeathed by Pusa. In the corpse of agricultural extension at Pardeep's village we see Etawah's child. Yet we see more than the failings of the culture of development; we see as well the tremendous impact it has had on the agriculturally most productive part of India. A new landscape is emerging; it is being shaped by the culture whose origins we have explored, and it is being shaped as though tradition did not matter, as though beauty could be dismissed because it is subjective, should be dismissed because it is a luxury.

Yet the tide of development does not wash over productive plains alone. On the contrary, it now washes over Asia's most remote mountain fastnesses. How shall I prove it? Let me choose Hunza as my example from the periphery.

Formerly part of Indian Kashmir but now in northernmost Pakistan, Hunza has never been better described than it was in 1899, when George Nathaniel Curzon made a short visit there shortly before his appointment as viceroy. Curzon saw Rakaposhi, the magnificent white pyramid that anchors the western end of the Karakoram Mountains, and he wrote: "Rakaposhi stands there and will stand as long as this orb endures, under the heavenly vault, under the eternal stars, ancestral, godlike, sublime, tremendous." He went on to describe the orchards in the Hunza Valley below—their "rich spoil of apricots, walnuts, apples, pears, melons, mulberries, peaches, and grapes." It's still true, despite precipitation averaging less than ten inches a year. Everything depends on irrigation—and has for a very long time.

Even before Curzon's visit Algernon Durand described the vital irrigation ditch that still today irrigates the fields around Karimabad, Hunza's largest settlement. "On this channel," Durand wrote, "the cultivation of Hunza proper entirely depends; should it fail, starvation stares the people in the face. It is not surprising, therefore, that the greatest care should be expended on its preservation. But what is wonderful is the excellence of the result arrived at. . . . The people have no proper tools, no crowbars and dynamite. . . . The use of mortar is unknown. . . . Yet with all these disadvantages, with nothing but their eye as a guide to levels, they have carried this great irrigation channel for six miles, and turned an arid desert into a garden. . . . It is a splendid work, and I admired it more every time I walked along it."

So have I. There cannot be many places where you can get up at dawn and walk directly from a hotel to irrigated terraces—walk past tiny fields of corn and stacks of unthreshed wheat, walk past gardens with grapes and apples. There must be a thousand paths here, some following the main ditches along contours, others winding downhill to the very cliffs that overlook the Hunza River, grim as the Indus. The houses are mostly of cobbles, with pueblo-style ladders leading to upper floors. Early in the morning, observant goats watch you through slatted doorways; all day in summer, halved apricots—moist at first, later like leather—lie drying on rooftops under the hot sun.

Although I have flown here from Islamabad—and the

mountain views are immense—I recommend the drive, especially if you can come indirectly from Islamabad to Peshawar to
Swat, then over the Shangla Pass and down to the Karakoram
Highway. Not far from Besham, where the Shangla Pass road
joins the highway at the Indus River, there is one notorious
slide near the village of Patan. At its start there is a small road-
sign masterpiece of understatement. It says only "Good
Luck."

Near Chilas—say four hours upstream from Besham and
halfway to Gilgit—the trees quit. So, too, of necessity, does the
spectacular logging that one sees farther downstream, where
timbers are skidded down ravines and swung on cables across
rivers. The Indus now looks like a river in California's Death
Valley, and a heavy roof of clouds I once saw there blocked out
the summits on either side and seemed to laugh at anyone
expecting rain.

A couple of hours farther on, we passed the road that leads
to Astor, a strange name to American ears but no relation. Astor
is significant chiefly because it marks the old route to Kashmir:
Curzon's route, built by the British when they established
themselves here in the 1890s. They did it to block imperial
Russia, and that is why Gilgit still has a major garrison and an
airstrip, used by civilian as well as military flights. You're always passing the airstrip on your way in and out, which means
that, once you know how often the flights are canceled because of bad weather, you're always wondering if the link to
the outside world is up today.

Coming in from the airport, you pass miles of shops along a
main street. Climb the great ridge that rises just south of town,
however, and much of the main street turns out to be false
front: highway frontage walled off from the irrigated fields that
stretch behind. The bazaar itself has little to offer a tourist
apart from dried apricots and unbelievably acidic apricot juice.
Both come from Hunza, across the Gilgit River and up the
Hunza River, which joins it here.

It was my first visit and I wanted to go to Chaprot, about
halfway to Hunza but a few miles off the Karakoram Highway.
Why Chaprot? The answer is a book by a Colonel R. C. F.

Schomberg, *Between the Oxus and the Indus*. Schomberg traveled here in the 1930s, when tourism was physically difficult and officially prohibited, and he speaks of Chaprot as "more beautiful than any other valley in the whole of the Gilgit Agency." Good enough; I hired a jeep and driver.

The Karakoram Highway is two lanes wide, but north of Gilgit you often see traces of the vertiginously narrow older roads on the opposite and near-vertical walls of the Hunza River's canyon. Some of them look impassable even by a mule, but a French expedition back in the summer of 1930 actually got some tracked vehicles over them—the first vehicles ever to reach Hunza. The trip was described in the *National Geographic Magazine* for March of 1932. Did that issue come to the attention of James Hilton? He was soon to write *Lost Horizon*, and his description of Shangri-La bears a very close resemblance to that issue's photograph of Karimabad.

An hour outside Gilgit I looked across at a natural terrace: cliff walled, level, green with trees and fodder. It was about a hundred feet above the Hunza River. We turned off the highway and crossed a one-lane wooden suspension bridge; on its far side the bridge nosed straight toward a cliff, at whose face the jeep made an amazingly abrupt ninety-degree turn to the left. Within a few hundred yards I was in the village of Chalt, to which the irrigated terrace belongs. I had no idea how far Chaprot was, and so we just drove on through.

The clouds laughed again and turned into uncompromising rain that stayed with us for the five or six slow miles to Chaprot. We crossed steep bridges, made hairpin turns, and went past terraced fields of young wheat and Lombardy poplars. We trashed thousands of pink apricot blossoms, knocked off the trees by the rain. Our tires buried them.

We finally came to a village and a collapsed bridge; the driver asked around and told me: "Chaprot." I asked for clarification: yes, this was it. There weren't a lot of people around, and the road was steep and slippery. Apart from their doors, which were built of planks so short that one had to stoop to enter, the buildings were built entirely of rock—some cleaved but most just unchinked river boulders: even the roofs were mantled with rock. So, too, were the paths between buildings, which were hardly more than rock slits opening upward to a gray-white sky above buildings so primitive that I could only distinguish homes from barns by listening for crying children.

Eventually some children came outside: the boys wore drab hooded jackets of Western style but the girls' attire boasted bright colors—the only color in Chaprot outside the village fields. Their mothers withdrew, but boys and girls posed. One girl stood on the main road with her back close to a stone wall neatly built of alternated slabs and blocks. There was a doorway a foot past her: it was open, and its wooden framework was visible, along with a tree in the courtyard. She wore that characteristic Pakistani dress: a colorful knee-length shirt over matching trousers, but she was wrapped in a magenta-pink shawl that framed the Tibetan features of her face and hung nearly to mid-thigh. It made a fine picture, but only she and I know how miserable the day really was.

Even now I find it therapeutic to remember this day: it helps me remind myself that Hunza isn't paradise. The average "farm," I could add, covers all of four acres. Low-earning wheat, moreover, is the main crop; it covers about half of the cultivated land, though it is followed at lower elevations by a corn crop. The average household supplements those grain crops with forty fruit trees, mostly apricot; it has about two hundred other trees, chiefly fast-growing poplars for roof timbers, fuel, and fodder for some fifteen animals. (The manure of those animals is absolutely essential to maintaining the fertility of the terraces, because the soil is hardly more than highly porous glacial silt.)

Apparently the British encouraged the Hunzans to build additional irrigation channels during the 1920s and 1930s. The population therefore began to increase, and despite infant mortality rates approaching two hundred per thousand, the population has more than doubled during the last thirty years alone. The British seem to have done little else in the way of development work, apart from providing a doctor who was withdrawn in 1947, when Pakistan needed him more elsewhere. So far as I know, the only other development work in

Hunza before 1950 was sponsored by the Aga Khan. The people of Hunza are chiefly Ismaili Muslims, a Shia sect devoted to him, and at the end of World War II he began paying for boys' schools.

Then an outsider came: an American geologist named John Clark. Like the extensionist Horace Holmes at Etawah, Clark had been in China during the war; like so many people at that time he saw the Chinese Communist victory and feared for his own country. After an exploratory trip through northern Pakistan and western China, he decided in 1949 to try bringing to Hunza a kind of development that would avert what he saw as the otherwise inevitable victory of Communism throughout Asia.

In a book published in 1956 about his work in Hunza—called simply *Hunza*—Clark explicitly states that his project was "a sort of pilot model for larger efforts." He explains how he formed a small foundation, the Central Asiatic Research Foundation, which provided him with twenty thousand dollars for an initial two-year period of residence in Hunza. Clark's strategy was to provide educational and medical services, set up a woodworking school to manufacture craft items from apricot wood, introduce American vegetable seeds, and generate some export income by catching butterflies for American museums and by planting wildflowers for their seed, which would be sent back to the United States for sale. Meanwhile he would rely on his professional skills to hunt for valuable minerals that would please the government of Pakistan and perhaps create some income for the people of Hunza.

Clark's matériel had to be flown to Gilgit, then packed to Hunza—the lead horse brandishing a small American flag. Plus, not surprisingly, Clark faced political problems from the start. There were rumors he was scheming to make Hunza part of the United States. Then, more seriously, the mir of Hunza and the government of Pakistan began to think that Clark would inevitably create discontent with the status quo. The mir feared that such discontent would undermine his authority (in fact, he survived until 1974, and his successor still resides as a private citizen in Karimabad). The government feared Clark's work would incline the people toward Communism, and for this reason, so ironic in light of Clark's purposes, Clark was forced to leave when his two years were finished.

Clark began those years, however, by setting up shop in the mir's palace at Karimabad. He prospected widely, without success. He established his crafts school, collected wildflower seeds, and planted his garden—too deeply: many of the vegetables never germinated. Most of his time was eaten up running his clinic: the job was so overwhelming that he writes, "I felt like a man trying to stop a thunderstorm." Sometimes he felt appreciated; at other times, the local people "were regarding me as just another foreign traveler to yield revenue as he passed by."

Finally, the government told him he could stay no longer: "I was raising their standards of living too fast. This would make Communists of them. . . . Although my motives were undoubtedly meritorious, from a military standpoint I was endangering the safety of the frontier—stirring up the local people." Clark tried to interest the Ford Foundation in taking over his work, but the foundation declined—oddly in view of its almost simultaneous commitment to expand the work done at Etawah. Perhaps Hunza was too remote and the political situation too precarious. Perhaps it was just bad luck. In any event Clark left; his final words lament the "tyranny I had not broken, ignorance I had not lifted, poverty that I had not relieved."

I found older people in Hunza today who remembered Clark, but his work is almost totally forgotten, especially because so much attention is being paid instead to the expanded efforts of the Aga Khan. Even the most casual tourist on the Karakoram Highway will notice the little green and white signs every few miles along its length, the ones with the letters AKRSP. They are never pronounced as an acronym, just as letters. But the letters come easily after a while, for the Aga Khan Rural Support Project was to the 1980s what Etawah was to the 1950s.

In fact, there is a direct linkage between Etawah and the AKRSP. It consists of one man: Akhter Hameed Khan, a Pakistani Muslim and holder of an M.A. degree in English literature from Agra University. In 1936, when he was twenty-four years old, Khan joined the elite Indian Civil Service. He spent two probationary years at Cambridge, then was posted as a subdivisional officer to Bengal. There he saw how the British, seeking to resist an apparently imminent Japanese invasion, confiscated all local boats and disrupted the rice industry so thoroughly that a great famine resulted—a famine greater than any in India since.

Like his peers, the young Khan followed instructions to exhort the farmers to greater food production: "I made patriotic speeches to rural gatherings. I inspected manure pits, inaugurated exhibitions, and gave away many prizes. Lecturing obsequious audiences and listening to flattering addresses, I imagined myself to be an engine of development. Later, after the flush of youth passed away, I realized that, notwithstanding official efforts, there was no perceptible change in production."

In 1945 Khan resigned from the ICS to become a locksmith. There cannot be another case quite like it, but there were few if any ICS members who, like Khan, were also both Sufis and Tolstoyans. Apparently Khan made good locks, but two years later he quit, unable to support his family or, in his words, to "live without books and leisure." This time he became a teacher in Delhi; then, in 1950, principal of the small Victoria College in Comilla, East Pakistan—an hour's drive east of Dhaka. It was there that he ran into the Americans.

In 1953 they were busy exporting community development from Etawah, and Khan was made director of the East Pakistan program. Community development at that time, he later wrote, was a rainbow. People thought that it "promised political peace by including everyone in a harmonious community." In fact, the program in East Pakistan was a disaster; Khan quit in a year and returned to his college. Two years later, however, the Americans were back, this time in collaboration with the Ford Foundation, which proceeded in 1958 to spend about two million dollars bringing East Pakistanis to Michigan State University and then, in the following year, bringing Michigan State professors to the newly created Pakistan Academy of Rural Development. It was located in Comilla just so Khan would agree to head it. Once again Khan left his college post. He induced the government to allot to the academy a hundred-square-mile block of Comilla District, which became the academy's laboratory. Despite his disavowals, Khan became "Mr. Comilla."

"In particular the Americans loved him." So writes a later head of the academy. "In him," this man continues, "they saw their Asian fantasies compounded of Gandhian, Sufistic and Buddhist ideals. For them he became the living prophet of rural development." How much of the Comilla Approach was really Khan's idea, however, is hard to say. The Americans considered him indispensable, but Khan writes that matters of policy were set by high officials in the government of East Pakistan: "We could, at best, slightly modify or refine and polish." Of the U.S. government and the Ford Foundation, Khan writes that "as paymasters they usually dictated the tune."

The central lesson of the Comilla Approach? In the words of a then vice president of the Ford Foundation who was soon to become a senior official of the World Bank, Comilla taught that "anyone who seeks to assist Bengali villagers must approach them ready to listen and learn, not to talk and instruct." It sounds good, like Allan Octavian Hume, like Albert Mayer. But Khan was no believer in Etawah, at least. He explained that "educated people will go to the village, only when the village is made fit for their habitation, that is, when it has schools and when it has medical services. Before that happens they will go there as the village-level workers are going today, that is, like people on a railway station platform; they just wait there for the next train home."

And so the Comilla Approach focused instead on hardware—mostly roads and tube wells for irrigation—and, simultaneously, on community training centers and cooperatives. More than three hundred of these cooperatives were formed by the late 1960s: most were agricultural, but others served merchants and masons, blacksmiths and bookbinders, rickshaw pullers and truck drivers. Americans working with the project at the time thought it was a tremendous achievement, and something of Khan's charisma may be seen in the words he spoke to members of those cooperatives in 1962: "Even if you don't eat, you must save your money. If you don't make your own capital, this whole society will vanish like the mist. Not a trace will remain. Money is the basis of all this work. And all this money will come from your hands. It will not come from outside."

As in India, there was great pressure to expand the program, and in 1964 Khan agreed to do so. As the "Integrated Rural Development Program," the work at Comilla seemed set to go national. In 1967, however, civil war came to Pakistan. By 1971 East Pakistan was Bangladesh, and Khan, originally from the Northwest Frontier Province, returned home. And the program? "In Pakistan," Khan would write, "where revolution is more popular than reform, the programme, after only seven years, was abolished instead of being improved. It needed re-direction. It was annihilated."

After two abortive starts with rural development projects in northern Pakistan, Khan moved to Karachi, where in 1991 he was still living and working with a community development project. At the same time, however, he became deeply involved with the expanding development program sponsored by the Aga Khan in Hunza. How could it have been otherwise, given his background? It was no coincidence, therefore, that the man the foundation chose to run the AKRSP was a Khan protégé who in years to come would turn to Khan in critical moments and who would call him the AKRSP's "mentor and guide."

What has the AKRSP accomplished? In an echo of the Comilla cooperatives, the AKRSP had tried to organize villagers into "VOs," village organizations. To do this, "SOs" or social organizers were sent to the field to meet with the villagers and discover the "social activist" who might play a leading role in each community. The AKRSP offered a cash incentive for creating a village organization. This incentive was applied to the village's "PPI" or "productive physical infrastructure." The AKRSP, in other words, would learn what the villagers believed they needed most. Perhaps it would be a new irrigation channel, perhaps a road; the only things categorically excluded were those, like domestic water supplies, that would not be "productive"—would not create wealth. Once the PPI had been determined, the AKRSP would provide not only technical guidance but money to cover the cost of materials and to pay for the labor provided by the villagers to build the PPI.

But completing PPIs was not the goal of the AKRSP: PPIs were the AKRSP's means of building village organizations that would go on to undertake other cooperative tasks. Those tasks would be built *without* subsidy and by borrowing against the security of the money in the village organization's savings account, which was required by the AKRSP in return for its contribution to the PPI. These savings accounts were so central to the AKRSP that by 1990 there was talk about the village organizations becoming self-sustaining village banks.

The echoes of Comilla grow still louder. Social organizers facilitated the establishment of over a thousand village organizations. Hundreds of PPIs were completed—mostly irrigation channels or short roads linking villages to the Karakoram Highway or other main roads. By 1990 some fifty-five thousand acres of land were being newly irrigated from completed PPIs; more than seventy thousand acres were getting additional or supplemental water supplies.

There were dozens of follow-on programs, too. Villagers could borrow against their savings to buy fruit trees, especially apple; alternatively, they might buy new wheat varieties that produced not only heavy grain crops but abundant straw for fodder. They could borrow to establish themselves in seed-potato production, particularly for sale to the lowlands of the Punjab. There were programs for artificial insemination of livestock, for vaccination, for cooperative purchase of electric churns. All were funded on a loan basis, with the village organization providing collateral in the form of its own cash savings and the AKRSP providing not only the loan but training in the activities.

The World Bank, not given to praise of other development organizations, sent a team to evaluate the AKRSP in 1986. The verdict? "Outstanding." Yet a critic might ask if the AKRSP's success was the result of the long local tradition of cooperation in matters such as irrigation-channel maintenance. How much of its success for that matter was the result of the villagers' deference to the Aga Khan? What would happen if the project were expanded and exported to non-Ismaili areas?

By the mid-1980s some VOs were dormant; others had split in two, apparently because groups larger than fifty households had trouble cohering. Could a group of this size run its own bank? Could a group of any size cohere for years to come? On a visit to one village, the AKRSP's general manager was bluntly told: "No one is honest. We fight when we get together because we are desperate. We would be happy to see everyone in adversity."

One afternoon I went to take a look at one particularly well-known PPI. I went down the Gilgit River toward its confluence with the Indus. There I turned off the Karakoram Highway and began going upstream against that great river, turbulent and khaki at the bottom of a rocky canyon. There are about seven inches of annual precipitation here, and there was nothing green except patches of tough brush. My destination was the Hanuchal Channel, described in the AKRSP's own files as "peerless and unique," in positively Persian diction as "beloved."

Now the village of Hanuchal stands on a patch of irrigated land on a right-bank bench. The villagers had traditionally relied for their water on the local Hanuchal creek; then, with the AKRSP's help, they decided to tap Maruk Creek, a few miles farther up the Indus. With five more cusecs of water available to them, the villagers could reclaim an additional three hundred acres of their bench. By the time of my visit the work was done; the villagers had distributed the first hundred acres of new land among some twenty-five of the village's hundred and ten households. They had taken out a loan for fruit trees to be planted on that land, which would be sown as well with two annual crops of grain, planted between the trees.

Looking up a cliff face about two miles past the village, I wondered if that notch I saw could possibly be what I wanted.

l doubted it, simply because the cliff face was so sheer, but here was a green AKRSP sign with the plain words "Hanuchal Channel." I started scrambling up a difficult slope of broken rock created from the rubble tossed down when the channel was built. At the top I was giddy. From perhaps three hundred feet above the road the Indus looked small, and I had whispers of vertigo whenever I looked away from the channel-side path. Worse: within a few hundred yards downstream I was forced to squat at a place where the cliff face was not vertical but overhanging. There could not have been more than three feet of vertical space between the channel and the rock ceiling that projected laterally perhaps ten feet beyond the cliff face.

It may sound odd that I was impressed to find that the channel was fitted with homemade escapes: there was nothing fancy here, nothing of metal—just wooden slats and wedges fitted into a gap in the channel wall, wedges that could be lifted up to open the escape in case of a channel break. I was impressed—and astonished: the escapes could be locally maintained and, if necessary, locally replaced. That's a great deal more than can be said for the thousands of more sophisticated gates installed by aid agencies elsewhere in the world.

I turned around and began walking all the way upstream to the channel head. It was a test of my none-too-strong resistance to vertigo, especially when the channel turned away from the Indus and began heading up the tributary Maruk. The path was perhaps two feet across, but the drop was a fatal one at many places, with boiling waters below. I would have turned around, but irrigation channels have a powerful allure, and half an hour later I came to the channel head. It consisted of nothing more than a few rocks placed to shunt water over to the right bank and into a channel which at first was only a few inches above the creek. It was the height of informality.

A few days later I visited a PPI with a very different history. This was at Passu, an hour's drive north of Karimabad. The morning was still cold when I headed upriver at six o'clock through shade-dark canyons—villages, each with their own irrigation channel, dotted here and there along the walls. Within an hour I was in open-sun Gulmit, and the day was warm. A man was cutting wheat with a sickle; a niece wearing a red machine-made sweater watched him. His English was good; it turned out he was a local schoolteacher, farming part-time. A new suspension bridge crossed the Hunza River here. It was a good one, according to a woman using it, and it was certainly carried on steel cables. The floor slats were crude, however, and laid according to a plan in which one slat was followed by two empty spaces. So long as the wind was calm and you had two free hands for the side-rail cables, it was okay.

Passu itself was another half hour up the road and around a good-sized hill. My first view of it came dramatically when, just short of the last curve, I got out and trudged over the ridge that the road encircles. At the top I looked down into a glacial valley with lateral moraines extending upstream to my left to a rocky glacial tongue a mile farther upstream. Passu lay to my right; a small place of perhaps sixty families, their homes surrounded by a few hundred acres of land patchily cultivated along the Hunza River.

Such water as Passu got was spread, unevenly as I say, over a broad terrace, its half-abandoned fields rimmed with stone walls. The village itself seemed mysteriously deserted of all but secretive women and children, who sequestered themselves among red hollyhocks behind garden gates. Channels ran through the village proper, some of them lined with concrete.

I had come to see Passu's PPI, a new channel almost three miles long. I nearly missed it, however: you have to go a few miles past Passu proper to see the terrace the new channel irrigates, and a few miles farther still to catch the channel at a point handy for walking to its head.

Once again the headworks hardly merited the name, but I grew chilly as I approached them along the rocky, almost lunar desolation of the channel's upper course. The day was hot, though, and I could see no ice ahead. It was only at the very head of the channel that I realized that the pile of boulders ahead was actually the rubbly snout of the Batura Glacier, over which the breeze blew and sent cool air downstream.

I wanted to return to the area irrigated by the channel, but

before doing so I crossed the Hunza River at another AKRSP
sign, pointing in this case to a new link road built as the PPI
of Shimshal village, which lies some miles upstream. Three or
four miles up the road a slide blocked the road. I walked stead-
ily for an hour through a canyon now very hot, the silt-choked
river as mocking as if it were salt. Twice there was some relief:
once when a clear trickle came in from the side, and once
again when the canyon choked down to an almost vertical slit
that funneled a cool breeze my way. Eventually I came to a
couple of work sites—mines I thought. Then I realized that
the road upstream disappeared; there was nothing but the
roughest of canyons ahead. The "miners" were, in fact, road
crews.

Near the good water along this walk there was a massive
boulder on which someone had written an invitation to stay at
a guest house in Shimshal. It's ironic, since Shimshal was the
traditional penal colony of Hunza. Times change. And how
would tourism change Shimshal, once the road was complete
and visitors such as me could drive in?

I ask the question because of what I found at Passu. The
fields—old and new—were being cultivated desultorily, for
the highway had brought new and easier ways to make money.
Passu's village activist had actually quit working with the
AKRSP the year the highway opened. He had opened a hotel.

The heavy guns had been brought in: not only the project's
general manager but also Akhter Hameed Khan. What happened then is described in the project files. "You have to decide," Khan told the villagers, "whether what Almighty Allah
has given you in these mountains is a blessing or a curse." The
villagers, he continued, must choose whether or not to develop
land "that has sustained generations of your ancestors." Depending on tourists, Khan said, was "false gold," for politics in
Pakistan were unstable: the road might be closed as abruptly
as it had been opened.

The villagers were unimpressed, and Khan turned punitive.
Tell them, he said (in Urdu to the translator who was speaking
to the villagers in Wakhi), that His Highness, the Aga Khan,
is planning a visit to the valley. If the villagers are not more

cooperative with the project "we will try our utmost that he doesn't visit Passu." Why should His Highness come, Khan said, "to grieve at what you have done?" The villagers sat stolidly. Khan said: "Tell them the AKRSP extended them its hand of friendship, assisted them in every way, gave them strength, and loved them, and they spat in our faces." There was no response, and Khan said, "Let us go." The minutes of the meeting state that at this point the "meeting broke up in pandemonium," with one villager "grabbing his shoe to use as a weapon."

Perhaps it was a glimpse of Akhter Hameed Khan's old ICS training; certainly it contradicts what the Americans thought was the chief lesson of Comilla. The relationship of the AKRSP to the villagers, Khan said on the drive back to Gilgit, should be not social but "like a teacher—who uses the rod occasionally." Ironically, the AKRSP's own first annual review had reviewed the history of community development in India and criticized the Gurgaon Experiment for its air of "superior wisdom."

Five years had passed from that Passu meeting to the time I came by; five years during which, as the project staff had correctly predicted, the project would stagnate. The new water was coming; it finally dropped over a bluff and bubbled happily down to a terrace unirrigated since the beginning of time. By now the terrace ought to have been green and golden: after all, the Passu villagers had gone beyond their PPI and borrowed another four thousand dollars for land development, fruit trees, and fertilizer. But there seemed little likelihood that the loans could be repaid from the patchy alfalfa and scattered fruit trees I saw. No one was at work. My own jeep driver was from a village closer to Karimabad, and on the nights I spent there he went home to sleep. Farming wasn't for him either.

With the highway open, in fact, some two-thirds of the Gilgit District's households now rely on nonfarm income, which provides about a quarter of the district's total household income. Those Hunza villagers who *do* farm are changing fast, too. There was a combine working on the wheat fields down in Gilgit, and even in small villages near Karimabad I saw wheat being threshed mechanically, great clouds of dust being thrown into the air, while off in the fields other men were doing the same thing more quietly, with wooden forks. What kind of wheat? For twenty years or so, improved varieties of wheat had been arriving from the lowlands. They hadn't been accepted very quickly, because the new varieties didn't produce as much straw as the old ones but required more fertilizer. The farmers who did adopt the new varieties were those who had off-farm jobs and who found that the rapid growth of the new varieties allowed them to stay at those jobs an extra week.

Rising expectations had come even to Chaprot. On a clear and hot July day I crossed the Hunza River once again, made that incredible cliff-face turn, and headed back through Chalt. The road had reverted from mud to dirt. On the cold days of spring I had not noticed the many spring-houses in Chalt; now I did, and I wondered what they were for, since channels led both in and out. Why bother with a covered pool? The channels might not run all the time, of course, but was there another reason? Perhaps it was a way of letting the dust in the glacial meltwater settle before one drank it. Then I noticed the long-handled wooden ladles parked outside the wells. I looked inside and saw wooden churns floating on the water.

This time I stuck my nose through open gates and saw brightly flowering gardens. Rakaposhi's snow, lost in the clouds on my last visit, was brilliant now against the blue sky, and the fields below were in knee-high corn. Often the mountain was juxtaposed even more lusciously against rooftops that were covered with apricots.

A mile farther along the road to Chaprot I got out to walk and came upon a man sitting outside his green-porched house. "Salaam aleikum." Picking up on my abominable accent, Malik Akhdar began speaking English. He was a teacher, a college graduate from Chaprot. He said he knew how beautiful the place was; it was famed, he said, for having everything one needed: water, food, wood, and fodder.

That was the theory; the practice was that he would leave if he could. Not that he was poor: he had electricity in his house—lights and a radio. (As he said this, his old mother sat spinning wool on the porch.) But he also had eight children. The education they could get locally was, in his phrase, "not competitive." Malik wanted his sons to become government officers and said that if he had a choice he would move to Islamabad. His oldest son was already in college in Karachi, but that success didn't persuade Malik to stay put. His four other boys still had to make the grade, and he wanted every advantage for them.

His daughters? It was a foolish question to ask, for the whole village of Chaprot is Shia rather than Ismaili. Malik expressed no surprise at my ignorance: "It is against our religion." His daughters, he went on, would leave school at fifteen or sixteen. (Later on, with an army officer, I would raise the question of whether Pakistan understood that it was trying to climb the ladder of development with one hand tied behind its back; his answer was yes but that resistance to female emancipation was fading slowly.)

Malik asked for a portrait of himself with his sons, and he insisted on posing with a solemnity that required a decent photographer. I took what I could, which turned out grim as lockjaw, and then drove farther up the valley. I parked at Chaprot and started walking again over the broken bridge and across the village creek. There was an intensely blue sky, there was snow at the horizon on all sides, there were rugged hills closer in—often just bare rock. Finally there was the village itself and its creek-hugging swath of cultivated land. It was dotted with stacks of wheat, some still unthreshed. And here, too, were the children with dirty faces, often marked with rashes. I walked for a while behind an old man who labored up a long, steep hill with at least a hundred pounds of lumber roped to his back. Within a few minutes a young guide attached himself to me, and I could not shake him without intolerable rudeness. Eventually I turned around.

The Aga Khan Foundation was sponsoring the Baltit Heritage Trust, which was restoring the abandoned castle of the mir of Hunza. Next to it, a traditional Hunza house had been made into a museum—simple but interesting. The foundation had also just brought over an American architect with a dozen students; they were working to map the complex pattern of houses surrounding the palace. From there, the architect said, they would fan out to study water supply and sewerage. (The local water was so full of silt that the manager of my hotel in Karimabad sent all the hotel's laundry fifty miles to Gilgit.)

The Aga Khan people had clout, too. A brick factory, for example, was under construction just upstream from Karimabad: Pakistani capital, Chinese labor. The American architect mapping Karimabad was opposed to it—said that brick houses would collapse in a seismically active area such as Hunza unless they were expensively reinforced. Word had been passed along, and the general manager of the AKRSP had just caught the ear of the prime minister of Pakistan. Work on the brick factory would be stopped.

I asked whether there was not an aesthetic as well as a safety argument to be made against brick, and the architect admitted that he preferred stone to "culturally inappropriate" materials. He, too, had observed the many new buildings going up in Karimabad not of traditional river boulders but of concrete blocks. Commercial buildings even had pull-down steel shutters. Still, the architect asked cuttingly if I had any idea how much more mortar was required by a building built of boulders than by one of rectangular blocks. Had I seen how steep the streets here were, and did I see how far down it was to the river? Did I think that in the villagers' place I would choose rock if a more convenient material was available?

What then, I asked, was both practical and beautiful? The architect suggested I look at the nearby Aga Khan Academy. This was a new girls' school made of concrete blocks whose ingredients were the natural color of the hillsides; its roof, though of corrugated sheet metal, had been painted the same shade of brown. The windows had an Islamic arch at the top; even the wall around the school grounds had been beveled to soften its edge. This was in extraordinary contrast with my hotel, which was painted white and which had a shiny metal roof that winked from miles away. The architect argued that the school was not only appropriate but would slowly be copied by villagers building houses—copied, that is, except for the windows, which he thought would prove too expensive.

He was right. A day later I came down an almost impossibly steep jeep trail and saw a house that looked very much like the academy. I stopped and found someone who said that the owner was a shopkeeper—I could find him down on the highway. It wasn't so easy, what with false leads to friendly and crowded shops where I was unable to make myself understood. An hour later, however, I did meet up with the owner, Khisro Khan, a middle-school teacher spending his vacation in a stationery shop that he had set up cooperatively with a dozen other teachers.

I told him that I was interested in his house, and he said that it had been built by his brother, who had indeed worked on the academy but who had now left Hunza for work elsewhere. Sure enough, the windows were rectangular, and to save more money the metal roof had been replaced by wood.

But the natural-color concrete block was there, and the house blended into the countryside far better than any other new building I saw in Hunza. I couldn't help asking whether conditions in Hunza were better or worse now that the highway was open and plenty of tourists were coming through. "Better," Khan said without hesitation. Why? Before, there had been nothing to buy.

I began to wonder if the Aga Khan Foundation's concern about cultural preservation might extend from architecture to whole landscapes. Might the builder of Hanuchal Channel have had an eye for the beauty of these places, as well as for their economies? Alas, the AKRSP engineer I talked with about this said that design decisions were driven solely by cost. He himself was equally proud of a PPI consisting of an electric pump that lifted water up to a bench. In fact he gave me some directions to a place called Soni-Kot, whose traditional water supply had now been diverted to supply domestic water to Gilgit. The pumping station, when I found it, consisted of a depressingly utilitarian setup, with two electric motors driving pumps. They pushed water through an eight-inch iron pipe stuck in the Gilgit River; the pipe ran through a crude pump house and, at about breast-height, continued some two or three hundred yards uphill, until it discharged into a rectangular pond rimmed with concrete.

Discouraged, I went some six miles west of Gilgit to Kargah, famous for its stone figure of the Buddha, which was carved on a cliff face some thirteen hundred years ago. An old irrigation channel took off nearby and ran for several miles along the ridge south of Gilgit town—ran on such a precise gradient that from Gilgit it looked like a geological intrusion.

An irrigation channel running in front of the wall and gate of a private house near Gilgit town, in the Northern Areas of Pakistan. The picture suggests that the terrain is level, but in fact the channel runs on a contour along a steep slope south of the town and many hundreds of feet above it. Hence the tiny grain mill just out of sight downstream, for the walk to the Gilgit market is daunting.

The weather had turned around: heavy clouds now replaced four or five brilliantly blue July days. The rain didn't start until I was well away from the jeep; I huddled next to a tree and stayed dry for a while. The rain grew heavier, and I got wet. But when the shower had passed, my shirt dried quickly. On the uphill side of the channel there was only broken rock, scree smooth as formica. On the downhill side, irrigated fields extended down to the valley floor. The fields had so many trees in them that from a distance the two sides of the contour-hugging canal looked like a coastline, with foamy green waters lapping a desert shore.

Just below that coastline there were homes with stone walls and wooden gates hiding fruit trees and flowers. At one point the channel ran right past such a gate; the residents could not help hearing the gurgling. Fifty yards downstream the channel parted, then came together again. It puzzled me until I saw the drop, saw the hut, saw the race in the current. Sensible for people who were several hours' walk from Gilgit: another gristmill, just like those of the Northwest Frontier Province— or those of the Eastern Jumna Canal.

I passed a half-dozen people. I felt that even if I could speak their language I could never make them see how much they stood to lose.

SOFTLY, SOFTLY

SOME TIME AFTER VISITING HUNZA FOR THE
second time I wrote to the Aga Khan Foundation in Geneva. I
knew no one there, but with some technical questions for
cover, I managed to ask what I really wanted to know: was the
foundation concerned about preserving the traditional rural
landscape of Hunza?

I received a long letter from Bob Shaw, the foundation's
general manager. Shaw explained that the AKRSP had been
conceived as a vehicle for agricultural development. It had
been reasonably successful in that regard—had done much to
stabilize villages that might otherwise have been abandoned.
Certainly that was a step toward preservation.

Beyond that, he went on, the AKRSP had to be careful.
There were other institutions within the foundation, such as
the Trust for Culture, which was working to preserve Baltit
and the old castle there. Turf wars had to be avoided. And
there was another problem. The Aga Khan encouraged "all of
his organisations to be concerned about the Rural Built Envi-
ronment," but "with the opening of communications to the
Northern Areas and the increases in income, the local people
tend to want to appear 'modern.' " Hence the concrete blocks,
the bricks, the bright sheet metal.

A few months later, in response to a reply I sent, Shaw wrote again and expanded upon what he called "the dilemmas of modernisation." He wrote of the "numerous conversations" he had had in northern Pakistan "with people who hark back nostalgically to the traditions and close relationships of an earlier era. And they will attack the crassness of modern commercialism and competitive relationships. Almost in the same breath, however, they will say how hard life was in the feudal days, and how much better it is today. I know people who are deeply concerned about, and active in, the preservation of local traditions. These same people think nothing of simultaneously asking me to bring them a video camera or cassettes!"

He asked if I had any ideas. Tit for tat. And I'm no planner. With a sense that I should have more arrows in my quiver, I suggested that a tourist-tax might be added to hotel bills in Hunza. The money could be assigned to community preservation: everything from subsidizing traditional building materials to traditional crop production methods. I got back a letter in which Shaw reminded me that the "AKRSP is *not*, of course, a government. Questions of taxation and subsidies fall outside its mandate." He acknowledged that recommendations could be made, but we let the matter lie.

What about the AKRSP's own staff? I suggested that they might be sensitized to the aesthetic implications of their work. A letter came back from Geneva: "*All* AKRSP engineers, without exception, are residents of, and originally from, the Northern Areas." The implication, I think, was that the AKRSP engineers cared for this place, knew its people—and would avoid the kind of arrogance that had plagued rural development in Asia from the days of the East India Company.

Of course it isn't so. It's fine to have local engineers, who, at least if they have village backgrounds, ought to understand what might and what certainly won't work here in northern Pakistan. But were these engineers from villages? And if they were, what kind of changes had come over them during their long years of schooling? Training does strange things to people, after all. Once certified as experts, would these new engineers remember how villagers thought and felt? Would they care?

This is a question that brings us up squarely against the

power of the culture of development. We've seen the origins of that culture insofar as they are expressed within the confines of particular professional disciplines, such as irrigation engineering, but we've skimped on seeing its broader outline, apart from quick looks at nineteenth-century utilitarians like Macaulay and at that walking apogee of imperialism, George Nathaniel Curzon. Let us therefore come closer to our own day and notice the preface that Lord Hailey of the United Provinces contributed to *The Remaking of Village India*, a book published in 1929 by Frank Lugard Brayne. Hailey wrote, "We have never made a direct and a concerted attack on this problem; we have never deliberately attempted to effect that change in the psychology of the peasant, and in his social and personal habits, without which it is impossible materially to improve his conditions of life." Hailey, I should say, was a most influential man; his authoritative *An African Survey* shaped development attitudes on that continent for decades. But Hailey wasn't saying anything original. I go back to 1928 and the Royal Commission on Agriculture in India, and I dredge up a witness, a career civil servant named W. H. Moreland. He testifies that "the will to live better must furnish the driving power without which improvements in agriculture and commerce will not give an adequate return. The dominant feature of rural India at the present day is that the will to live better is not a force to be reckoned with."

The mind races ahead, to that circle of girls we saw in a school near Allahabad: the girls who watched the strings of television commercials each night. In the space of a lifetime, "the will to live better" has become a force to reckon with.

You can see some of the intermediate steps. Here, to take a wonderful example, is Arthur Mosher. We met him some time ago, when he was principal of the Allahabad Agricultural Institute and the man who persuaded Albert Mayer to take up agricultural extension in Etawah. And here is Mosher appearing in 1950 before a group of foreign-aid workers in Washington; development workers, he says, "must dissolve the culture of rural India." Stunningly simple. His own institute, he continues, has succeeded because it attacks India's "root beliefs." Albert Mayer at Etawah had done the same thing, Mosher goes on to say. Mayer hadn't meant to, but he had done it anyway. Not to worry. "You have to recognize," Mosher concluded, "that disrupting of the culture is what you are going there for."

Such world-destroying confidence! John Clark, writing about Hunza, never mentions beauty, only the poverty that he works to conquer. (Nor is there any mention of beauty in the publications of the AKRSP: once again we hear only of "harshness.") Clark writes approvingly that "nothing is ever good enough to satisfy the West. At one blow, this [spirit] does away with tradition, fatalism, and apathy. It is the spur of all invention and discovery. Losing it, any culture ceases to progress." Nowhere in Clark's book do we read about the *cost* of progress.

Mosher returned to the United States, where he headed the Agricultural Development Council, an important private organization funded largely by Rockefeller money; in the 1960s he wrote a book crudely but significantly titled *Getting Agriculture Moving*. His appearance in 1950 before the American aid workers was hosted by the same American agricultural-extension specialist who would move to India the next year to take charge of the Ford Foundation's India office.

And if we're in Washington, D.C., we might as well wander around that cluster of buildings known sometimes simply by the original address: 1818 H Street. It's the World Bank. All that glass, all those guards at the doors, all those minds wrapped in steel! Not for a second do I slight the intelligence, the energy, the knowledge of the people so armored, but no one is more thoroughly blinkered than intelligent young specialists eager for professional advancement in an elite organization.

That's why I get so angry when British colonial officers are portrayed as pompous fools. We see it in Orwell's *Burmese Days*, in Forster's *A Passage to India*, and in countless lesser-known works like the Indian diary of Sidney and Beatrice Webb. We see it in movies, too, chiefly I suppose in Attenborough's *Gandhi*. It's such a caricature, a caricature of men whose education, whose breadth of vision was great enough that they could question the culture of development.

I think of Geoffrey de Montmorency, who rose to the governorship of the Punjab in 1928 but who as a young man served as the settlement officer for the canal colonies southwest of Lahore. In an early issue of the journal established by the Pusa Institute, de Montmorency wrote that those who knew this land "in its pristine condition and know it now as the most successful agricultural paradise in the Punjab, must experience a pang of regret at the passing of a desert of peculiar natural fascination and the sudden transition from the life of the book of Genesis to the vulgar modernity of successful agricultural exploitation." I am quite sure that the modern development professional will dismiss this as sentimental nonsense, rather than as fair comment on our ambivalent reaction to progress.

I think of Arthur Gaitskell, brother of the British politician Hugh. For many years, Arthur was the director of the Sudan Plantations Syndicate, which superintended all agricultural operations on the great Gezira Scheme. In the 1950s Gaitskell wrote of the displaced nomads who were more or less forced to settle as laborers there. "We hate these straight lines," they had said: "we would rather be hungry once every few years, with freedom to range with our cattle unconfined, than have full bellies and be fined if we stray outside these horrid little squares." Gaitskell tells the story without condescension but with the simple recognition that the nomads had yielded to force.

I think of people we have met on earlier pages, people such as Malcolm Darling, Frank Brayne's critic. In the late 1920s and in connection with a discussion about modernization, Darling was asked if "it was desirable to rouse . . . [the Indian peasant's] pathetic contentment?" Darling replied that "the peasant is still, I believe, the most contented man in the modern world. . . . If you are going to substitute the material progress that you have got in Europe, I should say on the whole, leave him where he is." He went on to argue elsewhere for a culture of what he called "sufficiency." He opposed it to the more extreme choices of Gandhian "poverty" and Western "gain."

Compare him, then, with the young animal scientist who returns home to the Sudan with a doctorate from a prestigious American university. He promptly starts a project to calculate how much weight nomadic livestock would gain if fed on sugarcane residues. Where are the residues? A hundred miles away. No problem: he proposes to truck them over a hundred miles of unpaved track. Is he joking? No; he's only extending his doctoral dissertation, which dealt, of course, with the nutritive value of cane waste as feed. (He would have done the work, too, if his degree had not helped him jump several rungs on the professional ladder. Within a year, he had a senior post in development administration.)

Or I think of an Egyptian village I once visited that depended for its irrigation supply on a canal rebuilt by the British. The water supply was imperfect, and so the Ford Foundation agreed to pay for wells to produce a supplemental supply. The Egyptian irrigation ministry, however, was not interested in conjunctive use. It was only interested in lowering the water table, which had risen dangerously high after construction of the High Aswan Dam. So it shut off the canal entirely and forced the villagers to use the wells. This was a risky business, for the wells might fail. Were the villagers consulted? Informed of what was happening? Not on your life. The villagers were pawns in the hands of university-trained engineers, whose professors had said nothing about talking to people.

We've seen it all before: the Indonesian engineers embarrassed by the rice offering at the dam, the Moroccan officer shouting down the farmers, Akhter Hameed Khan talking about the need to spank the villagers of Passu. But what shall we do about it? Prescribe a corrective dose? Perhaps a mandatory course for all development professionals? A critical review of the intellectual history of the culture of development and an assessment of the things it has destroyed? Such a course would be fascinating, but it would have almost no impact on students. What are three credit hours alongside a whole curriculum?

How much has changed in that curriculum this century! The proof is in the exams that were once used to screen young men applying to join the Indian Civil Service. They're still on file at the Library of Congress and the India Office Library in London. We can, for example, look over the thirty-eight exams that comprised the test in 1911. Most of them were worth several hundred points, and candidates had to take enough of them to total the six thousand points on which they were graded. But which to pick?

Most of the 232 young men who sat for the test that year began on August 1 with a three-hour examination in English composition. There was only one question. It asked for an essay. There were four subjects to choose from: pageantry, collaboration in literature, the treatment of poetry in science and philosophy, and an essay on this quotation from Macaulay: "The history of nations is often best studied in works not professedly historical." Manageable? Perhaps, but what's ahead? Many of the candidates took the next day's test, which was on political science. There they were asked, among other things: "What fresh light has been thrown on the origins of kingship by recent research and speculation?" Not so good.

On the fifth of August there was an exam on general modern history. "Give some account of the Caliphate of Cordova." "Illustrate the principle by which Napoleon organized his administration." "Estimate the chief characteristics of Einhard's work." This is discouraging. And things do not get much better on the seventh and eighth, with exams in English history. "Discuss the importance of the idea of the balance of power in determining the foreign policy of Henry VII and that of Wolsey." Getting a sinking feeling? On the eleventh there was a twelve-hour botany test, with sixteen questions. "Give a full account of the structure and development of the pollen-sac of an Angiosperm, and of the origin of the pollen-grain."

Well, perhaps there's hope for some of us up to this point. But on the sixteenth the subject was Latin prose composition. Candidates had to translate into Latin two passages, one from Machiavelli and another from Cowper. The next day is not much help: the test is in Latin poetry. You can put into Latin hexameters a passage from Spenser or, if that isn't your style, one from Matthew Arnold into Latin elegiacs. On the nineteenth there was a test in moral and metaphysical philosophy. Rotten luck: it asks about "the real service rendered to philosophy by Parmenides" and about "the relation of Hume's metaphysics to Locke's."

On the twenty-eighth there was a geography examination. That ought to be simple enough, but it's not. "State and account for the position of the chief areas naturally adapted to the cultivation of wheat. To what extent has the distribution of civilized man been affected by his efforts to extend those areas artificially." Then there's this puzzler: "Write an essay on the probable influence of the Baghdad railway on the regions through which it will pass."

There were other parts of the test, to be sure; they were in higher and lower mathematics, in physics, logic and psychology, geology, Greek verse, French and German, Roman law, and economics. But there were no giveaway questions.

I think back to the library Proby Cautley assembled at the Roorkee headquarters of the Ganges Canal—Ruskin, Irving, Melville—and I contrast those books with the stuff that development professionals read today, the books that all of us read today, if we find time to read. No doubt there are serious readers everywhere, including the ranks of those professionals, and of course there are always arguments in favor of education that is narrowly technical, but I still think we are witnesses to an unfortunate series of descending curves: curves tracking erudition, literacy, and—most important—the simple breath of education that enables a person to see beyond the walls of contemporary mass culture and a professional curriculum. Such declines make me deeply skeptical that we should expect development professionals today to show the least concern about the beauty they are helping to destroy.

Perhaps I am too pessimistic; perhaps there is hope in curricular reform; certainly I would not stand in the way of change there. Yet I am perhaps more inclined to see a glimmer of light in the public at large. I think back to Eruvellipet and to corpulent Mr. Appaji, that wealthy landowner sitting comfortably on the porch of his house. He could move to Madras, but he chooses to live here. I remember Venkata Naik, the London barrister now retired not to Hyderabad but to a simple home among irrigated fields near Shorapur. I think of Narayana Raju in the Godavary Delta—of his satellite dish and sandalwood doors—and of nearby Mr. Dikshitulu, that more modest man retired from the big city to Gunnavaram Island and taking me with satisfaction through his coconut grove. I think of Malik Akhdar, the man in Chaprot who said that this valley had everything one needed—even if he was eager to move to Islamabad for his children's sake. There are thousands of people like this in Asia, people who love the countryside.

To this faith in the people there is, of course, a quick and very sarcastic reply. Have I visited the fabled countryside around Guilin? Ah, the great tradition of landscape painting, with its karst towers rising above serene paddies. No doubt I've seen the tourists lined up by the thousands to motor down the river and bus back through the countryside. Have I by any chance managed to wander through the town of Guilin itself? Have I looked inside the department store? Why, then, with all this incomparable scenic beauty surrounding them, do the Chinese cluster around a display of boom boxes fitted out with flashing lights like diode-encrusted jukeboxes? And why is it that, if you tell the hotel clerk that the countryside is beautiful, she looks at you like you're crazy?

If I can't figure out the answer, I shall be told, I should get out of the tourist bus. I should watch a young man trudging behind a cow in the muck of a rice paddy. I should get in there with him. I should watch women coming down the road with buckets of human waste hanging from poles across their shoulders. I should take a turn helping the men who use a spoon to lift water from a ditch into paddies—a giant spoon hanging from a tripod at the paddy edge. Then comes the rhetorical climax. I should balance all my thousands of well-to-do people, the people who sit and enjoy the countryside, against the millions—the tens of millions, the hundreds of millions—who sweat in it every day of their lives. And I should report back—should say just when it is, please, that I think the culture of development will be turned around in response to public demand.

My reply will be a simple one, a question. How long did the culture of development take to become the juggernaut it is today? The answer, of course, is centuries. What was slow in coming will be slow in going. So slow that there will be nothing left to save? Perhaps. But that, of course, is a counsel of despair, and it is not any more predictable than my counsel of hope. Besides, these cultural pendulums do not swing with horological precision. Things can happen fast, so long as you admit the possibility of Asia growing rich.

The main problem, as I see it, is that pushing for change in the modern world is a very noisy business, and you can't talk about beauty at the top of your lungs.

I think of the Taj Mahal, rising weightless on its plinth as a chilly fog swirls up from the Jumna. At night, the dome becomes a universe so vast that mind and matter fuse. Here is a building that teaches us to see the world not as a million places but as one. Can you shout such things? How can you whisper and yet be heard? That is the question. And I suppose the answer is: "practice."

And so I remember coming down to Kurnool, some hundred and fifty miles south of Hyderabad. Near the Heaven Doors Bar I turned off the highway and checked into a hotel. A few minutes later I went out, as Thoreau might say, to saunter away the afternoon.

I was looking for a temple called Brahmagudem. It sits in a valley surrounded by scrubby hills. There's nothing fancy about it; no guidebook even mentions it. There is only a small Shiva temple, painted in crude vertical bands of red and white. Around the temple, however, there are huge shade trees, especially striking in this semiarid setting. What's most striking is the ribbon of paddy that lies in the bottom of the valley below the temple. It's kept emerald green with water from a temple spring. Long ago that spring was enclosed in a stone-walled pool perhaps twenty feet square; it stands there under the shade of the temple trees. A small channel runs out to the paddies below.

The people at the nearby village of Veldurti looked long
and hard at this foreigner driving his big rented car, but they
didn't follow me upstream to Brahmagudem. I parked in the
shade and looked around. In front of the temple there was a
humble white statue of Nandi, Shiva's bull. It faced a yellow
doorway in front of a room almost bare, a room all white except
for a black phallic emblem of the god.

Two teenage boys were jumping into the murkily green waters of the temple pool. I traced the irrigation channel for most
of its length, then returned to the temple and decided to wait
for dark.

Temples with lands of their own are a common thing in India: the fifteen hundred temples in Kurnool District together
own some three hundred thousand acres, about a tenth of it irrigated. The lands come as donations and are in turn leased out
to farmers whose payments support the temples in perpetuity.
The fields here were certainly *someone's* business: part of the
channel had been lined with concrete, and the spring had been
topped up with a well that was fitted with a diesel pump. It
dripped lubricating oil all over the neighborhood.

I set those things aside and waited. A man and woman
stopped to bathe in the tank. Another couple came by minutes
later in a bullock cart. They, too, stopped. The man removed
the yoke and let his animals drink. Slowly he put the yoke
back on, and the cart moved away. Another woman came by;
she was on foot, with a plastic pouch on her head and an alumi-
num pail in her hand. She ignored the tank, but in front of
the temple she stopped, put down her load, and prayed for a
moment. She picked her things up and moved on. The sun
finally set, darkness fell, and the priest locked up and went
home.

Perhaps it wasn't quite dark yet, but it was fully quiet. I had
the place to myself. I took off my clothes and got in the water.
It was too warm to be refreshing and what with the growing
darkness and the opaque water I couldn't see my own feet
even when they were only in a few inches of water. Fish nibbled.

I've never told a soul.

SOURCES

CHAPTER ONE: A CONTINENT AT RISK

So far as I know, nothing has been written during the last fifty years about the aesthetic costs of rural development in Asia, nothing except an opinion-piece of mine called "The Ecology of Our Lives," which constituted the germ of this book. It appeared in the National Geographic Society's *Research and Exploration* (7:1, 1991).

A longer description of what I saw at Luk Keng was published in the American Geographical Society's *Focus* (39:3, 1989) under the title "Bound and Adrift." As for Hengdi and Zhenxiong, I know of no literature whatever; my own knowledge rests entirely on what I saw on a trip arranged by Lee Travers, an agricultural economist then with the Ford Foundation but now with the World Bank. When I told him, afterwards, what I wanted to do with this trip, he said that I was tilting at windmills. While his opinion probably remains unchanged, I hope he yet sees some glimmer of merit in what I'm arguing about and for. A longer description of what we saw on that trip appeared in the American Geographical Society's *Focus* (41:1, 1991) under the title "Temples of Heaven."

The quotations from Sir Francis Bacon come from the latter part of *The New Atlantis* (1627) and from section eleven of the fifth part of Book One in *The Advancement of Learning* (1605). The quotations from Newman come from the eighth section of "Knowledge Its Own End," in *The Idea of a University* (London, 1873). The quotations from Arnold come from "Sweetness and Light," in *Culture and Anarchy* (London, 1869), except for the last quotation, which comes from "The Function of Criticism at the Present Time," which comes from *Essays in Criticism* (London, 1865).

The quotation from the 1943 conference organizing the Food and Agriculture Organization of the U.N. comes from the organization's own anonymous "FAO: the First 40 Years" (Rome, 1985).

CHAPTER TWO: THE SPIRIT OF THE PLACE

Despite my raptures, Ramappa has not made the list of India's great monuments. James Fergusson, the indefatigable architectural historian of the nineteenth century, gives it only a footnote in his monumental *History of Indian and Eastern Architecture*—and a rather disparaging footnote at that, since he implies that the "elaborately chased" pillars are "overdone." My own well-used *Murray's Handbook for Travellers in India* . . . (18th ed., 1959) is more complimentary, citing a 1922 Archaeological Survey of India publication that describes the temples as "the brightest stars in the galaxy of mediaeval Deccan temples." Contemporary guidebooks blow hot and cold, some mentioning the temples, others omitting them. George Michell's comprehensive and very useful *Penguin Guide to the Monuments of India* (London, 1989) allows the temples two respectful paragraphs of technical description but offers no appraisal.

There is, mercifully, an abridged edition of Oscar Lewis's *Village Life in North India: Studies in a Delhi Village* (Urbana, Ill., 1958): it is the chapter Lewis himself contributed to *Village India: Studies in the Little Community*, edited by McKim Marriott (Chicago, 1955). There, without explanation, Lewis dispenses with the fictitious name of Rampur that he uses without fail in his book-length treatment of Rani Kheri.

Gilbert Slater actually wrote of Eruvellipet twice, first in *Some South Indian Villages* (London, 1918) and then in *Southern India: Its Political and Economic Problems* (London, 1936). Curiously, two other pioneering studies of village economics were undertaken at the same time that Slater was working: Harold Mann's work appears in *The Social Framework of Agriculture: India, Middle East, England* (New York, 1967), while James Charles Jack's study of Faridpur was published as *The Economic Life of a Bengal District* (Oxford, 1916). Whether these three men knew of each other I cannot say.

In Bangladesh I began with Rumer Godden, who wrote of Dhaka in *A Time to Dance, No Time to Weep* (London, 1987) and, with her sister Jon, in *Two under the Indian Sun* (New York, 1966); the former has a confirming photograph of the Narayanganj house. For Nirad C. Chaudhuri I relied upon his two massive volumes of autobiography. Kishorganj figures mostly in the first, *The Autobiography of an Unknown Indian* (London, 1951), but it appears also in the second, *Thy Hand, Great Anarch! India, 1921–1952* (London, 1987), where Chaudhuri judges its countryside to be "like one of Constable's landscapes" (p. 210). In the later volume Chaudhuri also speaks of his longtime home in Delhi, which as of 1991 still stood, though no longer fronting a park. It was outside this apartment that Dom Moraes met Chaudhuri in an encounter amusingly described in Moraes's *Gone Away* (London, 1960), pp. 64–67. No one who has read much Chaudhuri will question my description of him as "peppery," but an interview-profile that was published in *The Financial Times* for 3–4 July 1993 shows him not the least mellowed at age ninety-six.

Finally, for Tagore I began with Nazimuddin Ahmed's *Buildings of the British Raj in Bangladesh*, edited by John Sanday, copyrighted by UNESCO, and published in 1986 by the University Press, Dhaka. The literature on Tagore himself, of course, is immense, though details of his years at Kushtia are exiguous. Discussing Tagore at length, Chaudhuri uncharacteristically sheathes his claws: Tagore is "the supreme Bengali." The English translations of Tagore's poetry, Chaudhuri contends, "are no approach to the originals" (*Thy Hand, Great Anarch!* pp. 632, 596), but they are still appealing.

A few other details. For the episode involving Wolf Ladejinsky, see *Agrarian Reform as Unfinished Business*, edited by Louis J. Walinsky (New York, 1977), p. 17. The Kipling piece on the Lahore "dairies" has been published as "Typhoid at Home" in *Kipling's India: Uncollected Sketches, 1884–88*, edited by Thomas Pinney (London, 1987), pp. 69–76. Sarah Lloyd's *An Indian Attachment* (New York, 1985) was hurt by a stupid review in the *New York Times* that condemned Lloyd for not staying with her man, and the book fell quickly out of print. It is now back in print and brings foreigners closer to rural India than any other book I can name.

CHAPTER THREE: THE WESTERN WIND

There are three basic sources for this chapter: Alan R. Beals's *Gopalpur: A South Indian Village* (New York, 1962); Eric Stokes's *The English Utilitarians and India* (Oxford, 1959); and Philip Meadows Taylor's *The Story of My Life*. There were two versions of the Taylor autobiography: a one-volume version (Edinburgh, 1882; reprinted Delhi, 1986), and a two-volume version published five years later (Edinburgh, 1887). Unless otherwise noted below, all quotations here are from the first edition. By the way, *Confessions of a Thug* (London, 1839) is still in print in India (Delhi, 1988). So, too, though long gone both in Britain and the United States, is Stokes's book (Delhi, 1992).

Details of the Upper Krishna Project, the huge irrigation project now being wrapped around Shorapur, are unfortunately restricted to the anointed few who have access to unpublished World Bank documents; they may begin with Staff Appraisal Report 7406–IN (Washington, D.C., 1989).

Unless noted otherwise, the quotations in the chapter come from the above-noted sources as follows:

"rock of doom," Lovat Fraser, *India under Curzon and After* (London, 1911), frontispiece

"I shall not be governor-general," Stokes, p. 51

"Mill will be the living executive," Stokes, p. 68

"breathe feelings," C. H. Philips, *The Evolution of India and Pakistan, 1858–1947: Select Documents* (London, 1962), p. 10

"if I were asked to sum it up," Stokes, p. 311

"now second-class citizens," Beals, p. 76

"the old order to the new," Beals, p. 78

"a very stronghold of freebooters," Taylor, p. 137

"dissolute to a degree," Taylor, p. 132

"gave himself up to fits," Taylor, p. 149

"seemed seventy," Taylor, p. 222

"no intrigue," Taylor, p. 204

"a coward and a fool," Taylor, p. 313

"and found it full of sand," Taylor, pp. 50–51

"it could not condescend" and other Macaulay quotes are from "Lord Bacon," which appeared in 1837 in the *Edinburgh Review*.

"his seemingly boundless knowledge," Taylor, p. 84

"his commencement of that system of progress," Taylor, p. 85

"the most practically useful," Taylor, p. 263

"I had to study road engineering," Taylor, p. 168

"planted many thousand of mango," Taylor, p. 237

"allow the women to be idle," Taylor, p. 272

"tolerably long dimensions," Taylor, pp. 171–72

"no society, no one to speak to," Taylor, p. 238

"a double row of fine young trees," Taylor, p. 237

"a noble sheet of water," Taylor, p. 205; I have simplified the etymology of the word *tank*, but even the OED is unsure which way the word moved. See also Ivor Lewis, *Sahibs, Nabobs, and Boxwallahs: A Dictionary of the Words of Anglo-India* (Bombay, 1991), p. 232

"the view was certainly very fine," Taylor, 1887, p. 222

"for nothing, for there was a lot," Taylor, 1887, p. 237

CHAPTER FOUR: IRRIGATION

So far as I know, the only writer ever brave enough to have chosen Indian irrigation as the subject of a book for laymen was the novelist Maud Diver, whose *The Unsung: A Record of British Services in India* (Edinburgh, 1945) deals partly with railways and chiefly with irrigation in what is now Pakistan. The most *famous* writer, on the other hand, ever to take up irrigation in a technical sense was a very youthful Sir Richard Burton: see his project proposals in Selections from the Records of the Commissioner in Sind, Compilation 7 of 1844–1847, *Economic Condition of Sind: State of Road, Canals, and Forests in 1846*, pp. 44–54.

For a comprehensive though militantly uncritical survey of Indian irrigation, one is forced to the Central Board of Irrigation and Power's *Development of Irrigation in India* (New Delhi, 1965). There is a much more critical treatment in *The Cambridge Economic History of India*, vol. 2 (Cambridge, 1982), pp. 677–736. Written by Elizabeth Whitcombe, it may be read alongside her *Agrarian Conditions in Northern India: 1860–1900* (Berkeley, 1972), which was generally damning in its assessment of irrigation's contribution to India's economic development. In turn, Whitcombe's work may be seen as the provocation for Ian Stone's *Canal Irrigation in British India* (Cambridge, 1984). Although I side with Stone in this debate, for the economic contribution of irrigation does seem irrefutable to me, his book is far more restrictive than its title suggests, and it is very hard sledding.

As for the broader question of irrigation management, probably the best single introduction is *Irrigation and Agricultural Development in Asia: Perspectives from the Social Sciences*, edited by E. Walter Coward (Ithaca, 1980). The World Bank has, during the last decade, become increasingly interested in the subject; an early sign was Anthony Bottrall's *Comparative Study of the Management and Organization of Irrigation Projects* (World Bank Staff Working Paper 458, 1981). More recently the World Bank has helped India develop and fund a National Water Management Project (those with access to such things may see the unpublished Staff Appraisal Report No. 6468–IN, 1987). The World Bank has also published Jeremy Berkoff's *Irrigation Management on the Indo-Gangetic Plain* (Technical Paper Number 129, 1990), which argues, untenably in my view, that irrigation-system performance is directly related to aridity, with project performance declining as farmers become less dependent on irrigation. Berkoff selects cases that support his thesis, but there are many others that do not; the truth, in short, is not so neatly deterministic. Meanwhile, the World Bank is now partially funding the International Institute for Irrigation Management, established in Sri Lanka a decade ago chiefly by the Ford Foundation, and the Bank's interest in better management in Indian projects may be seen throughout its *India: Irrigation Sector Review* (Report 9518–IN, 1991).

Apart from such general sources, I have relied for the first half of the chapter primarily on three books. They are the worshipful biography by Cotton's daughter, Lady Hope, under the title *General Sir Arthur Cotton, R.E., K.C.S.I., His Life and Work* (London, 1900), and two volumes by George Walch, at one time chief engineer for irrigation, Madras. Walch's books are *The Engineering Works of the Godavari Delta* (Madras, 1896) and *The Engineering Works of the Kistna Delta* (Madras, 1899). Apart from this trio, I have also quoted in this part of the chapter from Richard Baird Smith's pioneering *The Cauvery, Kistnah, and Godavery, Being a Report on the Works Constructed on These Rivers for the Irrigation of the Provinces of*

Tanjore, Guntoor, Masulipatam, and Rajahmundry, in the Presidency of Madras (London, 1856).

Unless otherwise noted, the quotations in the first half of the chapter come from the above-noted sources as follows:

"here are commemorated" is attributed to George Cunningham, last governor of the Northwest Frontier Province, by Norval Mitchell in *Sir George Cunningham* (Edinburgh, 1968), p. 6

"not the enterprises of your power," Hope, p. 54; Burke's speech, delivered 28 February 1785, was on the nabob of Arcot's debts; in the Nimmo edition of Burke's complete works (London, 1899), the quoted material appears in vol. 4, p. 68

"thought us savages," from Hope, pp. 50–51

"mass of rubbish," from Hope, p. 121

"good engineering," Hope, pp. 121–22

"I have given such a height," from Smith, p. 16

"boundary wall of an ancient temple," from Hope, p. 56

"the greatest blessing," from Hope, p. 46

"permanent prosperity of Tanjore," from Smith, p. 31

"run through Rajahmundry," from Hope, p. 85

"a strong body of police," from Walch (Kistna), p. 14

"my own impression," from Walch (Godavary), p. 9

"great sum of money," from Walch (Godavary), p. 21

"principal part," from Walch (Godavary), p. 29

"I think it will be advisable," from Walch (Godavary), p. 31

"boots or brushes," from Hope, p. 134

"except for periodical attacks," from Hope, p. 131

"for days together," from Hope, p. 137

"do something, my girl," from Hope, p. 484

"was never really happy," from Hope, p. 479

"within living memory," from Hope, p. 442

"taking all things into consideration," from Hope, p. 73

"I had not much time," from Walch (Godavary), p. 77

"grossly idle," from Walch (Godavary), p. 78

"a noteworthy achievement," from Walch (Godavary), p. 75

"works of this nature," from Walch (Kistna), p. 9

"want of proper instruments," from Walch (Kistna), p. 13

"and there the matter ended," from Walch (Kistna), p. 13

"I feel entirely satisfied," from Walch (Kistna), p. 29

"simply thrown into the river," from Smith, p. 59

"could no longer restrain," from Walch (Kistna), pp. 52–53

Turning now to the second half of the chapter: the Ganges Canal has been by far the most intensively studied of all British irrigation works in India: it dominates, for example, the books cited above of Elizabeth

Whitcombe and Ian Stone. For Cautley himself, see two works by Joyce Brown: the more personal is the sketch entitled "A Memoir of Colonel Sir Proby Cautley, F.R.S., 1802–1871, Engineer and Paleontologist," in *Notes and Records of the Royal Society of London*, vol. 34, 1978–80, pp. 185–225; the one more oriented to his work is "Sir Proby Cautley (1802–1871), a Pioneer of Indian Irrigation," in *History of Technology*, vol. 3, 1978, pp. 35–89. The upper Ganga irrigation modernization project is described in a World Bank staff appraisal report (4992–IN, 1984).

My own quotations in the second half of this chapter have been drawn primarily from other sources, namely:

"Canals of Irrigation in the N.W. Provinces," *Calcutta Review*, vol. 12 (1849), pp. 79–183. Ian Stone presumes the author to be Proby Cautley, but I see no evidence for this, and Brown does not include it in her list of Cautley's works. I believe the article is the work of several hands, including Cautley, Baird Smith, and an anonymous editor. Parts can be safely attributed, but other parts cannot be;

Richard Baird Smith, *Italian Irrigation: A Report on the Agricultural Canals of Piedmont and Lombardy* (London, 1852), specifically vol. 1, pp. 305–434, "Sketch of the Irrigation System of Northern and Central India," and vol. 2, pp. 333–64, "Concluding Remarks on the Legislation of Irrigation in Northern India";

Proby Thomas Cautley, *Report on the Ganges Canal Works from Their Commencement until the Opening of the Canal in 1854* (3 vols. and atlas; London, 1860);

Report of the Indian Irrigation Commission, 1901–03; part 1, General, and part 4, Appendix: Selected Evidence (London, 1903);

"*Minutes of Evidence, United Provinces of Agra and Oudh*," issued in connection with the preceding Commission (Calcutta, 1903);

The Life of Sir Colin C. Scott-Moncrieff, edited by his niece Mary Albright Hollings (London, 1917); and

William Willcocks, *Sixty Years in the East* (Edinburgh, 1935).

Unless otherwise noted, the quotations used in the second half of this chapter come from the above-noted sources as follows:

"it is very certain," *Calcutta Review*, p. 80
"famine in its most aggravated shape," Cautley, vol. 1, p. 18
"lined out nearly one hundred miles," Cautley, vol. 1, p. 29
"appeared to be perpetually," Cautley, vol. 1, p. 38
"to deal with the mountain torrent," Cautley, vol. 1, p. 101
"my health," Cautley, vol. 1, p. 37
"the power requisite," Cautley, vol. 3, p. 141
"marked by an uninterrupted," Cautley, vol. 1, p. 95, but see p. 76

"now as eager about aqueducts," *The Letters of the First Viscount Hardinge of Lahore to Lady Hardinge and Sir Walter and Lady James, 1844–1847*, edited by Bawa Satinder Singh (London, 1986), p. 210

"the word thorough," Willcocks, p. 47

"not grafts," Cautley, vol. 3, p. 155

"better qualified to magnify," p. iv of Proby Thomas Cautley, *Ganges Canal: A Disquisition on the Heads of the Ganges and Jumna Canals, North-Western Provinces, in Reply to Strictures by Major-General Sir Arthur Cotton* (London, 1864)

"men who were the Ishmaelites," Smith, vol. 2, p. 363

"this great tract," Smith, vol. 1, p. 382; also *Calcutta Review*, p. 165

"to attempt to regulate," *Calcutta Review*, p. 131

"make masonry outlets," *Calcutta Review*, p. 132

"to know, in fact, the true value," Cautley, vol. 1, p. 431

"as a rule believe," William Wedderburn, *Allan Octavian Hume, C.B.* (London, 1913), p. 140

"induced effect" from Richard Baird Smith, *First Revenue Report of the Ganges Canal, being for the Fussil Khureef of 1855–56* (Roorkee?, 1855), p. 25

"I am no sportsman," Scott-Moncrieff, p. 102

"cultivators . . . not used to irrigation," Irrigation Commission, part 1, p. 91

"quantity of water required," *Calcutta Review*, p. 131

"surface of land irrigated," Cautley, vol. 1, p. 427

"bad as it is," Cautley, vol. 1, p. 428

"every cloud in the sky," *Calcutta Review*, p. 128

"stealing water should be stamped," Smith, vol. 2, p. 353

"the stronger parties," Stone, p. 201

"seeing that the Government," Scott-Moncrieff, p. 58

"measurements have been dishonestly performed," Stone, p. 216

"water was consumed with much," Irrigation Commission, part 4, p. 138; testimony of A. W. Smart

"the distributary is 18 miles long," Irrigation Commission, part 4, p. 141; testimony of A. W. Smart

"the monsoon rains of 1877," Willcocks, pp. 57–58

"the number of outlets was reduced," Irrigation Commission, part 4, p. 280; testimony of H. Marsh

"in one year 1,700 outlets," Irrigation Commission, part 4, p. 281; testimony of H. Marsh

"the most noteable," *Minutes*, p. 53; testimony of M. Nethersole

"people say the irrigated lands," Irrigation Commission, part 4, p. 279; testimony of E. B. Alexander

"a scene of lamentation," Hollings, pp. 110 and 122

"do not you think it would be," *Minutes*, p. 55; testimony of M. Nethersole

CHAPTER FIVE: FARMING

The most comprehensive review of agricultural development during
the British Raj is the third volume of M. S. Randhawa's *A History of
Agriculture in India* (New Delhi: Indian Council of Agricultural Research,
1983). Randhawa is uncritical but a reliable factual reference. I, for example, have relied upon it in the latter regard for the material included in
this chapter on botanical gardens. Randhawa is weakest, not surprisingly,
in discussing the contribution of Christian missionaries to India's agricultural development: Sam Higginbottom, for example, receives no mention at all. Granted, missionaries are not a popular subject these days
even among non-Indians, but the pendulum should swing back; too
many of these men were too interesting and important to be forgotten. I
would recommend in this connection John Clough's autobiographical *Social Christianity in the Orient* (New York, 1914), which is the story of one
American Baptist mission in rural Madras.

The sources from which I have quoted more than once in the chapter
are:

Allan Octavian Hume, *Agricultural Reform in India* (London, 1879);
John Augustus Voelcker, *Report on the Improvement of Indian Agriculture*,
    (London, 1893; reprint Delhi, 1986);
William Wedderburn, *Allan Octavian Hume, C.B.* (London, 1913; re-
    print New Delhi, 1974);
Report of the Royal Commission on Agriculture in India (London, 1928);
Minutes of Evidence Taken before the Royal Commission on Agriculture, 13
    vols. (London, 1928);
E. J. Russell, "Science and the Indian Peasant," *Journal of the Royal
    Society of Arts*, vol. 87, 1939, pp. 662–74;
Sir Albert Howard, *An Agricultural Testament* (New York, 1943);
Sam Higginbottom, Farmer: An Autobiography (New York, 1949); and
Louise Howard, *Sir Albert Howard in India* (London, 1953).

Unless otherwise noted, the quotations used in this chapter come from
the above sources as follows:

"the foundation of the Temple of Humanity" and "Would my people,"
    M. Gopal Rao, *Nagarjuna Sagar* (Bombay, 1979), frontispiece and
    p. 33
"the water should be utilized in the upper taluks" comes from the
    testimony given on 13 February 1902, by Colonel A. W. Smart,
    Acting Chief Engineer for Irrigation, Madras, before the Indian

Irrigation Commission; it appears in the *Report of the Indian Irriga-tion Commission* (London, 1903), part 4, p. 136.

"with independence they would be saved," *Lok Sabha*, 6 April 1954

"if really good seed," Wedderburn, p. 145

"a steam plough," C. Benson, "The Saidapeth [*sic*] Agricultural Col-lege and Farm," *Agricultural Journal of India*, 4:4, 1909, p. 23

"the time is come," Randhawa, vol. 3, p. 173, quoting W. W. Hunter, *A Life of the Earl of Mayo, Fourth Viceroy of India*, vol. 2, p. 320

"their wheat-fields would," Hume, pp. 8–9

"first and foremost unquestionably," Hume, p. 45

"in *every* village," Hume, p. 51

"a thing that is entirely in accord," Hume, p. 51

"the cruel blunders," Hume, p. 69

"innumerable other minor matters," Hume, p. 88

"gigantic wind-power," Hume, p. 93

"there was to be as little writing," Hume, p. 26

"present is not a favourable," Randhawa, p. 179, quoting Sir H. M. Durand, military member of the Viceroy's Council

"dissent from the Statement," Randhawa, vol. 3, p. 180

"this paper, written many months," Hume, p. iii

"the orbit is not calculable," Hume, p. 2. For an expert appraisal of the collection consider these words of R. Bowdler Sharpe, writing in *The History of the Collections Contained in the Natural History Depart-ments of the British Museum*, 1906, vol. 2, p. 393: "The Hume Col-lection was one of the most splendid donations ever made to the Nation, and added to the Museum, which had previously but a poor series of Indian birds, the largest and most complete collec-tion of birds and eggs from the British Indian Empire the world has ever seen. The Hume Collection contained 258 types."

"in many parts there is little," Voelcker, p. vi

"the cultivator's chief wants," Voelcker, p. xi

"be the outcome of a study," Voelcker, p. xvi

"what have we been doing," Lovat Fraser, *India under Curzon and After* (London, 1911), p. 171

"escaped the fate of the majority," Albert Howard, p. 160

"in the entire history of international co-operation," Randhawa, vol. 4, 1986, p. 274

"a disaster of the first magnitude," Russell, p. 676

"the agricultural practices of the Orient," Albert Howard, pp. 9–10

"the NPK mentality," Albert Howard, p. 18

"the principle followed," Albert Howard, p. 37

"in the years to come, chemical," Albert Howard, p. 38

"insects and fungi are not," Albert Howard, p. 161

"the breakdown of a complex," Albert Howard, p. 169

"it is a great mistake," Louise Howard, p. 219

"in allowing science to be used," Albert Howard, pp. 198–199

"we cannot but regard it as a matter," Royal Commission, p. 46

"a new organization to which Pusa," Royal Commission, p. 48

"if the Research Council had been," Russell, p. 676

"the plant knows no division," Louise Howard, p. 39

"attempting to perpetuate," Russell, p. 676

"great problem in Indian agriculture," Russell, p. 672

"good farming seems to have disappeared," Russell, p. 676

"that is our greatest trouble," *Minutes of Evidence*, vol. 7, p. 581

"of what use it was," Higginbottom, p. 80

"go on living our lives," Higginbottom, p. 104

"they were sure I was mad," Higginbottom, p. 124

"Doctor, in many things," Higginbottom, p. 129

"regarded as avenues to employment," Royal Commission, p. 547

"a very large number of students," *Minutes of Evidence*, vol. 1, p. 48
    (testimony of Dr. D. Clouston)

"when I began this work," *Minutes of Evidence*, vol. 7, p. 564

"not regard it as a feather," *Minutes of Evidence*, vol. 7, p. 562

Albert Howard, I might add, was a fan of Franklin Hiram King, who wrote *Farmers of Forty Centuries* (New York, 1911), a study of Chinese agriculture. King spent many years in Madison as a professor of "agricultural physics" at the University of Wisconsin. During Theodore Roosevelt's presidency, he left Madison for a position in Washington, D.C., with the U.S. Department of Agriculture's Bureau of Soils. There, he no doubt heard much of the conservation movement then flourishing not only domestically but with the ambition of internationalizing America's new faith in efficient resource management. King's book reversed matters by arguing that the Orient had much to teach the West. As such, it was a major and acknowledged influence on Howard's thinking. King's book has recently been described by bibliographers at the USDA as "most influential . . . with far-reaching consequences for agricultural practices worldwide." (National Agricultural Library, *Bibliographies and Literature of Agriculture Number 72*, Beltsville, 1988.) I think it would be closer to the truth to say that his influence was great on the critics of modern agriculture.

CHAPTER SIX: VILLAGES

After writing this chapter I read Clive Dewey's *Anglo-Indian Attitudes: The Mind of the Indian Civil Service* (London, 1993), a study of Frank Brayne and Malcolm Darling. Dewey gives much support to the thesis that when it comes to slamming the British Empire there is no one quite like a postimperial Briton. Is it because these men know their erstwhile empire better than anyone else, or is it because they have not forgiven the empire for falling? I incline to the latter view. In any event Dewey goes a long way toward showing that Brayne's contemporaries saw him as a blowhard, tiresome beyond belief. I don't question Dewey's evidence, but since when have we required historic figures to be unfailingly good company?

The writing that poured forth during the 1950s and 1960s on the subject of community development in India remains truly disheartening, whether measured by its bulk or its palatability. Two standard works remain the old *India's Roots of Democracy*, by Carl C. Taylor et al. (London, 1965) and the newer *Rural Development in India: Some Facets* (Hyderabad: National Institute of Rural Development, 1981). Two newer and less ponderous studies, both of which review the history of community development, are L. C. Jain, *Grass without Roots: Rural Development under Government Auspices* (New Delhi, 1985) and S. R. Maheshwari, *Rural Development in India* (New Delhi, 1985). For a detailed study of a village that was part of an early community-development program near the Allahabad Institute, see Phillips Foster and Beverly Simmons, *Change in a Hindu Village: Bhanapur in 1955, 1968, and 1973* (University of Maryland Department of Agricultural and Resource Economics, 1978).

My quotations have been drawn from other sources, namely the following, of which the works by Brayne and Bowles are the most lucid, though not the most judicious:

Vol. 3 of the *Minutes of Evidence Taken before the Royal Commission of Agriculture* (London, 1928);

F. L. Brayne, *The Reconstruction of Rural India* (London, 1929);

Chester Bowles, *Ambassador's Report* (New York, 1954);

Malcolm Lyall Darling, *Rusticus Loquitur* (London, 1930);

Ministry of Agriculture, *Towards a Welfare State* (New Delhi, 1956);

Sadarshan Kapoor, *India Village Service: A Rural Development Programme in Uttar Pradesh* (Delhi School of Social Work, 1958);

Albert Mayer and Associates, *Pilot Project, India: The Story of Development at Etawah, Uttar Pradesh* (Berkeley, 1959);

Baij Nath Singh, *The Etawah Pilot Project*, pp. 95–426 of J. C. Kavoori and Baij Nath Singh, *History of Rural Development in Modern India*, vol. 1 (Delhi: Gandhian Institute of Studies, 1967);

Ministry of Community Development, Panchayati Raj and Cooperation, *Evolution of Community Development Programme in India* (Delhi, 1963);

S. K. Dey, *Power to the People?* (Bombay, 1969);

Chester Bowles, *Promises to Keep: My Years in Public Life, 1941–69* (New York, 1971); and

Gerald E. Sussman, *The Challenge of Integrated Rural Development in India: A Policy and Management Perspective* (Boulder, 1982).

Unless otherwise noted, all the quotations in this chapter come from the sources listed immediately above:

"in one of the poorest districts," *Minutes*, p. 76

"we are beginning," *Minutes*, p. 74

"would insist with all my power," *Minutes*, p. 57

"better seed, better implements," Brayne, p. 3

"to jerk the villager," Brayne, p. 2; also quoted by Randhawa, p. 360

"the dignity of labour," *Minutes*, p. 62

"heart and center," *Minutes*, p. 57

"deluge the area," Brayne, p. 3

"cannot hitch," *Minutes*, p. 84

"who look at village life," Darling, p. 154

"it is utterly useless," *Minutes*, p. 57

"At Gurgaon we have got," *Minutes*, p. 100

"in order to enable Hissar," *Minutes*, p. 69

"lazy and superlatively unthrifty," quoted from a famine report of 1879 by the *Gazetteer of the Gurgaon District, 1883–4* (Lahore, 1884), p. 68

"a magnificent hall," *Minutes*, p. 63

"deliberately attempted to effect," F. L. Brayne, *The Remaking of Village India* (London, 1929), p. xvii

"The moment you disappear," *Minutes*, p. 91

"a convenient beast of burden," *Minutes*, p. 60

"Now, seven months later," Darling, p. 155

"by order and through fear," Darling, p. 125

"so long as they prefer rings," *Minutes*, p. 76

"I suppose some sort of a Mussolini," *Minutes*, p. 82

"is the chief cause," Darling, pp. 156–58

"the people's own," Ministry of Community of Development, p. 19; the writer was Spencer Hatch

"no lasting improvement," Ministry of Community Development, p. 39; the writer was V. T. Krishnamachari

"a desire in the villagers for improvement," Singh, p. 96

"in the spirit of *humility*," Kapoor, p. 18

"I am not really enamoured," Dey, p. 57

"I pulled out a ten-page project," Sussman, p. 7

"over here our Department of Agriculture," Mayer, p. 11

"at long last, one of the villagers," Singh, p. 130

"you will be called upon to work," Singh, p. 152

"when we first visited Etawah," Bowles 1954, p. 198

"it is not difficult to foresee," Bowles 1954, p. 206

"so far experience indicates," Bowles 1954, p. 202

"India slumbers in her villages," Ministry of Agriculture, p. 124

"this is how it is with 'development,'" Kusum Nair, *Blossoms in the Dust* (London, 1961), p. 73

"we must fight against the possibility," Mayer, p. 115

"a few individuals of the middle," Mayer, p. 111

"seem to work with mercenary motives," Mayer, p. 112

"the first-aid man in all fields," Ministry of Agriculture, p. 124

"our colleagues looked at us as fools," Sussman, p. 48

"you forgot the farmer," Sussman, p. 51

"it was impractical in India," Bowles 1971, p. 549

"there was tremendous pressure," Sussman, p. 88

"Jawaharlalji had unquestioned faith," Dey, p. 116

"when out of consternation," Dey, p. 119

"a great protagonist of centralisation," Sussman, p. 58

"had what his mind and heart had been after," Dey, p. 119

In connection with *Behind Mud Walls,* by William and Charlotte Wiser, see also Charlotte Wiser's *Four Families of Karimpur* (Syracuse University, Foreign and Comparative Studies/South Asian Series 3, 1978). ("Karimpur" was the pseudonym the Wisers consistently used for Karimganj.) For the "Green Revolution" and matters such as the development of new seeds and fertilizers, the best source is the fourth volume of M. S. Randhawa's *A History of Agriculture in India* (Delhi: Indian Council of Agricultural Research, 1986). For more recent statistics on fertilizers and crop production, I have relied upon the 1992 edition of the *Hindu Survey of Indian Agriculture* and upon the government of India's *Economic Survey 1991–92, Part II, Sectoral Developments* (Delhi, 1992).

CHAPTER SEVEN: THE HEARTLAND

Alkalinity in Karnal has been a problem for a long time, but Denzil Ibbetson, who studied the district a century ago, noted only the easier-to-remedy accumulation of "saline efflorescence." See his *Report on the Revision of Settlement of the Panipat Tahsil and Karnal Parganah of the Karnal District, 1872–1880* (Allahabad, 1883), pp. 66–67. Is it possible that the alkali was a result of excessive irrigation? Such would have been Albert Howard's judgment, I think.

For the Hissar Livestock Farm, see the farm's undated pamphlet "Production of Hariana Pedigree Bulls at the Government Livestock Farm, Hissar" (Hissar, 1960?).

For the general organization of agricultural research and education in India today, see *National Agricultural Research, Education and Extension Education Systems in India,* by K. V. Raman and others (Hyderabad: National Academy of Agricultural Research Management, 1988). The operation of the Train and Visit (T&V) extension system has been analyzed in-house by the World Bank's Gershon Feder and Roger Slade: *Aspects of the Training and Visit System of Agricultural Extension in India: A Comparative Analysis* (World Bank Staff Working Paper 656, 1984).

All the numerical data concerning Khaluwas I owe to Professor M. H. Qureshi of Jawaharlal Nehru University in New Delhi; quite by chance he had only recently taken a class to Khaluwas and with his students had spent some weeks there studying the village.

Sources of the chapter's quotations are as follows:

"come inside India," Malcolm Lyall Darling, *Rusticus Loquitur* (London, 1930), title page

"the peripatetic system," E. Shearer, "Steam Threshing in India," *The Agricultural Journal of India*, vol. 2, 1907, p. 250

"it is useless to select," J. W. A. Morgan, "The Government Cattle Farm, Hissar, Punjab," *The Agricultural Journal of India*, vol. 2, 1907, p. 367

"Machete EC," from *Haryana Farming*, vol. 21, June of 1992, p. 17

CHAPTER EIGHT: THE PERIPHERY

The historical sources I have quoted more than once in this chapter are:

George Nathaniel Curzon, *Leaves from a Viceroy's Note-Book* (London, 1926); the quoted parts have been reprinted in *A Viceroy's India: Leaves from Lord Curzon's Note-Book*, edited by Peter King (London, 1984);

Algernon Durand, *The Making of a Frontier* (London, 1899; reprint Karachi, 1977);

Reginald C. F. Schomberg, *Between the Oxus and the Indus* (London, 1935; reprint Lahore, undated); and

John Clark, *Hunza: Lost Kingdom of the Himalayas* (New York, 1956; reprint Karachi, 1980).

Probably the simplest place to begin reading about the AKRSP is the World Bank's highly complimentary Operations Evaluation study: *The Aga Khan Rural Support Program in Pakistan: An Interim Evaluation* (Washington, D.C., 1987); a second interim evaluation was prepared in 1990 for official use only (Report No. 8448–PAK). Shoaib Sultan Khan, in charge of the AKRSP from its inception, has written, in collaboration with Mahmood Hasan Khan, his own account of the project: *Rural Change in the Third World: Pakistan and the Aga Khan Rural Support Program* (New York, 1992). For Akhter Hameed Khan, see Arthur Raper, *Rural Development in Action* (Ithaca, 1970), as well as two works of Khan's from which

I have quoted: *Rural Development in Pakistan* (Lahore, 1985) and *The Works of Akhter Hameed Khan*, vol. 2 (Comilla: Bangladesh Academy of Rural Development, 1983).

The Karimabad Girls' Academy was the subject of an illustrated article by Brian Brace Taylor in *Mimar*, Number 31, March of 1989, pp. 20–27.

Unless otherwise noted, the following quotations come from the above sources:

> "Rakaposhi stands there," Curzon, p. 178
> "rich spoil," Curzon, p. 193
> "on this channel the cultivation," Durand, p. 162
> "more beautiful than any other valley," Schomberg, p. 97
> "a sort of pilot model," Clark, p. 3
> "I felt like a man," Clark, p. 74
> "were regarding me as just another," Clark, p. 100
> "I was raising their standards," Clark, p. 227
> "tyranny I had not broken," Clark, p. 262
> "I made patriotic speeches," Khan 1985, p. 7
> "live without books and leisure," Khan 1985, p. 300
> "promised political peace," Khan 1985, p. 189
> "In particular the Americans," Akbar S. Ahmed in Khan 1985, p. iv
> "we could, at best, slightly modify," *Works*, p. 159
> "anyone who seeks to assist," David E. Bell in Raper, p. vii
> "the educated people will go to the village," *Works*, p. 68
> "even if you don't eat, you must save," Raper, p. 284
> "In Pakistan, where revolution," Khan 1985, p. 49
> "mentor and guide," Khan 1992, dedication page
> "superior wisdom," AKRSP, *First Annual Report* (Gilgit, 1983), p. 2

CHAPTER NINE: SOFTLY, SOFTLY

The quotations in the chapter come from the following sources:

"we have never made a direct," in Brayne, *The Remaking of Village India* (London, 1929), p. xvii

"the will to live better," W. H. Moreland, quoted in the *Report of the Royal Commission on Agriculture in India* (London, 1928), p. 499

"you have to recognize," in "How Do You Work with Another Culture?", address given by Dr. Arthur Mosher before the Point IV Seminar held on 20 December 1950 (mimeo), p. 4

"nothing is ever good enough," in John Clark, *Hunza* (New York, 1956; reprint Karachi, 1980), p. 267

"in its pristine condition," G. F. de Montmorency, "The Chenab Canal Colony," in *The Agricultural Journal of India*, vol. 3 (1908), p. 197

"We hate these straight lines" comes from W. P. Clarke, quoted by

Arthur Gaitskell in *Gezira: A Study of Development* (London, 1959), p. 202

"is was desirable to rouse," comes from vol. 7 of the *Minutes of Evidence Taken before the Royal Commission on Agriculture* (London, 1928), p. 630

"the peasant is still, I believe," Malcolm Lyall Darling, *Rusticus Loquitur, or The Old Light and the New in the Punjab Village* (London, 1930), pp. 378–79

The ICS exams were shared with two other agencies, and the full title is, therefore, "Open Competition Examination for Home Civil Service, Indian Civil Service, and Eastern Cadetships in Colonial Service." Since one often reads about people cramming for the tests, I might add that cramming would hardly be possible unless the questions were repeated year after year. They were not, at least not in the years around 1911, which I have examined. It is true, on the other hand, that the best scores were attained by men who chose to enter the Home Civil Service rather than go to India. In 1911, for example, the highest score attained by a man going to India was the eleventh highest score of all. Twenty-odd years later, Arthur Beatson was officiating secretary in the government of India's Department of Education.

INDEX

BRET WALLACH is professor and chair of geography at the University of Oklahoma and author of the acclaimed book *At Odds with Progress: Conservation and Americans* (1991). He has received numerous grants and fellowships, including a MacArthur Foundation Fellowship between 1984 and 1989. He contributes regularly to the American Geographical Society's *Focus* magazine and to other professional journals. Professor Wallach was born in Twin Falls, Idaho, and was educated at the University of California, Berkeley.

Library of Congress Cataloging-in-Publication Data

Wallach, Bret, 1943–
   Losing Asia : modernization and the culture of development / Bret
Wallach ; drawings by Susan Trammell.
     p.   cm.
   Includes bibliographical references and index.
   ISBN 0-8018-5170-X (hardcover : alk. paper)
   1. Rural development—Asia.   2. Rural development—India.   3. Asia—
Rural conditions.   4. India—Rural conditions.   I. Title.
HN655.2.C6W35   1996
307.1'412'095—dc20   95-12863